CHILDREN'S
RIGHTS RE-VISIONED

PHILOSOPHICAL
READINGS

CHILDREN'S
RIGHTS RE-VISIONED
P H I L O S O P H I C A L
R E A D I N G S

Rosalind Ekman Ladd

Wheaton College

Wadsworth Publishing Company

I(T)P™ An International Thomson Publishing Company

Belmont • Albany • Bonn • Boston • Cincinnati • Detroit
London • Madrid • Melbourne • Mexico City • New York
Paris • San Francisco • Singapore • Tokyo
Toronto • Washington

Philosophy Editor: Tammy Goldfeld
Editorial Assistant: Kelly Zavislak
Production: Ruth Cottrell
Print Buyer: Barbara Britton
Copy Editor: Ruth Cottrell
Cover Designer: Harry Voigt
Compositor: TCSystems, Inc.
Printer: Malloy Lithographing, Inc.

Printed in the United States of America

1 2 3 4 5 6 7 8 9 10—01 00 99 98 97 96

For more information, contact Wadsworth Publishing Company.

Wadsworth Publishing Company
10 Davis Drive
Belmont, CA 94002
USA

International Thomson Editores
Campos Eliseos 385, Piso 7
Col. Polanco
11560 México D.F. México

International Thomson Publishing Europe
Berkshire House 168–173
High Holborn
London, WC1 7AA
England

International Thomson Publishing GmbH
Königswinterer Strasse 418
53227 Bonn
Germany

Thomas Nelson Australia
102 Dodds Street
South Melbourne 3205
Victoria, Australia

International Thomson Publishing Asia
221 Henderson Road
#05-10 Henderson Building
Singapore 0315

Nelson Canada
1120 Birchmount Road
Scarborough, Ontario
Canada M1K 5G4

International Thomson Publishing Japan
Hirakawacho Kyowa Building, 3F
2-2-1 Hirakawacho
Chiyoda-ku, Tokyo 102
Japan

 This book is printed on recycled paper.

Library of Congress Cataloging-in-Publication Data
Ladd, Rosalind Ekman.
    Children's rights re-visioned : philosophical readings / Rosalind
Ekman Ladd.
        p.   cm.
    Includes bibliographical references.
    ISBN 0–534–23532–8
    1. Children's rights.   2. Children's rights—Moral and ethical
aspects.   I. Title.
HQ789.L33 1995   95–3845
305.23—dc20   CIP

CONTENTS

PREFACE

T hose who teach courses in applied ethics, social philosophy, and philosophy of law recognize the challenge of finding materials that are current, accessible to a wide range of students, and of high scholarly quality. This anthology is intended to meet that challenge, drawing from philosophy published within the past ten years on topics that have generated intense public interest.

The collection is new in another sense, as well, for the readings re-vision issues about the rights of children by introducing some feminist perspectives as well as traditional ethical theory.

Classroom dialogue and interaction are a vital part of teaching ethics, so the introductions to each topic offer short case descriptions drawn from recent newspaper accounts, which can be used to trigger discussion and to introduce additional topics not directly addressed in the readings.

If this book succeeds in its purpose, students and teachers alike will find themselves rethinking questions about the moral status of children, as well as appreciating the ways in which philosophical thinking can prepare one for participating in the public debate.

Acknowledgments

I would like to thank the reviewers who were generous with their time and expertise, helping to make this book a more useful tool for those who will teach and learn from it: William Aiken, Chatham College; Alison Bailey, Illinois State University; Lori Gruen, Lafayette College; Anne Minas, University of Waterloo; Sally Scholz, Purdue University; Rosemarie Tong, Davidson College; Jennifer Welchman, University of Maryland; and Carl Wellman, Washington State University.

My thanks, too, to Kenneth King, former Philosophy Editor at Wadsworth, for giving the first encouragement for this project and to Tammy Goldfeld, Editor, who has guided its development.

Most of all, my thanks to John Ladd, with whom I have shared many conversations on the rights of children, both theoretical and applied.

Introduction

In the Bible the story is told about Solomon, the king, who was asked to decide the fate of an infant claimed by two women. Both had given birth to sons at the same time in the same house. One child died and each woman accused the other of having replaced her own dead child with the live child. Solomon said, "Bring me a sword. Divide the living child in two, and give half to the one, and the other half to the other." One woman seemed satisfied that justice was to be done, but the other cried out, "Give her the living child and by no means slay it." Solomon then decided that the real mother was the one who would save the life of the child and gave the child to her.

Thus we see that moral issues about the rights of children, the rights of parents, and the role of the state have a long history, indeed. We praise the woman who was willing to put the best interest of the child before her own claim to motherhood, but it is perplexing that the issue cannot be settled by the usual moral principles of fairness and justice.

The Solomon story and its many variations are being reenacted on the current stage as well. Custody battles over adopted children, children who want to divorce their parents, parents who want to restrict the content of their children's education or refuse medical treatment for their children on religious grounds—all these controversies are being debated in the public arena. Newspapers and TV specials highlight the drama, and the national political agenda is sharply focused on family values, education reform, and heightened concern for the well-being of children.

These issues capture the attention of college and professional school students, whether they are reflecting on their own experiences as they move from adolescence to independence, preparing for careers working with children, or anticipating their own future roles as parents. Philosophical discussions offer an opportunity to step back from the sensationalism of newspaper articles and TV specials and to take a reflective, reasoned approach to the problems.

Among philosophers, the rapid growth of applied ethics and the demand for the teaching of ethics in professional schools is bringing about thoughtful discussions whose goal is not only insight for its own sake but also guidance in finding solutions to practical problems. The selections reprinted here make important contributions to the field.

About This Book

This anthology addresses the need for philosophical reflection on issues concerning the status and treatment of children. The selections were all published within the past 10 years and were chosen to be clear and accessible to beginning students but rich enough to challenge the more advanced.

Introductions to each section begin with short discussions of recent cases that raise important philosophical questions about the relationships among children, parents, and the state. Each Introduction provides an outline of the most important issues addressed in the readings on that topic and an overview of the arguments typically advanced for and against different ways of resolving the issues. A brief statement about the content of each selection and suggestions for further readings complete each introduction.

Consideration of cases, issues, and arguments demonstrates that although cases usually arise in courts of law, they are settled only by reasoning about values and ethics. If students understand all sides of an issue, they can be encouraged to develop their own positions on controversial topics and to support their views with careful, disciplined thinking.

Background Issues: Protectionists Versus Liberationists

The movement for children's rights emerged in the 1960s, riding the wave of concern for unfairly treated groups. Although it did not result in as many changes as the civil rights movement or equal rights for women, it did result in dropping the legal age of majority from 21 to 18, thus lowering the age for voting, financial independence, and other such factors. While everyone recognizes that any legal age is necessarily arbitrary, debate continues about whether younger minors should be allowed to make more decisions for themselves.

Controversy about children's rights reflects a tension between two concerns for the welfare of children: protecting children from their own mistakes, even at the expense of restricting their choices and behavior, versus giving children more freedom, even at the risk of their choosing what is not in their own best interest. Protectionists emphasize that children have a right to assistance and care from adults, whereas liberationists emphasize that children have a right to self-determination.

Debates over child labor laws illustrate the two positions. Those in favor of safeguarding children want to limit the number of hours children may work, especially during the school week, and to restrict their employment to nonhazardous jobs. Those in favor of liberties for children want to let the individual child or teen decide when and where to work.

A long philosophical tradition addresses the role of children in society and the duties of parents and society to them. Plato recommends communal child rearing instead of separate families. Aristotle describes children as belonging to their parents, whereas Locke, Hobbes, and Rousseau all try to justify the authority of parents over children and to develop ideals of education and theories about how to raise children to be rational, responsible adults. Mill distinguishes between children and adults on the basis of maturity, which he thinks warrants denying to children the liberties accorded to competent adults.

More recently, a connection has evolved between feminism and increased interest in children, and it has both a pragmatic and an academic aspect. Typically, housewives and mothers in the United States have provided as unpaid labor what most other industrial nations have subsidized in terms of infant and after-school child care. However, as women enter the workforce in unprecedented numbers and children increasingly live in other than traditional two-parent families, society at large is forced to reconsider its responsibilities to children.

In academic circles, issues in the private, domestic sphere are receiving recognition as legitimate subjects of inquiry as part of the acceptance of new scholarship in women's studies. Feminist writers have pointed out, for instance, that divorce reduces the average standard of living of women and their dependent children by 73 percent in the first year, that domestic violence affects the children in a household as well as the woman victim, and that concern for actual and possible fetuses has led to discriminatory practices against women in the workplace. Scholars as well as legislators are thinking about ways in which society must change to resolve these issues.

On a more theoretical level, one significant contribution of feminist philosophy to the study of ethics is a serious challenge to framing questions of ethics and values exclusively in terms of rights. The language of rights, it is said, implies an adversarial relationship between parties; generally no one raises questions of rights unless making a complaint against another. For instance, it is appropriate to claim your rights are being violated by your landlord, to whom you stand in a purely formal, legal relationship, but odd to claim your rights against a friend—at least if you intend to keep that friendship. Among family members where ties are even closer than simple friendship, it is suggested, the language of rights should give way to models that stress connection, care, intimacy, and relationship rather than separateness, individuality, and independence. Thus, although much of the current philosophical literature about children is written in the language of children's rights, it is important to consider insights that may result from alternative conceptual frameworks. As the title of this volume suggests, questions about children's rights are being re-visioned in new theoretical approaches.

Philosophical Themes and Concepts

A number of important themes and concepts are used throughout the literature on children's rights. Although each author develops arguments in a particular way, it will be useful for the reader to have some general background. For example, different writers share the same general conception of what rights are in order to argue intelligibly for or against giving more rights to children.

Rights

A useful, basic definition of a right is that it is a justified claim. Whereas a privilege is something that may be offered or taken away, a right must ordinarily be fulfilled unless the individual whose right it is chooses to waive it. Rights may be negative or positive. Negative rights are liberties or freedoms to do something without interference from others, that is, claims to noninterference. Positive rights are claims to some performance, sometimes referred to as welfare rights or entitlements. To illustrate the distinction: If children have a negative right to be free of abuse, others are prohibited from treating them in certain ways; if children have a positive right to adequate food and shelter, these services can be claimed on their behalf.

From these examples, we may assume that for every right that a person has, someone else has a duty. Thus the child's right to be free of abuse implies a duty for parents and all others to refrain from certain behavior. A child's right to food and shelter implies that someone has the obligation to provide it. This principle, that every right implies a corresponding duty, is called the correlativity of rights and duties.

This principle of rights and duties can present problems for children's advocates, for while it is easy to draw up lists of rights that should apply to all children, the claims are empty if no one specifies who has the duty to fulfill these rights. Various human rights documents of the United Nations are sometimes criticized on these grounds, for the United Nations has neither the authority nor the funding mechanisms to provide all children adequate food, shelter, and education.

One way to implement rights for children is to make them into legal rights by legislation within the jurisdiction of one nation or one state. Many of the controversies about children's rights are about changing laws that currently exclude children from rights accorded to adults. How does one go about changing laws? Often it is by appeal to moral arguments. For example, the argument that a certain law is unfair can be a powerful method of convincing people that it needs to be changed. Thus arguments that try to show that children have a moral right to certain freedoms or entitlements can serve as the basis for changing laws that deny them those freedoms. For example, arguing that every child has a right to decent health care has as its goal the institution of tax-supported insurance systems that cover all children, or at least all children whose parents cannot pay for it themselves.

Moral rights are sometimes referred to as human rights, universal rights, or natural rights. These terms refer to the theory that moral rights are based simply on the fact that the rights-holder is a human being, that the rights apply to all human beings, and that the rights apply to human beings in a natural state—that is, they are not dependent on people being citizens or residents of a certain state. Legal rights, by contrast, depend on one's status as a citizen or by virtue of certain qualifications, and they can vary from place to place or time to time. Moral rights, it is claimed, should be granted to everyone, wherever or whenever they live, regardless of what their legal rights are.

Having rights bestows a special moral status, and it implies that the rights-holder's claims must be met. Some theorists hold that only human beings can be rights-holders, or even that only mature, rational beings can have rights. Others argue that although only rational beings can be moral agents with free choice and moral responsibility, nonrational beings can also have rights. Nonrational beings might include children, incompetent adults, and animals.

Saying that they have rights implies that they must be treated in certain respect-
ful ways.

Unfortunately, different people's rights sometimes conflict, and not all of
them can be fulfilled. For example, parents may have the right to practice their
religion, but if this practice includes clitoridectomy of female infants, it can
be argued that children have a conflicting right not to be abused and that
clitoridectomy is a form of abuse. Some of the most difficult issues concerning
children, families, and states arise when actual or purported rights conflict with
one another and it is not easy for philosophers, lawyers, or those who make
public policy to decide which rights should override the others.

Mill and Liberalism

Many of the basic principles on which arguments about children's rights are
based use as their source the theory of liberalism developed by John Stuart
Mill (1806–1873). Mill's theory has been enormously important in developing
social norms and ideas about the role of government that guide many of the
Western, industrialized nations, and philosophers often defend or criticize laws
and social policy on the grounds of whether or not they are consistent with
Mill's principles. As a political theory, liberalism may be contrasted with various
sorts of authoritarianism—for example, communism and dictatorships.

Two aspects of liberalism are important to questions about the role of
children in society.

1. Mill develops the theory of utilitarianism, which measures the rightness
of any act in terms of the consequences it brings to society, or to the greatest
number of people. For Mill, the most important value that contributes to a
good society is individual freedom. He says in his essay, *On Liberty,* "Over
himself, over his own body and mind, the individual is sovereign," and "The
free development of individuality is one of the leading essentials of well-
being. . . ." His reasons for saying this are his belief that individuals know
their own best interests better than anyone else and his view that even if they
make mistakes, it is still to the overall benefit of society to have liberty for
individuals. "All errors he is likely to commit against advice and warning are
far outweighed by the evil of allowing others to constrain him to what they
deem his good."

Mill places two qualifications on individual freedom, however. First, the
harm principle says that government or other citizens may interfere with a
person's liberty if it causes harm to others.

> The object of this essay is to assert one very simple principle,
> as entitled to govern absolutely the dealings of society with the
> individual in the way of compulsion and control, whether the
> means used be physical force in the form of legal penalties or
> the moral coercion of public opinion. That principle is, that
> the sole end for which mankind are warrented, individually or
> collectively, in interfering with the liberty of action of any of
> their number, is self-protection. That the only purpose for

which power can be rightfully exercised over any member of a civilized community, against his will, is to prevent harm to others.

If a person is causing harm only to himself, however, others may not interfere. "His own good, either physical or moral, is not a sufficient warrent." Mill, then, rejects what is generally referred to as strong paternalism, the theory that it is justifiable to interfere with persons' liberty against their will for their own good.

The second qualification on individual freedom is that it applies only to mature, rational, or competent adults.

It is perhaps hardly necessary to say that this doctrine is meant to apply only to human beings in the maturity of their faculties. We are not speaking of children, or of young persons below the age which the law may fix as that of manhood or womanhood. Those who are still in a state to require being taken care of by others, must be protected against their own actions as well as against external injury.

Mill, then, does defend what is generally referred to as weak paternalism, the theory that it is justifiable to limit persons' liberty against their will for their own sake if those persons are incompetent. Furthermore, he assumes without argument that children—that is, anyone considered a minor by law—are immature or incompetent in the relevant sense.

Mill's principle of individual freedom is often used to support claims that parents make against state intervention in the family, and it is the source of much conflict between family and state. The counterargument is based on the principle that some of the things parents do are harmful to children and that the state has legitimate authority to intervene in the case of harm to others.

2. The theory of utilitarianism says that one should always act to produce the greatest good for the greatest number. Thus moral rules and laws are determined, directly or indirectly, by the general interest. Individual liberties are protected in the "portions of a person's life which affect only himself." These include:

. . . first, the inward domain of consciousness; demanding liberty of conscience in the most comprehensive sense; liberty of thought and feeling; absolute freedom of opinion and sentiment. . . . Secondly, the principle requires liberty of tastes and pursuits; of framing the plan of our life to suit our own character . . . without impediment from our fellow-creatures, so long as what we do does not harm them, even though they should think our conduct foolish, perverse, or wrong.

When it comes to actions that affect others, then society may interfere, either by legal penalties or by "general disapprobation," that is, social disapproval. Governments may prohibit or require certain actions, based on harm or benefit to others in society.

Mill is aware, however, of the danger of this general policy, and he warns against what he terms the tyranny of the majority, the possibility that those in the majority may force their opinions on others.

> Protection . . . against the tyranny of the magistrate is not
> enough; there needs protection also against the tyranny of the
> prevailing opinion and feeling, against the tendency of society
> to impose . . . its own ideas and practices as rules of conduct
> on those who dissent from them.

Oppression of minorities is wrong, according to Mill, because it violates the
principle of individual freedom and also because the free expression of opinion
is necessary for achieving and appreciating truth.

Some of the most interesting and perplexing conflicts between parents,
children, and states arise when parents subscribe to minority beliefs and prac-
tises, such as religious or cultural patterns out of the mainstream, and want to
bring their children up accordingly, because majority opinion is that this type
of upbringing is harmful to children. How should the balance be struck between
differing views about children's best interests?

The Incompetency Argument

Mill does not try to defend his distinction between adults and children,
which is the foundation of denying liberty to children, but other philosophers
have developed a number of versions of what may be called the argument
from incompetency. One of the most picturesque is stated by John Locke
(1632–1704):

> The Freedom then of Man and Liberty of acting according
> to his own Will, is grounded on his having Reason. . . . To
> turn him loose to an unrestrain'd Liberty, before he has
> Reason to guide him is . . . to thrust him out amongst Brutes,
> and abandon him to a state as wretched, and as much beneath
> that of a Man, as theirs. This is that which puts the Authority
> into the Parents hands to govern the Minority of their
> children.

Jeremy Bentham (1748–1832) also draws out what he sees as some of the
reasons why children should be under the authority and protection of adults.

> The feebleness of infancy demands a continual protection.
> The complete development of its physical power takes many
> years; that of its intellectual faculties is still lower . . . Too
> sensitive to present impulses, too negligent of the future, such
> a being must be kept under an authority more immediate than
> that of the laws . . .

A fuller version of the incompetency argument might read like this: In order
to exercise liberty, one must have autonomy—that is, the ability to make
decisions by oneself—and those who exercise autonomy must fulfill two conditions: they must have relevant knowledge and not act out of ignorance, and
their decisions must be voluntary and not coerced. However, the argument
continues, children lack knowledge, and this can be seen in several ways. The
influential psychologists Jean Piaget (1896–1980) and Lawrence Kohlberg

(1927–1988) show, based on empirical research, that cognitive abilities develop in chronological stages, and only after the age of 12 or so are children capable of abstract, logical thinking. Children also lack what Aristotle calls practical reason: Because of limited experience, even if they know abstract principles of morality or prudence, they are not good at seeing how it applies to themselves, and without experience one cannot predict the consequences of one's actions. In addition, it can be argued that children, in general, do not know their own interests, may confuse what they want with what they need, and thus lack the important characteristic on which Mill rests his theory of liberty for adults.

It is also said that children also lack independence or voluntariness in their actions. They are strongly influenced by their parents and teachers, and, for older children, by their peers. In their eagerness to please others on whom they are physically and psychologically dependent, their actions are not "their own" in the fullest sense. Some also say that children tend to be victims of their passions, choosing immediate gratification and finding it difficult to resist temptation. While all of these failings can also be failings of some adults, these characteristics are truer of children as a class than of adults as a class.

One these grounds, then, it is argued that children are incompetent. They will choose badly and they will harm themselves. Therefore, they should not have autonomy or liberty rights.

There are ways to challenge the incompetency argument, however, and those who argue in favor of more rights for children often deny some parts of the argument. First, of course, it is necessary to distinguish infants and young children from school-age children and both of these groups from adolescents. Many theorists accept some form of Piaget's developmental theory and assign greater rights to older children and teens as they increase in cognitive skills and experience.

A different argument is that knowledge is task-specific: A child may be incompetent about some things but not about others, depending especially on experience. Thus, for example, a child raised in the country may know about the dangers of snakebites or hypothermia but not about crossing busy streets, which a city child knows. Thus some children should be allowed to decide about certain things but not about others.

Of course, one can raise doubts about whether anyone, child or adult, ever has true voluntariness. Since all people are socialized by parents and community, they tend to adopt the values they are taught, or at least they are limited to choosing among those values with which they have some familiarity. Furthermore, everyone has passions and thus is influenced by them, so either no one ever acts voluntarily or else children act with as much or as little voluntariness as adults.

If the incompetency of children is successfully challenged, then the door is open for according them more rights. The more children, or at least older children and adolescents, are perceived to be like adults, the less justified are the measures that are designed to protect them, but which in reality function as restrictions on their liberty.

Suggested Readings

Aiken, William, and Hugh LaFollette, eds. *Whose Child? Children's Rights, Parental Authority, and the State* (Totowa, N.J.: Rowman and Littlefield, 1980).

Archard, David. *Children: Rights and Childhood* (London: Routledge, 1993).

Blustein, Jeffrey. *Parents and Children* (New York: Oxford Univ. Press, 1982).

Cafagna, Albert C., Richard T. Peterson, and Craig A. Staudenbauer, eds. *Philosophy, Children, and the Family* (New York: Plenum, 1982).

Cohen, Howard. *Equal Rights for Children* (Totowa, N.J.: Rowman and Littlefield, 1980).

Guggenheim, Alan, and Martin Sussman. *The Rights of Young People* (Toronto: Bantam Books, 1985).

Houlgate, Laurence D. *The Child and the State: A Normative Theory of Juvenile Rights* (Baltimore: Johns Hopkins, 1980).

Koocher, Gerald P., and Patricia Keith-Spiegel. *Children, Ethics, and the Law* (Lincoln: University of Nebraska, 1990).

O'Neil, Onora, and William Ruddick, eds. *Having Children: Philosophical and Legal Reflections on Parenthood* (New York: Oxford Univ. Press, 1979).

Purdy, Laura. *In Their Best Interest? The Case Against Equal Rights for Children* (Ithaca: Cornell, 1992).

Scarre, Geoffrey, ed. *Children, Parents, and Politics* (Cambridge: Cambridge Univ. Press, 1989).

Some Theoretical Issues

Cases for Discussion

Curfew Laws

In November 1990, the city of Atlanta, Georgia, enacted a curfew law prohibiting anyone under the age of 17 from being out after 11 P.M. on weeknights or midnight on weekends unless they had work, school obligations, or parental permission. Dallas, Texas, enacted a similar law, adding a fine of up to $500 to be levied on parents or proprietors of businesses who allowed teens to break the curfew. Skeptics doubt that curfews lessen street crime, but Atlanta's records show that aggravated assaults dropped 14 percent for the first five months of 1991 compared to the same period for the previous year. The American Civil Liberties Union is appealing the curfew laws, claiming that Supreme Court rulings have upheld the right of teens to "hang out."

The usual justification for restrictions on minors is that it is for the protection of those too young to protect themselves. In the case of curfew laws, however, the purpose appears to be primarily to protect society and only incidentally to protect the minors who are restricted.

Prior restraint—that is, restrictions on people before they have actually committed any crime—is defensible when there is evidence of clear and present danger to self or others. Thus, for example, psychiatrists must report to police a patient who has made threats against specific victims. Curfew laws, however, differ from this principle in that they apply not to particular individuals on the basis of clear evidence of danger to others, but to a whole group of people, based solely on age. Shouldn't children, like adults, be treated as innocent until it can be shown that they have broken a law? Shouldn't children have some, or all, of the legal rights that adults have?

Adult Trials for Juveniles

Cameron Kocher is a nine year old accused of murdering a seven-year-old girl. Because of the unusually serious nature of the offense, controversy arose about moving the trial from juvenile court to criminal court, where the boy would be tried as an adult. Advocates of a "get tough" policy think that if children are capable of committing adult crimes, they should be punished as adults. Those who defend keeping all minors within the juvenile court system emphasize the possibility of rehabilitation and treatment.

The juvenile court system, established in 1899, has come under serious criticism in recent decades. Originally established to focus on education and reform, not just punishment, the motives behind the establishment of special procedures for children are protectionist and paternalistic: Judges are allowed broad discretion in deciding the fate of the children who appear before them, invoking the standard of the best interest of the child. Children are called juvenile delinquents, not criminals, and they may be sent to training schools or detention centers but generally not to jails or prisons. Children are given a "second chance" in that in many states arrest and other records are sealed and may not be used for any purpose once the offender reaches the age of 18 or 21.

Not all of the provisions of juvenile court, however, work to the benefit of minors. Rules of evidence are informal, jury trials are typically not available, and behaviors that are not considered criminal or illegal for adults can be defined as such for minors. Such behaviors are referred to as status offenses. For example, children can be brought before juvenile court for such things as "wayward" behavior, meaning not obeying their parents. Because these provisions seem unfair to children, critics have called for changes in the system so that minors will be treated more like adults.

Yet children are not adults, and it seems bizarre to many to think of trying a nine year old in adult court. Did he really know what he was doing? Can he understand legal concepts such as self-incrimination? And, while older teens may be enough like adults to warrant their inclusion in adult courts, are the formal procedures of law courts appropriate for young children? Won't it distort the caring relationship that adults should have with children to put them into a system designed so that one party is the adversary, almost an enemy, of the other?

The Issues

1. One way that society places restrictions on individuals is by establishing laws—for example, requiring payment of taxes or limiting how fast one may drive. However, there are constitutional guarantees of freedoms, which limit the kinds of laws that can be established. Thus constitutional guarantees, say, freedom of speech, rest on certain moral claims, especially on the principle that individuals should be free to do what they want as long as they do not harm others.

It is not clear, however, that constitutional guarantees of freedom apply to children. Laws that distinguish minors from adults, such as child labor laws and laws that support the placing of children under the guardianship of their parents or other adults, demonstrate that society generally does not accord these rights to children. It took a special Supreme Court decision, *In re Gault* in 1967, to interpret the Constitution in favor of minors, determining that rights of due process should apply to juveniles. Only then were minors guaranteed the right to have a lawyer, not to incriminate themselves, and to cross-examine their accusers.

Challenges to social policies that restrict children more than adults raise a more general question about children's rights. Because of the connection between laws and morality, there are two parts to this important question. As a practical matter, one can ask: Should children have legal rights? This question is answered by trying to answer a more basic question: Do children have moral rights? Do they have moral claims—that is, natural rights or human rights—that should be fulfilled by legislating them as legal rights?

2. Those who are concerned about children—both those who want special protections for children and those who want greater liberties for children—phrase their concerns in terms of rights. Protectionists say that children have the right to be taken care of in special ways, and liberationists say that children have the right to greater freedom to choose for themselves. However, simply talking about rights implies certain ways of characterizing relationships between individuals, seeing people more like antagonists in a court of law than partners in cooperative activities. This has led some philosophers to raise a very basic philosophical question: Is the language of rights appropriate for talking about children? Is there a better theoretical framework to use in talking about the relationship between children, parents, and the state?

The Arguments

Against the Language of Rights

One of the great values in life, it is claimed by the contemporary philosopher Ferdinand Shoeman and others, lies in the intimate relationships that exist between adults and children, notably within a family. This kind of relationship is possible, however, only if it is free of outside interference and intrusion. If the adult-child relationship is characterized in terms of rights that one may claim against the other, then the door is open to state intrusion in order to ensure compliance with these rights. Thus the positive value of intimate relationships is threatened by applying the language of rights to children.

A similar argument stresses that rights language is necessary and appropriate when adjudicating conflicts between strangers, as in the law courts, but it works by setting the parties up as adversaries. The adult role, however, should be as parent or parent substitute, guiding, educating, helping, and supporting the child. This role is perverted, then, by applying a model of rights.

A further argument tries to show that characterizing the adult-child relationship in terms of rights is too narrow. Whereas very specific claims of rights can be made by or on behalf of a child against specific adults for certain things—for example, claims to financial support for the necessities of life—there are more general obligations that cannot be stated as specific rights, such as everyone's duty to be kind to children.

For Rights Language

If it is denied that children have rights, it is feared that parents or the state can do anything they want to children without being accused of violating their rights. If rights language cannot be applied to children, then the least powerful members of society are open to oppression without any recourse. Without rights, they cannot claim—on either moral or legal grounds—that anything is due to them. The language of rights makes possible claims to liberty or protection for individuals, however weak a position in society they occupy.

The language of rights is also a powerful political tool. It is one thing to exhort people to do more for children, but like appeals to charity, they can be ignored with relatively little guilt. Claims based on rights, however, cannot be set aside so easily, and if they are recognized as legal rights, they will be strengthened by state enforcement. Thus the language of rights may be indispensable in fighting against such things as curfew laws.

Even if one could always assume harmony, love, and altruism toward children, some say there is reason to assign rights to them, for recognizing someone as having rights is a way of showing respect. To be without rights is to be a nonperson, to be lower on the scale of moral importance.

For an Alternative Theory

Is there a way to recognize and respect children as persons without distorting the whole picture of adult-child relationships into nothing more than a kind of wary coexistence?

Some new feminist theories are emerging as alternatives to the language of rights. Many are influenced by the work of psychologist Carol Gilligan, who identifies a "feminine voice" that emphasizes the value of relationships and connection rather than the autonomy and independence of single individuals. While the readings in this section raise critical questions about the language of rights and take some steps toward developing alternative theories, it must be remembered that this approach is fairly recent and the overwhelming majority of the literature on children, even within the last ten years, has been developed in the context of the language of rights. Thus almost all of the readings in this book reflect a theory of rights.

The Readings

"The Philosopher's Child," Judith Hughes, Professor of Philosophy and International Women's Studies, University of Newcastle upon Tyne, England.

Hughes sets the stage by considering why society does not give children the same rights as adults. She does not accept the argument from incompetency, saying that it is not lack of rationality that distinguishes children from adults. Instead, she attributes to society a protectionist attitude, saying that society does not acknowledge children as autonomous persons, hoping thereby to protect them from the burden of responsibility for their own decisions.

"Children's Rights and Children's Lives," Onora O'Neill, Philosopher and Principal, Newnham College, Cambridge, England.

O'Neill addresses the appropriateness of using the language of rights in talking about children. She rejects rights language (despite her title) and proposes focusing on the obligations adults have to children rather than the rights children may have. She argues that this allows a broader scope, including not only perfect obligations that specify what is owed to whom and by whom, but also imperfect obligations, such as the duty to be kind to children. Imperfect obligations are general duties applying to everyone but may be fulfilled in different ways.

"Rights for the Next Generation: A Feminist Approach to Children's Rights," Martha Minow, Professor of Law, Harvard University.

Minow discusses the legal treatment of children and claims that there are many inconsistencies, which she attributes to overemphasis on questions of competency and rights. As an alternative to the language of rights, she develops a feminist analysis, suggesting changes in the juvenile court system that would serve to strengthen children's relationships with parents and community, not pit one against the other in an adversarial way.

The Philosopher's Child

Judith Hughes

Some of Our Children Are Missing

Children have served philosophy very well. That is the first thing which anyone surveying the literature would notice. Along with a selection from a list including women, animals, madmen, foreigners, slaves, patients and imbeciles, children have served in that great class of beings, the "not-men," in contrast with which male philosophers have defined and valued themselves. Unlike the others who appear and disappear as fashion and progress dictate, children occupy a permanent place in the list partly because of their continuing presence as a potential sub-class, partly because they have never protested and mainly because it is assumed that in favourable circumstances they will become men and therefore require attention. They have received it in the shape of detailed educational theory carefully worked out to see them through the maturation process from infancy to adulthood. Generations of philosophers have documented this process. Perhaps the best known version is Shakespeare's seven ages of man which is a poetic statement of what had already been received wisdom for centuries and was to remain so for centuries to come. Education was to guide the infant through the transition to manhood including such stages as childhood, boyhood and youth. That is the second thing to notice; the philosopher's children are boys. The fact that at least half of the world's children would not actually go through this process beyond the first two stages is conveniently forgotten or ignored and, no doubt, the reasons for this were largely social. But the neglect of girl children through the centuries of theorising is more than a social injustice, though many might think this real and bad enough.

Education has an end. Although it is fashionable to talk about its value "for its own sake," what prompts the theorising is the strong and well-founded belief that the experiences of childhood affect the kind of adult which the child turns out to be. Where the end is person- rather than role-oriented—that is, where the end is the development of the human mind and spirit rather than the production of, say, information technologists—then education is valued in relation to some conception of worthwhile human existence which it is meant to serve. Such an ideal does not stand isolated from the practices which strive towards it but interacts with those practices, helps to construct them, and is in turn constructed by them.

The great philosophers have always produced such a person-oriented account at least for those whose education was thought to matter. Education has been

From *Feminist Perspectives in Philosophy*, Morwenna Griffiths and Margaret Whitford, ed., Indiana University Press, Bloomington and Indianapolis, 1988, 72–89. Copyright 1988. Reprinted by permission of the publisher.

directed at the production of the rational, the free, the independent of mind, the dignified, in short, the autonomous human being. Yet because the philosopher's adult has traditionally been male, his children boy children, and his educational programmes designed to facilitate the transition between them, the ideal of the fully human person has been masculinised to the point where otherwise thoughtful and sometimes good and wise men have unashamedly admitted that this defining ideal is not applicable to half the species. Rationality turns into narrow intellectualism, freedom into licence, independence into isolationism, dignity into selfish pride; the autonomous human being turns out to be no more than a social atom after all.

The degeneration occurs, not because men are congenitally or even incorrigibly narrow, libertine, isolated or selfish, but because in defining themselves as autonomous beings in opposition to other human beings they have had to seek what separates them as a group from others. It is a curiously paradoxical foundation upon which to build a theory of autonomy. Moral autonomy is concerned with individuals not with groups; a conception of autonomy which depends upon group membership displays its own contradiction.

This paper is partly about the rejection of certain accounts of autonomy though not with the rejection of the ideal of autonomy itself. It is also about children.

Women Philosophers and Girl Children

Why should women in general and women philosophers in particular be specially interested in the nature and status of children? There are, of course, the familiar and obvious reasons connected with women's traditional role in child-rearing but there are less obvious reasons too. When philosophers dismiss women as "not-men" they frequently do more than simply lump them together with children or lunatics. Explicitly or implicitly the suggestion is that women *are* children or lunatics or whichever other company they keep. It would be well to know just what this entails. Schopenhauer said that women remain big children all their lives; it would be interesting to know what he thought children were like. A common result of this is that when the philosophers deny autonomy to women, they do so for the same sorts of reason that they deny it to children and cite lack of rationality, capriciousness and vulnerability among their characteristics. We can do more than to reject such descriptions of ourselves; we can ask further questions: are children like this? is this why children are not autonomous?

Again, women well know what it is like to be treated as children and they find it offensive. It would therefore be reasonable to consider whether children find it offensive to be treated like children. Is being treated as a child an intrinsically humiliating and self-denying experience? What is it to be treated as a child? Women philosophers are in a special position to consider such questions for in the image of the philosopher's child they see themselves. It is no accident that the liberation of women, such as it is, should form part of a wider movement of liberation in general; liberation for one part of the "not-men" is bound to have a knock-on effect when your fellow groups are sometimes quite literally identified with you.

The assumption that all groups in the "not-men" class are identical with each other is so firmly rooted that, as we shall see in the fourth section, it is readily assumed even by modern libertarian thinkers that showing that, for example, some ground for distinguishing between men and women is false or irrelevant, immediately commits us to the view that the same ground is irrelevant in distinguishing men from children. "That's what they used to say about women" is not a proof that saying it about a child is false. But it should make us very suspicious. That when women are given the vote it follows that children should be given it too is no argument at all, but a version of it occurs in modern debates over the justice or injustice of Mill's famous disclaimer in his essay *On Liberty*. Having denied that we may ever legitimately interfere with the liberty of another except on the grounds of self-protection, Mill (1910) asserts:

> this principle is meant to apply only to human beings in the maturity of their faculties. We are not speaking of children or of young persons below the age which the law may fix as that of manhood or womanhood. Those who are still in a state to require being taken care of by others must be protected against their own actions as well as against external injury. (p. 73)

This view, as we shall see, has been attacked on the grounds that it rests on the false assumption that the distinction between adults and children is identical with the distinction between rational and non-rational beings. The attacks are based on empirical observation; most women and older children are actually quite as rational as most men while some men are actually less rational. If we agree that in that case women should be embraced by the liberty principle then so should children. I shall suggest that this does not follow because rationality is not in fact the grounds for the distinction in the first place.

Partly to redress the balance and partly because talking about "children" covers such a wide range of potential images, I shall try to keep before my mind an ordinary 10-year-old of our society. She is the child of this paper unless I indicate otherwise. Throughout we should ask ourselves, does *this* (whatever is being said) apply to *her*? First of all, let us remind ourselves of the traditional picture of children drawn for us by some great philosophers of the past. One thing they are all quite sure about is that children are not like adults; in particular they agree that children lack some capacity for rational thought which adults have.

Now We Are 6—or 10—or 18 . . .

> the slave has absolutely no deliberative faculty; the woman has but its authority is imperfect; so has the child, but in this case it is immature. (Aristotle, 1959, 1260A)

> Children . . . are not endued with Reason at all, till they have attained the use of speech but are called Reasonable Creatures for the possibility apparent of having the use of Reason in time to come. (Hobbes, 1914, p. 21)

[Children] . . . love to be treated as Rational Creatures sooner than is imagined . . . [by which] . . . I mean, that you should make them sensible by the Mildness of your carriage, and the composure even in your correction of them, that what you do is reasonable in you and useful and necessary for them. (Locke, 1968, p. 181)

In training for youth, the child must be given reasons; in the training of the infant for childhood this cannot be done. Young children ought merely to have things shown to them as they are, or they get puzzled and ask question after question. But as we approach the age of youth reason appears. At what age ought the education for youth to begin? Roughly at the age of ten years, when by nature the child enters the stage of youth and begins to reflect . . . The youth . . . is capable of having principles; his religious and moral ideas can be cultivated, and he is able to attend to his own refinement. (Kant, 1930, pp. 250–1)

If a society lets any considerable number of its members grow up mere children, incapable of being acted on by rational consideration of distant motives, society has itself to blame for the consequences. (Mill, 1910, p. 139)

What are the philosophers' children like? They have an "immature" deliberative faculty (Aristotle), are not "endued with Reason" (Hobbes), until roughly the age of 10 (Kant) and are "incapable of being acted upon by rational consideration of distant motives" (Mill). But they are not completely lost causes. The immature deliberative faculty will mature; children have the "possibility apparent" of turning into rational beings (Hobbes); they love to be treated as though they were rational though they are not so yet (Locke); you can give the prerational child reasons for acting in certain ways and he will turn into the youth who is capable of having principles (Kant). Until the time when these things happen then Mill's disclaimer comes into operation. Children must be taken care of by others and protected from external injury and against their own actions.

The traditional view is encapsulated in the claim that children are not autonomous; that is, on a standard interpretation, they lack the capacity to act rationally in pursuit of their own self-chosen goals. It is then a matter of preference whether you say that they cannot choose the goals or that they cannot form strategies to achieve them or both. In either case, the political implication is that denying rights to children is entirely justified, and there the matter rests. In all this, there are perhaps a couple of things which look plausible when we compare the philosopher's child with our mental picture; Aristotle's observation that children are immature and Mill's suggestion that they might need protection. Beyond that, the similarities seem remote.

There is obviously something wrong with a portrayal of children as totally lacking in reason until they leap out of bed on their tenth birthday announcing that they are now able to act on principle. Apart from being false, such an account leaves no room in our thinking about children for things like teaching and learning, or development in understanding and character and all those other concepts which refer to processes and not to states. The tension between these theoretical views of children as non-rational, non-autonomous beings and the practical knowledge of real children is evident in those quotations from Hobbes and Locke and Kant and Mill.

Children, according to Hobbes, have the "possibility apparent" of becoming reasonable. In what does the possibility consist? Hobbes is not using an inductive argument here; the "possibility apparent" is not an inductive argument from observations about past children but is meant to refer to some discernible feature of present ones. But what? Hobbes does not tell us, but whatever it is it had better be something which a monkey does not have. It is not language since Hobbes is here talking about the prelinguistic child. Perhaps it consists in the ability to respond intelligently to the language of others. But then, either Hobbes has failed to distinguish the child from at least the higher and domesticated animals or the force of "intelligently" must be explained in such a way as to exclude animals. In any case, if such a qualification is called for it is hard to see how a creature with no rationality at all could possess it.

Locke's remarks are just as puzzling. Children are definitely not rational but love to be treated as if they were. How is this possible? Apparently they like having things explained to them without understanding either the explanation or even what an explanation is. Perhaps he just means that they like the sound of my voice? Well, maybe they do, but making any old noises is clearly not sufficient to enter the rationality stakes; I must at least *say* something. Is it just that I talk to them that they love? Maybe, but I can also, if I like, talk to my car, but yelling at it in the approved Basil Fawlty manner is hardly treating it as rational. Lockean children have the added amazing ability to recognise reason in you without possessing any themselves, while Kantian kids, two stages back from rationality, have the disconcerting habit of getting puzzled and asking questions.

Mill's minors are a little more complicated. Part of the time he sees them in the familiar way as creatures who lack rationality to at least some degree. But in the disclaimer his children need above all to be protected from the ghastly consequences of their own actions. Their problem seems to be not one of the inability to choose goals or to form strategies for achieving them, but an incorrigible propensity to choose the wrong ones and an awesome efficiency in achieving them unless adults intervene.

All in all, it is a pretty unconvincing picture. If you say that children are completely non-rational then you have to account for the fact that they become rational, and to do that it appears from these examples that you have to assume that they already are. If, on the other hand, you allow rationality to children, then you cannot use their lack of it as a criterion to distinguish them from adults. Hobbes *et al.* are not aware of the unreality of their original pictures which is why, often in the same sentence, they produce these contradictions. The one thing they do not do is to re-examine the original for the tell-tale signs of forgery.

Illegitimate Inferences

The recognition that children cannot simply be written off in the rationality stakes and cannot therefore be denied autonomy on this account has led some writers to conclude that they cannot, therefore, be denied it on any account. We should notice that this view is not just a flight of fancy from the loony left, the pederast lobby or children themselves. It is also to be found in stronger or weaker versions of more cautious academic thought.

In *Escape from Childhood* (1974), John Holt notes that children are, in fact, capable of a great deal more than modern society allows them to be. He sees childhood as a fairly modern invention designed to fit adult rather than children's needs, and an oppressive invention at that. He suggests that children should be given a comprehensive range of civil and legal rights including the right to vote, to manage their own financial affairs, to direct and manage their own education and to control their own sex lives and

> **to make and enter into, on a basis of mutual consent, quasi-familial relationships outside one's immediate family—i.e. the right to seek and choose guardians other than one's own parents and to be legally dependent on them. (Holt, 1974, p. 16)**

This is also the view put forward by John Harris, though in less specific terms. Like Holt, Harris believes that the so-called incompetence of children is an adult invention imposed on children for adults' convenience. He makes a firm proposal that the age of majority should be gradually reduced to 10 years, and remarks:

> **We must remember that to deny someone control of their own lives is to offer them a most profound insult, not to mention the injury which the frustration of their wishes and the setting at naught of their own plans for themselves will add. Perhaps we should conduct annual examinations from an early age to be sure that we do as little of this sort of damage as possible? (Harris, 1982, p. 49)**

Now Holt and Harris both have many wise, enlightened and humane observations to make about some of the injustices which we inflict upon children, but as these remarks show, putting them right without inflicting equally grave injustice is no easy matter. Both of them appear to suffer from a form of mental myopia in imagining the consequences of such proposals, and I am not here referring only to Mill-type consequences of harm brought about by unwise decisions.

What, we may ask Holt, happens to the child who, dissatisfied at home, seeks in vain for guardians who would suit him? What if no one wants him? Our papers are currently full of "hard-to-place" children in local authority care advertising for foster or adoptive parents. In such a situation the skilled care of social workers is crucial to ensuring that an unwanted by-product of success for some children is not the total destruction of self-esteem for others. What, we may ask Harris, happens to the child who repeatedly fails his annual examination? To impose such a test on children would be a particularly invidious way of discriminating against them, unless Harris has in mind that we should all undergo such examination. He might then be open to bitter objections from many adults. These two suggestions, far from being enlightened liberation of all children, are actually oppression of a deeply damaging kind to at least some, and Harris's suggestion contains a capacity criterion in disguise.

In any case, it would be dishonest to pretend that Mill-type consequences are not relevant here. Suppose Holt's 6-year-old does opt out of school? What happens to her then? What happens if her father is unwilling or unable to stay at home with her? Is it any better to oblige her to go abseiling or butterfly-catching instead? However much she may enjoy such pursuits, there will be times when she would actually rather wander the streets unaccompanied. Given that Holt is presumably not volunteering himself to take care of her, who will? His view that letting children run in and out of busy airports smartly avoiding the traffic is perfectly reasonable depends upon a conception of a child which is far narrower than even the sex divide. Holt's child is actually the Artful Dodger; mercifully, not all children are.

There are other difficulties too. It is not clear whether or not Harris thinks that children of 10 should be obliged to take on full political status whether or not they want to, but Holt clearly does not. He proposes that "the rights, privileges, duties, responsibilities of adult citizens be made available to any young person, of whatever age, who wants to make use of them" (Holt, 1974, p. 15). If Holt thinks that this proposal would remove an arbitrary boundary line between adults and children, then he is mistaken.

The point about an adult citizen is that he has these rights, privileges, duties and responsibilities whether or not he wants them. He may not exercise his rights or he may shirk his duties, but he cannot forgo them. They are not just *available* to him, they are his. That is what being a citizen involves. Rights and privileges do not pose any particular problems in the case of children. Holt can and does believe that children should have them as adults do, and then leaves it up to the child to decide whether or not to exercise them. But the same cannot be said for duties and responsibilities. Failure to exercise one's rights may be morally neutral; failure to carry out one's duties is not. It would be perfectly possible to give the rights to children without imposing the duties on them, the one does not entail the other, but we would then still be distin-guishing between adults and children as citizens. Children still would not have full political status. Duties and responsibilities are not merely *available* to a citizen; they are an integral part of being a citizen. Holt does not want children to be obliged to take on any of these responsibilities and he manages to make his point by concentrating solely on the rights so that he can remark:

> I do not say, either, that these rights and duties should be tied into one package, that if a young person wants to assume any of them, he must assume them all. He should be able to pick and choose. (Holt, 1974, p. 16)

If he can "pick and choose," I suggest, he is not a citizen, he does not have full political status and he is quite distinguishable on these grounds alone from the adults around him who do not have this option.

Holt and Harris both, in the end, face the same problem. They attack the status quo by pointing out that the reasons given for denying rights to children are *bad* reasons, and then explicitly or implicitly deny them duties for no reason at all. Whatever else such a strategy may achieve, it certainly does not manage to produce a situation in which children are politically indistinguishable from adults and it rests on premises which, unless they can be defended, gain nothing for any defence to the charge of arbitrariness.

When in Doubt, Go Back to Aristotle

The trouble with all the views which we have looked at is that they tie the notion of autonomy firmly and solely to that of knowledge interpreted in either a broad or narrow sense.[1] That it is firmly tied must be correct; the inhabitants of Brave New World are not autonomous precisely because they are denied access to relevant information. Relevant knowledge is a precondition of autonomy but it is not synonymous with it.[2]

Aristotle said something very interesting in that extract from the *Politics* which I quoted earlier; he said that women have a deliberative faculty but that it lacks full authority. What did he mean?

What he did not mean is that women lack rationality; they can and do deliberate. At first sight what he seems to be saying is simply that no one is going to take any notice of the conclusions which a rational woman reaches after deliberation. On further reflection, I think this is exactly what he is saying, and its significance is immense. His view is that the judgements which women make have no standing. Keeping to the domestic front for the moment, what this means is that the conclusions which women reach, not matter how carefully and intelligently they are worked out, can never have the status of decisions. You cannot decide, though you may desire, to divorce your husband if the law does not allow; you cannot order the wine if only his signature makes the order legitimate. And you inability to decide or to order has nothing to do with your mental powers. But Aristotle is not just making a sociological point about what is and is not permitted to women in his society. His remark goes deeper than that. It refers not to power but to authority, and what I think he means is that although a woman can make good and wise judgements, she cannot be the arbiter of that goodness or wisdom. For that she needs the ratification of men, and that is enough to conclude that her judgements lack authority. Now that is quite different from saying that women always make *bad* judgements, that is to say, that they suffer from some deficiency of rationality. Aristotle only produces spurious suggestions about a woman's incapacity to think or to stick to principles when he is obliged to say something about *why* their judgements lack authority. It then looks as though the argument runs:

(1) Women lack some moral or cognitive capacity
therefore (2) Women (must) lack authority.

In truth this version is the argument on its head; its real form is:

(1) Women lack authority
therefore (2) Women (must) lack some moral or cognitive capacity.

The important point here is that Aristotle's women are not autonomous, not because they lack abilities or capacities but because they lack authority; that is, their right to make decisions, to speak for themselves is not acknowledged. This acknowledgement is absolutely essential, for without it no mental act which they perform, however well, will count as a decision at all.

The point I am making here is based on an observation by Stanley Cavell (1979, p. 460) and repeated by him in many contexts: "a human being could not fail to know, confronting me, that I am a human being." Why not? Because to see someone is to see them as a human being and to see them as a human being is to acknowledge them as such. This acknowledgement is not derived from a prior knowledge of facts, rather it is a precondition of there being any facts. We do not, on the Cavell model, first discover certain truths about an object and then conclude that it is a person; we first acknowledge the person and only inquire into facts later if necessary. The point was put graphically by my colleague, Ian Ground. Faced with a row of objects we do not, he said, lampooning Wittgenstein, perform appropriately by pointing to one after the other saying that's a tree, that's a tree, that's a man, that's a tree. Rather we will say (pointing) that's a tree, (pointing) that's a tree, (waving) hello! (pointing) that's a tree. What makes us *greet* the man is not an albeit swift chain of inference, it is his presence which commands the acknowledgement while the presence of the tree does no such thing. Of course, if the man is clearly carved from stone then pointing is in order, and if we subsequently discover that "he" is an inflatable rubber doll we are suitably embarrassed. But we are embarrassed because we got it wrong when usually we do not. In our viewing of the other we see ourselves being viewed; the recognition is mutual.

How then is it possible to withhold acknowledgement? Cavell's answer is that it is not. There is no way of seeing another human being except as another human being. In a poignant discussion of the hypothesis that Southern slave owners did not see their slaves as human beings he disagrees:

> When he wants to be served at table by a black hand, he would not be satisfied to be served by a black paw . . . Everything in his relation to his slaves shows that he treats them as more or less human—his humiliations of them, his disappointments, his jealousies, his fears, his punishments, his attachments. (Cavell, 1979, p. 376)

Treating people as if they were not people is not a possibility; to try to do so requires all the resources of evil which the human mind can muster, but it always breaks down.

What is possible is to treat people as more or less human. We can withhold acknowledgement from them on limited or selective fronts. This may not be downright evil, but in the absence of potential disbarments (like possibly being a rubber doll) it requires a considerable amount of bad faith. It is very *hard* to do. This is what Aristotle appears to do to his women. They are human, and are acknowledged to be, they can think but they are not to be acknowledged as authoritative, and if their presence demands such acknowledgement, they are bad women who should have been taught to hide or repress such demands. Rousseau's blueprint for the education of Sophie is directed at this end, and if it is truly successful, she will internalise the lesson until neither her behaviour nor her demeanour will demand the acknowledgement. Then she has been infantilised and she is no longer autonomous. But Rousseau's blueprint contains its own contradiction. If you need to teach people or compel them in some other way to repress their natural demand for acknowledgement as rational, competent, authoritative human beings then you have no answer to the charge of some malefaction between bad faith and dreadful wickedness.

Is this unfair to children? When we deny autonomy to our 10-year-old, are we too guilty of bad faith? What reason could we produce to allow that she may have the capacity to act autonomously while denying her the capacity-to-act-autonomously? Whatever it is we should first notice that while the capacity to act autonomously is construed as a psychological capacity, the capacity-to-act-autonomously is not. It is a social capacity which depends upon the acknowledgement of others. What we need to do is to show that withholding this acknowledgement is neither arbitrary nor unjust; we have to ask, does her being demand it.

Carrying the Can

To do this we need to consider another element in the picture of autonomy which was so meticulously side-stepped by Holt. That is, the matter of responsibility. In *Freedom and Resentment* (1974, p. 19) Strawson talks not of a child's emerging autonomy but of "the progressive emergence of the child as a responsible being." Responsibility is an aspect of autonomy to which lip-service is commonly paid but which takes a back seat in most discussions about children. I believe it to be central.

In his essay, "In Defense of Anarchism" (1970), R. P. Wolff does give responsibility a central place in his brief analysis of autonomy. He argues that freedom of choice makes a man responsible for his actions while the capacity to reason about those choices places him under a continuing obligation to *take* responsibility for those actions. To *take* responsibility is to accept the duty of deciding for oneself what is right. A man, Wolff argues, can forfeit his autonomy by not *taking* the responsibility on himself; by, for example, obeying commands blindly; but he cannot abnegate the responsibility which the possibility of choice confers upon him. Since being autonomous includes both freedom of choice and the capacity to reason about those choices, the impairment of either is a bar to autonomy.

Against this background he makes two remarks about children:

> It is quite appropriate that moral philosophers should group together children and madmen as beings not fully responsible for their actions, for as madmen are thought to lack freedom

of choice, so children do not yet possess the power of reason in a developed form. It is even just that we should assign a greater degree of responsibility to children, for madmen, by virtue of their lack of free will, are completely without responsibility, while children, insofar as they possess reason in a partially developed form, can be held responsible (i.e. can be required to take responsibility) to a corresponding degree. (Wolff, 1970, pp. 12–13)

All men refuse to take responsibility for their actions at some time or other during their lives, and some men so consistently shirk their duty that they present more the appearance of overgrown children than of adults. (Ibid., p. 14)

There is a striking similarity between Wolff's way of talking about children and the views we saw put forward by Hobbes, Locke and Kant. Wolff begins with the assurance that children are not rational and then immediately backpedals to say that actually they are, partially at least. Four paragraphs later where the second quotation appears, the child is not unable to take responsibility but is refusing to take it. She is not an incompetent but a degenerate. Having denied that she is incompetent, I am certainly not going to concede that the only alternative is to make her a degenerate; there must be another choice available.

What is missing from Wolff's analysis, though it is present in his terminology, is the recognition of the public face, the mutuality of responsibility. He talks of *assigning* responsibility to children, *holding* them responsible, *requiring* them to take responsibility and these are natural ways of speaking. What they do is to introduce a new element into the concept of responsibility which involves more than free will and reason; now a third party is present and is an active participant in the language game in which responsibility has a role. People are not only responsible *for* something, they are responsible *to* God, other individuals, society or themselves, and this latter Kantian notion is derived from the primary social context in which it makes sense for the concept of responsibility to be invoked. This is just what I was claiming for authority. To say either that someone acts authoritatively or that someone is responsible for his actions may depend upon the possibility of ascribing mental states or capacities but neither is merely a shorthand way of ascribing them. In the case of the fully autonomous person, authority and responsibility go hand in hand. The capacity-to-act-autonomously *is* the coming together of the two. If both or either is impaired then so is this capacity, and both depend upon the psychological capacities of the agent *plus* the recognition of other members of the moral and political community. This raises a difficulty.

Passing the Buck

The problem here seems to be this: am I saying that a child is responsible if and only if we declare her to be so, given that she knows what she is doing? This view has some historical clout. Given the knowledge it is always possible

to hold someone responsible for their actions. Children were still being impris-
oned and deported when Mill wrote that disclaimer. Is it then just a matter
of fashion, of the times in which we live? Not entirely; to begin with we might
take a pragmatic line in the light of new knowledge about the long-term effects
of such treatment on a child's subsequent development. We might argue that
while we *can* hold her responsible, the consequences of so doing turn out to
be unacceptable. But the horror which writers such as Dickens expressed at
the cruelty of his times was prompted by no such knowledge. Dickensian child
victims grow into upright citizens if they grow up at all. What Dickens saw
was what most of us see, the *inhumanity* of treating a child in certain ways.
In what does the inhumanity consist? Not just in harsh action; increased
concern about children is almost always part of a larger concern about people
in general, but when horrible things are happening to people it is not unusual
to focus on children and try special pleading on their behalf. This special
pleading is, no doubt, partly emotional but it might very well include reference
to children's lack of knowledge and understanding. Yet the inhumanity does
not consist in the ascription of certain cognitive states either. We may be quite
right to ascribe agency to a child for his acts. The inhumanity seems to lie in
allowing the full weight of responsibility to fall on the child. Responsibility is
not only about agency. "When we say a person is responsible for what he does
we mean not just that he was the agent . . . we also say that the act reflects
(back) on the agent," writes David Wood (1973, p. 191). How much reflecting
goes on depends upon the reflective capabilities of the child and also on the
strength and direction of the beam which we, the adults, determine.

Perhaps now we can take Mill's insight on board without opening ourselves
to the charge of arbitrariness. Mill wanted to protect children against the harm
which they might do themselves. The problem which was supposed to bring
liberal theory crashing to the ground was that we do not wish to justify interfering with adult liberties on these grounds. It may be that what we are protecting
children from is not so much the awful consequences of their ignorant decisions
but of the burden of responsibility for those decisions which children are not
yet ready to bear and which, for entirely non-political reasons, we cannot
choose to impose upon them. If giving or withholding this responsibility were
possible options in a one-person game, then this criterion would do nothing
to counter the charge of arbitrariness but I have already argued that they are
not and could not be. We can only *play* at ascribing responsibility outside this
mutual interaction; making the horse a senator, blaming the toy which the
child trips over are games which do not fool the horse or the toy.

Growing up, maturing, emerging into autonomy is the process of the child
taking from the adult more and more of the responsibility for those actions
which she does knowingly. Respect for the dignity and freedom of the child
consists in the recognition that the burden of responsibility shifts from the
adult to the child as she herself demands it. We leave unhappy teenagers who
"don't want to talk about it" alone; the tearful 5-year-old comes and dumps
the problem in your lap. In between, we say, we "play it by ear" and what we
listen for is the child's own claim to have its decisions treated as authoritative
and to be ready to bear the responsibility. This claim is not a conscious, spoken

claim; if it gets to that stage, we have already left it too late. The claim is implicit in the child's own social interactions and unless we are blind or acting in chronic bad faith we can do no other than acknowledge it. But neither can we impose it. Holding a child responsible is not the same as making her responsible; we may succeed in the former, without her cooperation we can never succeed in the latter.

Now it can still be objected that this is also true of adults and that I have still, therefore, failed to distinguish them from children. However, there is a difference. With children, the presupposition is that we take the responsibility until they show us that they want it; with adults we assume that they take the responsibility unless they show us that they don't. (We are surprised when the "man" turns out to be a robot.) That is what membership of the moral and political community is, and it is a serious business which deserves more attention than I can give here.[3] It is quite correct that children's application for membership should be taken seriously; once accepted there is no turning back, resignation is not an option.

To end, a word about voting. Voting is not just a matter of knowing how to put a cross on a piece of paper, nor of having a rough or even quite refined view of the policies of the major political parties. It also, in a democracy, involves being responsible to some degree for the society which we have. Maybe "I didn't vote Tory," but even that does not enable me to opt out of that responsibility entirely. Why else would I buy the sticker?

Let us ask our 10-year-old's mother if her daughter is ready to take that responsibility. What would she say? Perhaps that, yes, her child is intelligent and thoughtful and even knowledgeable; yes, she would be as competent as many adults in coming to sensible conclusions. Also, perhaps, that sometimes at night, she finds her crying for the starving of Africa or unable to sleep with the terror of the possibility of nuclear war or desperately seeking a denial of the reality of the horror of the Holocaust. Perhaps she would be angry if, by trying to impose responsibility on her daughter by giving her the vote, we were also taking from her the only comfort which she has, namely that when she is older she will change all that. Or perhaps she would just tell us that her child is not yet ready; she would be right.

Denying the vote to children is not based on some false assumption about 10-year-olds' political knowledge, nor to deny that they have interests, nor to protect them from the harm their votes might do. It is to take responsibility to ourselves for the way the world is. And that really does belong to us.

Notes

1. For accounts which include emphasis on experience and understanding see Scarre (1980) and Schrag (1977).
2. I am grateful to Michael Bavidge of the Department of Adult Education in the University of Newcastle for sharing his time and his ideas with me on the main point of this section.
3. Some interesting and illuminating remarks about what constitutes membership of a political society are to be found in Easton and Dennis (1969).

References

Aristotle (1959), *Politics,* Everyman series (London: Dent).

Axtell, James L. (ed.) (1968), *The Educational Writings of John Locke* (Cambridge: Cambridge University Press).

Cavell, Stanley (1979), *The Claim of Reason: Wittgenstein, Scepticism, Morality and Tragedy* (Oxford: Oxford University Press).

Easton, David and Dennis, Jack (1969), *Children in the Political System* (New York: McGraw-Hill).

Harris, John (1982), "The Political Status of Children," in Keith Graham (ed.), *Contemporary Political Philosophy* (Cambridge: Cambridge University Press), pp. 35-55.

Hobbes, Thomas (1914), *Leviathan,* Everyman series (London: Dent).

Holt, John (1974), *Escape from Childhood: The Needs and Rights of Children* (Harmondsworth: Penguin).

Kant, Immanuel (1930), *Lectures on Ethics,* trans. Louis Infield (London: Methuen).

Locke, John (1968), "Some Thoughts Concerning Education," in J. Axtell (ed.), pp. 111-325. (First published 1705).

Mill, John Stuart (1910), *On Liberty,* Everyman series (London: Dent).

Scarre, Geoffrey (1980), "Children and Paternalism," *Philosophy,* vol. 55, pp. 117-24.

Schrag, Francis (1977), "The Child in the Moral Order," *Philosophy,* vol. 52, pp. 167–77.

Strawson, P. F. (1974), *Freedom and Resentment and Other Essays* (London: Methuen).

Wolff, Robert Paul (1970), *In Defense of Anarchism* (New York: Harper Torchbooks).

Wood, David (1973), "Honesty," in Alan Montefiore (ed.), *Philosophy and Personal Relations* (London: Routledge & Kegan Paul), pp. 191–223.

Children's Rights and
Children's Lives*

Onora O'Neill

A friend who lived in New York could not see the sky from her windows. To discover the day's weather she had to peer at a glass-fronted building opposite, which offered a blurred reflection of part of the sky above her own building. I shall argue that when we take rights as fundamental in looking at ethical issues in children's lives we also get an indirect, partial and blurred picture. If no more direct, clearer and fuller account can be had, we will have to rely on any oblique and partial light which a theory of children's fundamental rights provides. If a clearer, more direct and more complete view of ethical aspects of children's lives is available, we would have good reason to prefer it.

We may begin with a reminder of the appeal and importance of thinking in terms of children's rights. Children easily become victims. If they had rights, redress would be possible. Rather than being powerless in the face of neglect, abuse, molestation and mere ignorance they (like other oppressed groups) would have legitimate and (in principle) enforceable claims against others. Although they (unlike many other oppressed groups) cannot claim their rights for themselves, this is no reason for denying them rights. Rather it is reason for setting up institutions that can monitor those who have children in their charge and intervene to enforce rights. The Aristotelian thought that justice is a relation between equals, so inappropriate in dealings with children, is to be rejected. The lives of children are no private matter, but a public concern which can be met by fostering children's rights.

Many aspects of this view seem to me plausible. I shall not query the thought that children's lives are a public concern or the aim of securing *positive* (legal, institutional, customary) rights for children. I shall, however, query whether children's positive rights are best grounded by appeals to fundamental (moral, natural, human) rights. This conclusion does not threaten children's positive rights, which may have other grounds; nor does it deny that children have fundamental rights. Rather I shall claim that children's fundamental rights are best grounded by embedding them in a wider account of fundamental

* It is a pleasure to thank the readers for this journal, as well as Hillel Steiner, Bob Goodin, Sara Ruddick, William Ruddick, Jerry Schneewind, Richard Lindley, and especially Sheldon Leader, for helpful and discerning comments.

obligations, which can also be used to justify positive rights and obligations. We can perhaps go *further* to secure the ethical basis of children's positive rights if we do *not* try to base them on claims about fundamental rights.

Theories of fundamental rights are most frequently queried from one or another consequentialist perspective. In those perspectives rights cannot be fundamental; if they were they would sometimes obstruct goals of maximizing benefit or of minimizing harm. Since the whole point of appeals to fundamental rights is to "trump" appeals to other considerations (e.g., welfare, convenience, happiness), there is no denying that insistence on respect for fundamental rights is only contingently and at times not closely connected to good results. This is as true of adult's as of children's rights and is independent of any particular account of fundamental rights. The only view of rights which can be assimilated into consequentialist thinking takes them not as ethically fundamental "trumps" (as appeal to statutory rights is in legal thought) but as rules of thumb for maximizing good results. All of this is well known.

The arguments against theories of fundamental rights offered here neither depend on nor support any form of consequentialism. The perspective from which I shall argue, like that chosen by some writers on rights, is *constructivist.*[1] It differs from those approaches because it offers (in the first instance) an account of the construction not of rights but of obligations. I shall develop a view of obligations that is (broadly) Kantian, indeed more strictly so than numerous accounts of rights that are labeled Kantian. This account of obligations offers, I believe, a fruitful alternative to theories of fundamental rights in all contexts. In the last section of the paper I hope to show that there are particularly strong reasons for adopting it in our thinking about children.

The strategy of argument will be simple. I shall first argue that theories that take rights as fundamental and those that take obligations as fundamental are not equivalent. The scope of the two sorts of theory differs and does so in ways that matter particularly for children. Then I shall argue that a constructivist account of obligations has *theoretical* advantages which constructivist accounts of rights lack, although rights-based approaches sometimes have *political* advantages which obligation-based approaches do not. Finally, I shall argue that in the specific case of children, taking rights as fundamental has political costs rather than advantages. I conclude that taking rights as fundamental in ethical deliberation about children has neither theoretical nor political advantages and suggest how we could obtain a more direct, perspicuous and complete view of ethical aspects of children's lives by taking obligations as fundamental.

Scope: The Problem of Imperfect Obligations

When we have an obligation, we are required to do or omit some type of action. Sometimes we are required to do or omit this type of action for *all* others. Sometimes we are required to do or omit it for *specified* others. Sometimes we are required to do or omit the action for *unspecified* others, but not for *all* others. Obligations of the first two sorts may be thought of as having corresponding rights. Obligations of the third sort cannot plausibly be thought of as having corresponding rights.

It may help to fix ideas if we have in mind examples of obligations of each sort; however, these examples are no more than provisional illustrations. If a fully developed theory of obligations suggests that any of these illustrations is spurious, the illustration can be replaced by an example of a genuine obligation.

First, we are obliged to refrain from abuse and molestation of children, whether or not they are specifically in our charge. This obligation is owed by all agents to *all* children: the right holders—all children—are specified. *Universal* obligations may be said to be *perfect* or complete obligations: they specify completely or perfectly not merely who is bound by the obligation but to whom the obligation is owed.[2] Universal obligations may also be *fundamental,* in the sense that they are not derived from any more basic ethical claim or relationship and do not depend on specific social or political arrangements or on prior acts of commitment. If a universal perfect obligation is fundamental, then the rights that correspond to it are also fundamental rights.

Second, those who have undertaken to care for specific children will have obligations to them, and those specifc children will have a right to care of an appropriate standard. Here too the obligation specifies completely or perfectly from whom performance is due and to whom performance is owed, and the obligation is a *perfect* obligation. However, it is not a universal obligation but one owed by specified agents to specified children, whose counterpart rights are special rights. Special rights depend on special relationships. Hence special obligations and rights are not fundamental: rather they are positive obligations and rights whose specific content depends on the specific social and political arrangements and the roles and commitments agents undertake. For example, the specific acts required to fulfill the obligations that teachers or parents may have to children in their charge depend on the specific definitions of these roles in a given society. Such roles and practices and their component obligations and rights are open to ethical criticism and justification in terms of fundamental obligations and rights.[3]

Third, we may have a fundamental obligation to be kind and considerate in dealing with children—to care for them—and to put ourselves out in ways that differ from those in which we must put ourselves out for adults. This obligation may bind all agents, but is not one that we owe either to all children (such an "obligation" could not be discharged) or merely to antecedently specified children. What it will take to discharge this fundamental obligation will differ with circumstances; these circumstances will in part be constituted by social and institutional arrangements that connect specific children to specific others. Fundamental obligations that are not universal (owed to all others) are, when considered in abstraction from social and institutional context, *incomplete* or *imperfect*. This is not just a matter of the indeterminacy of the act or omission enjoined by the principle of obligation, but more fundamentally of the fact that, so long as the recipients of the obligation are neither all others nor specified others, there are no right holders, and nobody can either claim or waive performance of any right. If there are any fundamental obligations that are imperfect in this sense, then there are some fundamental obligations to which no fundamental rights correspond.[4]

Once imperfect obligations are institutionalized, certain positive special obligations are established to which certain positive rights correspond. For example, one aspect of institutionalizing a fundamental obligation to care for children in particular social circumstances might be to assign social workers a positive obligation to monitor specific children at risk. The children so at risk would then acquire a corresponding positive right to be monitored by those social workers. However, the rights so institutionalized will not exhaust the content of a fundamental imperfect obligation. The obligations of roles such as parent or teacher or social worker are commonly taken to require more than meeting those rights which are institutionalized with the role.[5]

Although imperfect fundamental obligations lack corresponding rights, their fulfillment was not traditionally thought optional: the very term "imperfect obligation" tells us that. What is left optional by a fundamental imperfect obligation is selection not merely of a specific way of enacting the obligation but of those for whom the obligation is to be performed. Those who do only what the children they interact with have a (universal or special) right to will do less than they ought. They will fulfill their perfect but not their imperfect obligations. In particular parents or teachers who meet only their perfect obligations would fail as parents or teachers. They would not merely fail to be saintly or heroic parents or teachers, that is, omit supererogatory action. They would fail in much that we take to be straightforwardly obligatory for parents and teachers.

Provided the distinction drawn here between perfect and imperfect obligations is retained, various other distinctions are easily accommodated. Because perfect obligations require action for all or for specified others, they have correlative definite, assigned rights, which can be claimed or waived and are in principle enforceable—even in a state of nature. Imperfect fundamental obligations, whose performance is not owed to all or to specified others, do not entail assigned rights and so are not claimable or waiveable by right holders or enforceable in abstraction from an institutionalized context which allocates recipients to agents. Imperfect obligations can be enforced only when they are institutionalized in ways that specify *for whom* the obligation is to be performed, so defining who holds the counterpart institutional rights and can claim or waive them.

Contemporary ethical writing that is rights based has difficulty in capturing these distinctions. If rights are taken as the starting point of ethical debate, imperfect obligations will drop out of the picture because they lack corresponding rights. The omission would be unworrying if advocates of rights also provided a broader ethical theory which could ground imperfect obligations. Unfortunately, a broader approach to the grounding of obligations is impossible within certain approaches to fundamental rights and repudiated within others. Those who argue that there is an open-ended "right to liberty," so that any act which violates no other's rights is permissible, clearly leave no room for any obligations other than perfect obligations to respect others' rights. What they leave room for is in fact nothing more than the pursuit of individual preference, even if it is given a dignified gloss by being classified as an "exercise of the right to liberty" or as "pursuit of a conception of the good."

Those who repudiate an open-ended "right to liberty" and so could allow for imperfect obligations also surprisingly often deny that the space so provided is governed by any obligations.[6] Modern "deontological liberals" take pride in being agnostic about the good for man and argue that insofar as action is not required by respect for others' rights, it is legitimately devoted to pursuit of our varied subjective conceptions of the good, that is, to action that reflects individual preferences. Liberal theorists who allow space for imperfect obligations but then allocate that space to the pursuit of personal preferences do not offer *any* account of imperfect obligations. It is no wonder that some of them characterize action that might traditionally have been thought a matter of (imperfect) obligation in jocularly trivializing terms, for example, as "frightfully nice," a matter of "decency" or of being "morally splendid."[7] Sometimes such action is seen as a matter of individual preference or style; sometimes it is promoted as supererogatory and so (once again) not obligatory. Recent rights-based thinking, whether libertarian or nonlibertarian, obscures the differences between mere expressions of individual style or preference, ordinary acts of kindness and consideration which may (in a given context) be matters of imperfect obligation, and truly saintly or heroic action. Without an account of imperfect obligations all of these may seem no more than ways in which we have a right to act, since others' rights are no constraint.[8]

This narrowing of ethical vision makes it hard for rights-based approaches to take full account of ways in which children's lives are particularly vulnerable to unkindness, to lack of involvement, cheerfulness or good feeling. Their lack may be invisible from the perspective of rights. This may not seem significant if we think only of children in danger but is vital if our concern is the quality of the lives children lead. Cold, distant or fanatical parents and teachers, even if they violate no rights, deny children "the genial play of life": they can wither children's lives.[9] Children can hardly learn to share or to show "the unbought grace of life" if we are concerned only with their enforceable claims against others.

If imperfect obligations could be set aside, theories of obligations and of rights would have the same scope. They would offer two equivalent descriptions of a single set of ethical relationships. When we speak of (perfect) obligations we adopt the perspective of the agent and consider what must be done if there is to be no moral failure; when we speak of rights we adopt the perspective of the recipient (of perfect obligations) and consider what must be received or accorded if there is to be no moral failure. We would be dealing with two perspectives rather than with distinct accounts of ethical relationships, and the only reason to prefer either idiom would be that the audience for a particular discussion was either in a position to act (so that discussion of its obligations was relevant) or in a position to be affected by others' actions (so that discussion of its rights would be relevant). Many audiences would be in a position both to act and to be affected; for them both perspectives would be important. However, if we think imperfect obligations important, we cannot see a choice between obligation-based and rights-based theories as mere choice of perspective, since the scope of a theory of fundamental rights is narrower. Nor, as we shall see, is a preference for rights-based perspectives vindicated by more theoretical considerations. . . .

Imperfect obligations are traditionally thought to comprise matters such as help, care or consideration, and the development of talents, to whose specific enactment others have no right, but which agents are obliged to provide for some others in some form. These can be incorporated within a universalizing construction by a simple extension of the basic construction. The basis of the universalizing construction is rejection of action which reflects principles that cannot be universally acted on by a plurality of distinct rational beings. Human beings are, however, not merely distinct rational beings: they are also *vulnerable* and *needy* beings in the sense that their rationality and their mutual independence—the very basis of their agency—is incomplete, mutually vulnerable and socially produced. Our agency is vulnerable to one another in multiple ways, and particularly vulnerable at certain stages of our lives. Unless children receive both physical care and adequate socialization, they will not survive; if they merely survive they may not become competent agents: without education and instruction appropriate to their society they will lack capacities to act that are needed to function in the specific contexts available to them. A plurality of distinct rational beings who are also needy cannot therefore universally act on principles of mutual indifference. If they did, agency would fail or diminish for some, who then could adopt no principles of action, so undermining the very possibility of action on principles that can be universally shared. Rational and needy beings cannot universally act on principles of refusing all help to one another or of doing nothing to strengthen and develop abilities to act. However, it is impossible to help all others in all ways or to develop all talents or even some talents in all others. Hence obligations to help and to develop others' capacities must be imperfect obligations; they do not mandate specific acts of helpfulness to specified others or any specific contribution to developing talents in specified others. The construction of imperfect obligations commits rational and needy beings only to avoiding *principled* refusal to help and *principled* neglect to develop human potentialities. The specific acts required by these commitments will vary in different lives. Those who live or work with children are likely to find that they must take an active part both in their care and in their education if inaction is not to amount to principled refusal of those commitments.[10]

Fundamental imperfect obligations cannot be identified with any counterpart set of fundamental rights. Unless and until they are institutionalized, these obligations have no allocated right holders. When we consider them in the abstract, nothing can be said from the perspective of recipience; no rights holders are specified; there is nobody to claim or waive performance. However, if a constructive argument shows that universal indifference to helping others and universal neglect to develop human capacities for action are matters of (imperfect) obligation we will have reason to act to try to further these obligations. In particular we will have reason to construct and support institutions that realize and foster the discharge of these obligations.[11] For example, where we can foresee the incidence of need in broad outline (as we can for children) and the incidence of opportunity to meet or deny needs (as we can for those who in a given society are charged with the care of children) we may find strong reasons to establish a legal and social framework that secures certain positive obligations and so positive rights to care and education of a certain standard for children. The argument behind such a grounding of children's statutory and customary rights will appeal to a combination of perfect and imperfect obligations, and use these to work out how the actual practices of caring for and educating children of a particular society at a given time should be developed or modified. An argument for the same legal and social changes which appealed directly to children's fundamental rights would have the more daunting task of demonstrating in abstraction from particular institutions and practices that each child has a fundamental right to specific forms of care and education.

Politics: The Rhetoric of Children's Rights

None of these arguments shows that it is always pointless to talk about children's fundamental rights. Whatever we say about fundamental perfect obligations can, after all, be stated just as accurately in terms of the counterpart fundamental rights. However, since children depend so much on others who perform their imperfect obligations, a shift to the idiom of rights in discussions of children risks excluding and neglecting things that matter for children. Yet we all know that the idiom of rights has become a common and respected way of approaching ethical issues to do with children. The success of this idiom, we have seen, cannot be attributed either to its being the only or obvious nonconsequentialist approach to fundamental principles that matter for the treatment of children, or to its preeminent theoretical coherence. What then accounts for its present prominence? Why does so much current discussion of fundamental ethical issues focus on children's rights and not on obligations to children?

I believe that a large part of the answer to this question is historical and that a short consideration of that history suggests good reasons for caution in using the rhetoric of rights to think about ethical issues on children's lives.

The rhetoric of rights was separated from its parent theories of natural law and human obligations in the eighteenth century. The discourse of rights is an entirely legitimate descendant of older discussions of obligation and justice, of virtue and happiness, which have been ubiquitous both in popular and in philosophical discussion in ethics since antiquity. Rights can readily be derived from a theory of obligations merely by considering perfect obligations from the perspective of recipience. However, the legitimacy of the discourse of rights becomes problematic when it aspires to become the sole or fundamental ethical category.

The shift to the perspective of recipience may sometimes have a liberating force. On the surface it may seem strange that a shift away from the perspective of agency to that of recipience could liberate or energize. Since rights will be unmet, indeed violated, unless those who hold the counterpart obligations do what they ought, it may seem puzzling that an idiom which addresses recipients rather than agents should be at all important. However, the rhetoric of rights had powerful uses in its original context of confrontation with absolute monarchies and other undemocratic and oppressive institutions. By adopting the perspective of the recipient of others' obligations, it insists that the recipient is no mere loyal *subject* who petitions for some boon or favor but, rather, a *claimant* who demands what is owed and is wronged if a rightful claim is denied. Of course, claims, like petitions, may go unheeded by the powerful; but unlike petitioners claimants construe such rejection as injustice. The rhetoric of rights disputes established powers and their categories and seeks to empower the powerless; it is the rhetoric of those who lack power but do not accept the status quo. Those who claim their rights deny that the powers that be may define who they are, what they may do, or what they are entitled to. Although the rights of the powerless can only be met, as they can be thwarted, by the action of the powerful, the powerless in claiming their rights assert limits to others' power (which they may fail to establish). The charters and declarations of the human rights movement from the grand eighteenth-century documents to the UN Universal Declaration of Human Rights, as well as the activities of contemporary movements for civil rights, women's rights, and minority rights, constantly appeal over the heads of the powers that be, urging those who are powerless to claim their rights and so to take the first step away from dependence.

If the powerless gain recognition for the rights they claim, those on whom the counterpart obligations fall must acknowledge and fulfill them. Sometimes these obligations will be fulfilled with little urging from those whose rights are acknowledged; sometimes enormous "pressure from below" is needed before there is change. The political point of the rhetoric of rights is therefore evident: rhetoric has to be one of the main weapons of those who lack power. This also explains the easy and frequent misuse of that rhetoric to claim spurious rights even when no corresponding obligations can be justified. Many of the rights promulgated in international documents, including the International Declaration of the Rights of the Child, are perhaps not spurious, but they are patently no more than "manifesto" rights,[12] that cannot be claimed unless or until practices and institutions are established that determine against whom claims on behalf of a particular child may be lodged. Mere insistence that certain ideals or goals are rights cannot make them into rights; but a proleptic rhetoric of rights may be politically useful in working to set up institutions that secure positive rights that constitute (one possible) realization of fundamental imperfect obligations.

We have already seen that a constructivist account of fundamental rights faces *theoretical* difficulties in dealing with ethical issues to do with children. A rights-based approach suffers not only from the *general* difficulty that its construction is indeterminate, but from the specific problem that it cannot ground the imperfect obligations whose fulfillment is so important in children's lives. Such theoretical difficulties might, however, not lead to political failure. The perspective of rights may be ideologically and politically important in spite of its theoretical difficulties because its rhetoric empowers the powerless. Can appeals to children's fundamental rights be politically significant, in the way that other appeals to rights have been? Do they or can they help empower children or their advocates to wring recognition and fulfillment of obligations from the powerful?

Appeals to children's rights might have political and rhetorical importance if children's dependence on others is like that of oppressed social groups whom the rhetoric of rights has served well. However, the analogy between children's dependence and that of oppressed groups is suspect. When colonial peoples, or the working classes or religious and racial minorities or women have demanded their rights, they have sought recognition and respect for capacities for rational and independent life and action that are demonstrably there and thwarted by the denial of rights. No doubt oppression takes its toll, and those who have been treated as dependent all their adult lives often lack confidence and are more subservient and less autonomous than they may become: but the potential for empowerment is there, and activity and agitation to claim rights that are denied may itself build confidence and autonomy. But the dependence of children is very different from the dependence of oppressed social groups on those who exercise power over them.

Younger children are completely and unavoidably dependent on those who have power over their lives. Theirs is not a dependence which has been artificially produced (although it can be artificially prolonged); nor can it be ended merely by social or political changes, nor are others reciprocally dependent on children. The dependence of oppressed social groups, on the other hand, is often limited, artificially produced, reducible and frequently matched by the reciprocal dependence of the privileged on the oppressed, who provide servants, workers and soldiers. It is not surprising that oppressors often try to suggest that they stand in a paternal relation to those whom they oppress: in that way they suggest that the latter's dependence is natural and irremediable and their own exercise of power a burden which they bear with benevolent fortitude. The vocabulary and trappings of paternalism are often misused to mask the unacceptable faces of power. It is not mere metaphor, but highly political rhetoric, when oppressors describe what they do as paternalistic.

Child-rearing and educational practices are often harsh and ill judged. Yet they are fundamentally different from other exercises of power in that (with few exceptions) parents and educators seek to reduce (some or all of) children's incapacities and dependence. Even when they are reluctant to lose their power over children, they do not want specifically childish dependence to continue indefinitely. This is not because parents or educators are always high minded but because children's dependence is a burden for those on whom they depend. When power over children is systematically used to perpetuate forms of dependence or subservience which are not peculiar to childhood, we criticize not just those child-rearing and educational practices but also whatever wider social relations keep those who have left childhood in positions of economic and social dependence. The rhetoric of rights may have relevance and resonance for the *adults* of such societies, who find themselves still dependent and powerless even when they lose the peculiar dependence of childhood. Yet an appeal to rights will have little chance of empowering those who are still children: if they are too young they will be wholly unable to respond to the appeal; if they are old enough to respond they will probably find themselves well on the way to majority and to the ending of the forms of disability and dependence that are peculiar to children.

The crucial difference between (early) childhood dependence and the dependence of oppressed social groups is that childhood is a stage of life, from which children normally emerge and are helped and urged to emerge by those who have most power over them. Those with power over children's lives usually have some interest in ending childish dependence. Oppressors usually have an interest in maintaining the oppression of social groups. Children have both less need and less capacity to exert "pressure from below," and less potential for using the rhetoric of rights as a political instrument. Those who urge respect for children's rights must address not children but those whose action may affect children; they have reason to prefer the rhetoric of obligations to that of rights, both because its scope is wider and because it addresses the relevant audience more directly.

Since the ranks of childhood are continuously depleted by entry into adult life, no "children's movement" on the model of the women's movement or of civil rights movements can be envisaged. However, "mature minors" can find themselves in a position partly analogous to that of oppressed social groups.[13] Their minority may sometimes be prolonged unnecessarily by civil disabilities and modes of life that damage their social development and postpone competence. Mature and maturing minors who are restricted and damaged by civil liabilities and infantilizing social practices can use the rhetoric of rights to help secure greater recognition and independence. This rhetoric may galvanize and empower those who find themselves with many mature capacities but still with the burdens of minority; it may even hasten the maturing of capacities. Vicarious action to secure rights may be valuable for other minors, whose maturing has been delayed or undermined by infantilizing (even if well-meant) treatment. For the majority of children, however, the rhetoric of rights is merely one indirect way of reminding others of some of their obligations.

If we care about children's lives, we will have a number of good reasons not to base our arguments on appeals to children's fundamental rights. Some of these reasons are the theoretical difficulties of theories of fundamental rights. To look at rights is to look at what is ethically required indirectly by looking at what should be received. Constructivist accounts of what should be received are radically indeterminate, hence blurred. All rights-based approaches are incomplete in that they tell us nothing about what should be done when nobody has a right to its being done: they are silent about imperfect obligations. The view we get from the perspective of rights is not merely indirect, but blurred and incomplete.

Other reasons against invoking children's fundamental rights are political. The rhetoric of rights is mainly useful to agents who are largely powerless but able to exert at least rhetorical pressure from below. Children are more fundamentally but less permanently powerless; their main remedy is to grow up. Because this remedy cannot be achieved rapidly they are peculiarly vulnerable and must rely more than other powerless groups on social practices and institutions that secure the performance of others' obligations. The great disanalogies between children's dependence and that of members of oppressed social groups suggest that the rhetoric of rights can rarely empower children.

These conclusions will be uncongenial to some of those who have hoped to add the momentum of the human rights movement to activism on behalf of children. I think that hope is illusory because it exaggerates the analogies between children's dependence and the dependence of oppressed social groups. Nor do I think we should be surprised that rights-based approaches have not proved congenial or illuminating ways of handling the full range of fundamental ethical issues that face those who live with children. Theories of rights were born and developed in large part in repudiation of paternalistic models of just political and social relations. Their proponents have repudiated the justice of familial analogies which liken kings to fathers, see colonial powers as mother countries, women and underdeveloped peoples as childlike, and just social relations as patriarchal. However, it is no mere analogy when we speak of mothers and fathers as parents, and children are not just metaphorically childlike. There are good reasons to think that paternalism may be much of what is ethically required in dealing with children, even if it is inadequate in dealings with mature and maturing minors. Nothing is lost in debates about the allocation of obligations to children between families and public institutions if we do not suppose that fundamental rights are the basis of those obligations. However, a fuller account of fundamental obligations to children and of their appropriate institutionalization in families and in public institutions is a further story. The task of this paper has been to show why that story needs telling.

Notes

1. The term "constructivist" is particularly associated with Rawls's project of giving an account of justice whose justification is neither foundationalist nor subjective nor merely stipulative. Here I use the term without close examination to cover approaches which seek to justify ethical principles by reference to an account of agency and rationality, without relying on claims about desires or preferences. Compare John Rawls, *A Theory of Justice* (Cambridge, Mass.: Harvard University Press, 1971), and "Kantian Constructivism and Moral Theory," *Journal of Philosophy* 77 (1980): 515–72, as well as, e.g., Ronald Dworkin, "Justice and Rights," in *Taking Rights Seriously* (London: Duckworth, 1977), pp. 150–83, esp. pp. 160 ff.; Alan Gewirth, *Human Rights: Essays on Justification and Applications* (Chicago: University of Chicago Press, 1982): Henry Shue, *Basic Rights: Subsistence Affluence and U.S. Foreign Policy* (Princeton, N.J.: Princeton University Press, 1980).

2. They are not and cannot be completely specific about the act or forbearance that is owed: no act description can be fully determinate. Some accounts of the distinction between perfect and imperfect obligations suggest that the difference is only or mainly that the latter leave more "latitude" to act in various ways. Although it is plausible that imperfect obligations leave *more* latitude, I shall rest nothing on this difference since it does not provide a clear demarcation between perfect and imperfect obligations. *Any* principle of obligation must leave action underdetermined: deliberation and adjudication are indispensable in the application of principles of perfect as well as of imperfect obligation.

3. H. L. A. Hart, "Are There Any Natural Rights?" *Philosophical Review* 64 (1955): 175–91.

4. Although fundamental perfect obligations, like fundamental imperfect obligations, often

need institutional embodiment (cf. Shue) this does not obliterate the difference between them. It is only in the case of perfect obligations that right holders are identifiable prior to institutionalization.

5. There are various reasons for thinking that the content of fundamental obligations cannot be completely institutionalized. First, the positive obligations of institutions are specified not only by the positive rights they create or confer, but by their mandates, goals and purposes as well. (We understand well enough that institutions like individuals can fail in their obligations without violating any rights, that there can be positive as well as fundamental imperfect obligations.) Second, and more specifically, the obligations of institutions charged with securing public goods, or averting public harms, cannot be exhaustively decomposed into obligations to respect individual rights. Third, certain obligations may be premised on the discretion of the obligation bearer to allocate the performance of the obligation: those who see charitable giving as obligatory commonly think that there are no corresponding rights since the allocation of such giving is at the discretion of the one who gives. I am indebted to Sheldon Leader for clarification of these points.

6. Ronald Dworkin, "What Rights Do We Have?" in *Taking Rights Seriously*, pp. 266–78, specifically denies that there is an open-ended "right to liberty," yet he also insists that liberalism is agnostic about the good for man; see Ronald Dworkin, "Liberalism," in *Public and Private Morality,* ed. Stuart Hampshire (Cambridge: Cambridge University Press, 1978), pp. 113–43.

7. These phrases are taken from Judith Jarvis Thomson, *Rights, Restitution, and Risk* (Cambridge, Mass.: Harvard University Press, 1986), esp. pp. 13–18; also pp. 58, 64; similar turns of phrase are used by many other writers.

8. Compare further arguments to some of these conclusions in Joseph Raz, "Right-based Moralities," in *Theories of Rights,* ed. Jeremy Waldron (Oxford: Oxfod University Press, 1984), pp. 182–200, esp. pp. 185–86.

9. See Edmund Gosse. *Father and Son* (Harmondsworth: Penguin, 1984). For variations on the theme of withering parenting, see F. M. Mayor. *The Rector's Daughter* (Harmondsworth: Penguin, 1973): and Molly Keane, *Good Behaviour* (London: Sphere Books, 1982). Recent philosophical writing on ethical issues affecting children often stresses the danger of relying too much on *positive* rights, which typically come into play in adversarial contexts and so are destructive of intimacy and family life. See, e.g., O. O'Neill and W. Ruddick, eds.. *Having Children: Legal and Philosophical Reflections on Parenthood* (New York: Oxford University Press, 1979), esp. pt. 2; Jeffrey Blustein, *Parents and Children: The Ethics of the Family* (New York: Oxford University Press, 1982): Francis Shrag, "Children: Their Rights and Needs," in *Whose Child? Children's Rights, Parental Authority and State Power,* ed. William Aiken and Hugh La Folette (Totowa, N.J.: Rowman & Littlefield, 1980), pp. 237–53; Ferdinand Shoeman, "Rights of Families, Rights of Parents, and the Moral Basis of the Family," *Ethics* 91 (1980): 6–19. The objections raised in this article to rights-based approaches to children's issues are not objections to children's *positive* rights. On the contrary, one of the aims of the approach is to ground positive rights adequately (while accepting that there is much to be said against overemphasizing adversial contexts in thinking about children's lives). However, we are ill placed to object to an overemphasis on *positive* rights unless and until we can offer an account of *fundamental* obligations to children. Given the dearth of obligation-based approaches, and in particular the lack of accounts of the grounds of fundamental imperfect obligations, in recent philosophical discussions of children's issues, I believe that the literary illustrations are revealing and not redundant. Some recent discussions of "rights to do wrong" are, I believe, also a sign of the failure of modern liberal political theory to show what, apart from appeals to fundamental perfect obligations and their corollary rights, could ground judgments of wrongdoing. This is not an unavoidable situation: we have only to look back to the structure of the Kantian enterprise, or to the tradition of civic humanism (cf. Quentin Skinner, "The Idea of Negative Liberty: Philosophical and Historical Perspectives," in *Philosophy in History,* ed. R. Rorty, J. Schneewind, and Q. Skinner [Cambridge: Cambridge University Press, 1984]) to see that a serious account of imperfect obligations is compatible with taking perfect obligations, and so rights, seriously.

10. The background to these points lies in Kant's treatment of the "contradiction in the will" version of the Formula of Universal Law. I have offered an interpretation of the argument that connects it to considerations of human need and vulnerability in *Faces of Hunger,* chaps. 7 and 8, as well as in "Between Consenting Adults" and "Rights, Obligations and Needs," *Logos* 6 (1985): 29–47.

11. It is a point of controversy whether imperfect obligations should ever be legally enforced. I shall take no stand on the matter. All that is claimed here is that in institutionalizing

such obligations we make them *enforceable;* the modes of enforcement may use social or psychological sanctions rather than legal ones. It may be the case that certain sorts of sanction that are available ought not to be used to enforce certain types of obligation. If it is the case (it seems plausible, but I have not argued the point here) that the act descriptions in principles of imperfect obligation are less determinate than those in principles of perfect obligation, legal enforcement of imperfect obligations may have to be indirect—that is to say, it may work only by way of constituting certain institutions on whom specific interpretations of principles of imperfect obligation are laid as positive obligations.

12. The phrase is Joel Feinberg's in "The Nature and Value of Rights," in his *Rights, Justice and the Bounds of Liberty: Essays in Social Philosophy* (Princeton, N.J.: Princeton University Press, 1980). Although manifesto rights cannot be claimed or enforced as they stand, they propose principles to be institutionalized. For example, the *United Nations Declaration of the Rights of the Child in Having Children,* pp. 111–14, includes the rights "to grow and develop in health" (principle 4), "to an atmosphere of affection and of moral and material security" (principle 6), and to "an education which will promote his general culture and enable him on a basis of equal opportunity to develop his abilities and his sense of moral and social responsibility" (principle 7). None of these "rights" is well formed as an enforceable claim, but they can be seen as ideals that should inform the construction of institutions that secure enforceable claims.

13. See *Having Children,* pt. 3, for discussions of the situation and predicaments of "mature minors."

Rights for the Next Generation:
A Feminist Approach
to Children's Rights

Martha Minow*

> And though one says that one is part of everything,
> There is a conflict, there is a resistance involved;
> And being part is an exertion that declines:
> One feels the life of that which gives life as it is.
> —*Wallace Stevens*[1]

"Children's Rights" is a new, but recognizable topic. Law schools offer courses on the subject; casebooks and other publications herald its arrival.[2] Yet the topic presents conceptual, practical, and political difficulties. What exactly is a right that can be exercised by a five-year-old, or a two-year-old—and does it rest on different premises than rights for adults? How are rights for children to be enforced: do they require adult supervision, and if so, by which adults? Won't many adults politically oppose suggestions that children—perhaps their own children—should have legal liberties and powers that constrain the liberty and authority of adults?

Behind the answers to these questions—and behind the issue of children's rights generally—lie assumptions about the differences between children and adults. Although societies throughout time have drawn distinctions between children and adults, the specific line drawn has shifted; in our culture and legal system, there is no one line or single characteristic commonly understood to signify adulthood. Different demarcations result from focusing on age, behavior, biological development, indications of mental status, and relationships between the individual and other persons, not to mention any combination of such factors.

Critics and reformers concerned with children's legal status have drawn on these competing theories about childhood in both defending and challenging

---

* Assistant Professor, Harvard University. The author thanks Bill Rubenstein, Kathleen Sullivan, and Sarah Walzer for their help, and Mary Joe Frug for her inspired and constant conversations. An earlier version of this Essay was a background paper for the Harvard Executive Sessions on The Future of Juvenile Justice at the John F. Kennedy School of Government.

---

separate treatment for children. Yet no theory specifically resolves the practical—and political—issues about when to treat a given individual as a child or as an adult. Whatever a chosen theory may point to as the distinguishing characteristics of childhood, the choice to label an individual as a child or as an adult often entails sharp differences in the treatment that individual will receive. In a powerful sense, the debate over where to draw the line between childhood and adulthood represents a debate over the kind of relationship any given individual should have with the larger community.

The current pattern of drawing lines between childhood and adulthood in our society is marked by inconsistencies and contradictions. These inconsistencies, I will argue, arise not from anything intrinsic to children, but instead from legal conceptions affecting children—legal conceptions insensitive to the relationships children have and those they need. The inconsistencies cannot be rationalized by a notion of variable competence that would adjust legal status in light of a range of competencies demanded for contrasting situations. Variable competence is an idea toward which the varied legal treatment of children might aspire, but this Essay offers an explanation of why this aspiration has not been achieved, practically and theoretically. Nor can the inconsistencies be explained as expressions of an incomplete march toward children's independence, for competing legal trends invoke children's dependencies. I suggest that we need to develop a perspective on children's rights that refrains from comparing the abilities of children and adults and instead addresses their mutual needs and connections.

In Part I, I show how the current legal lines drawn between children and adults have little rationale and I offer explanations of why that is: first, because the lines we presently draw seldom focus on children at all; and second, because when we do focus on children, legal rules embody competing principles about how the state should treat them. I then turn to consider how this line-drawing task misses the challenge of children's rights. In Part II, I provide a more complex conceptual framework, one that goes beyond merely drawing lines according to competency notions. The starting point for this framework is a recognition of the relationships children have with parents and with the state—and the relations also arising between parents themselves and the state. Pursuing the preconditions for these relationships, the framework offers a basis for understanding what children's rights have meant and could entail.

This exploration offers special importance for those interested in women's rights. Children's rights owe some portion of their origins to struggles for women's rights, and the conceptual and practical problems raised by children's rights help to illuminate obstacles encountered by women's rights as well. In addition, the historic roles played by women as advocates for children's needs and interests closely link women's own political struggles with political reforms on behalf of children.[3] Finally, rights for children, as developed later in this Essay, epitomize feminist concerns about the importance of connection, caretaking, and social relationships; pursuing a theory of children's rights holds promise for a wider feminist approach to new forms that rights could take. By thinking through steps toward a jurisprudence of children's rights, this

Essay seeks to clarify not only what rights could mean for a new generation, but also what a new generation of rights could mean.

I. Contradictions in the Legal Treatment of Children

How does our society draw the line between childhood and adulthood? An overview of the legal treatment of children reveals what seem to be patterns of inconsistency. In many places, an eighteen-year-old may consent to her own abortion without telling her parents, but the truancy laws and school regulations require that she obtain parental permission to miss school to see the doctor. A seventeen-year-old may be treated as an adult on charges of committing a violent crime; he may even be subject to the dealth penalty; but the same person could well be treated as a child for purposes of employment and other contractual relations, including marriage. A six-year-old may not consent to her own medical care, but she may be forced to testify in court against her parents. The law may compel the payment of child support for an individual past the age of eighteen who is still attending school, but allow nonpayment if school attendance ceases. What accounts for these varied legal treatments of young people?

A. *Rational Line-Drawing Gone Awry?*

An initial explanation of these seemingly inconsistent treatments could build on a notion of rational line-drawing based on assessments of varied kinds of competencies any given child may have. Thus, legal rules may treat children variously because lawmakers recognize that a child may have developed some, but not all, of the competencies society deems relevant to a range of tasks or responsibilities. From this vantage point, children need custody and care when they are incompetent, and rights and autonomy when they are competent. Variations in legal treatment could be justified on the basis that each individual progresses through stages of development. At any given time in a child's development, he or she may be competent for some purposes and incompetent for others.

However appealing this view may be as a normative theory,[4] it fails to describe the current legal universe. It seems bizarre to justify the variable treatment of young people currently manifested in the patchwork of legal regulations as though it expressed careful judgments about their competencies for various tasks and responsibilities. Why would an eighteen-year-old be competent to consent to her own abortion but not be entitled to miss school for her doctor's appointment without parental permission? Why would the seventeen-year-old be competent to be treated as an adult in criminal court but not competent to sign a contract at that age? A theory of variable competence may make theoretical or programmatic sense, but it does not supply the rationale for the particular choices the law has made up to this point.

Besides descriptive failure, this effort to understand the current legal universe in terms of rational line-drawing presents a theoretical defect: it pretends that competency is the only issue, and that there are knowable boundaries between competence and incompetence for any given societal task. Instead, it is more honest to disclose that competence and incompetence are used here as proxies for a variety of concerns about what societal decision-makers think children may need, and about what they simultaneously think allows adults to choose for themselves. Additionally, competence and incompetence are a crude set of proxy ideas. There are no uncontroversial principles to pinpoint the kinds of competencies crucial to accord an individual independent decision-making power and to relinquish paternalist control. Granting someone independence is a political or moral choice made by each society to fulfill its own purposes—not a rational decision gauged by psychological or other scientific measures. Moreover, competence to act with "independence" as a political or moral status is quite distinguishable from the psychological, physical, and social involvements that connect any individual to others. Legal rules that imply that only independent people may enjoy rights fictionalize the actual grant of rights to people who remain dependent in many ways.

From this perspective, the inconsistent legal treatment of children cannot be attributed solely to the general problem of drawing boundaries. Even though there seems no obvious line between childhood and adulthood, the many, and many inconsistent, lines drawn by this society to signify legal distinctions between children and adults invoke competing conceptions of the individual's relationship to the community and the state, not merely competing definitions of adulthood versus childhood. A more candid and comprehensive analysis, then, should turn to the conceptions of the child's relationship to the state—and to adults—that govern our legal system.

B. Children Neglected in the Public Sphere

Locating children within the larger legal system, I suggest, yields the conclusion that children simply are not the real focus of the varied laws that affect them. Instead, other powerful social goals are the focus of these laws. Traffic safety, control of violent crime, and regulation of abortion, for example, are social goals in which children may have incidental roles, and the laws affecting children in these areas actually play out political and practical debates which make children quite beside the point. Law reformers may in fact mix some concern for children with these other concerns. Yet it is noteworthy that laws against child labor, for example, did not pass legislatures until organized labor joined in their support—and realized that child labor laws could improve the ability of adult workers to command higher salaries by constricting the available labor pool. Children here were only one of many social concerns, and perhaps not even a central one. Because children are not the dominant focus of many legal reforms, it should not be surprising that laws treat them inconsistently.

Put somewhat more contentiously, let me suggest that the inconsistent legal treatment of children stems in some measure from societal neglect of children. The needs and interests of children, difficult enough to address when highlighted, are too often submerged below other societal interests. The dominance of these other interests helps to explain the inconsistent treatment of children.

It may seem odd to talk about societal neglect of children, given the occasional outpourings of rage over particular problems confronting them.[5] Yet here are some facts. Despite the wealth of this nation, twelve countries do better than we do in keeping their infants alive.[6] Over twenty percent of all children in this country live in families whose incomes fall below the poverty line.[7] The same point, put another way: nearly forty percent of people in poverty in this country are children.[8] Over one million children come to the attention of public authorities each year as victims of serious abuse by adults—and these are just the children whose abuse becomes known by others.[9] Massachusetts spends about the same daily fee for a child in foster care as a kennel charges per day to house a dog.[10] Only thirty-five percent of all mothers raising children alone receive any child support from fathers.[11] Nearly one million children under age five have no adult supervision during the day.[12]

Adolescent suicide for children aged eighteen to nineteen increased from three out of one hundred thousand in 1950 to ten out of one hundred thousand in 1977.[13] The risks of injury and violence for fifteen- to twenty-four-year-olds has grown more serious in recent years. The issues for children in this country are especially severe for racial minorities: about fifteen percent of white children suffer some nutritional deficit—compared with about one-third of all Black children.[14]

Why might these problems facing so many children seem so unfamiliar in public debate? What set of beliefs could permit social conditions placing children at such risk while allowing legal rules that instrumentally use children to achieve other social goals? Here, the basic legal framework governing children deserves another look. That basic framework rests on a sharp distinction between public and private responsibilities for children. Using this public/private distinction, the framework assigns childcare responsibilities to parents, and thereby avoids public responsibility for children. Public power becomes relevant only in exceptional circumstances, when parents default. The government is not supposed to "intervene" in the private realm of the family, where children's needs and interests are managed by their parents.[15] At a societal level, the basic framework essentially authorizes public neglect of children while assigning duties to parents entrusted with children's care.

Children's rights—in contrast simply to laws affecting children—represent a challenge to this basic framework of governance. The proponents of rights for children may seek to direct governmental attention to what children say they want for themselves, or to secure specific governmental rules restraining parents, teachers, and other authority figures from imposing their wills on children. These very different forms of governmental attention that reformers may seek suggest a new explanation for the pattern of inconsistent legal treatments of children. Indeed these inconsistencies could be understood in part as clashes between policies erected by Progressive Era reformers, and those created by more recent advocates for children's independence.

C. Children Spotlighted in the Public Sphere: A Short History of Children's Rights in America

Reformers advocating rights for children have cut against the basic legal framework that assigns responsibility for children to the private sphere. Yet sharp contrasts arise between claims of public protections—initiated by the Progressives—and claims of publicly conferred autonomy for children, advanced more recently. Both kinds of claims now compete for legal enforcement and complicate the meaning of children's rights.

1. Progressive protections   The Progressive Era reforms implemented protective notions—compulsory schooling, child labor laws, and the juvenile court system—which furthered children's dependence on adults and legally removed children from the adult spheres of the marketplace and the civic community.[16] Progressive reformers offered a variety of reasons for these early efforts to concentrate public attention on children. Some expressed revulsion at the risks to children in industrial labor settings; others identified the economic and political needs of an industrial society for people with formal educations, and at minimum, literacy.[17] In effect, the reformers helped to invent adolescence—a new stage after infancy but before adulthood—and thereby prolonged childhood.

Contemporary commentators have observed how the child became the focus for humanitarian reforms that otherwise occupied the Progressives. Many women reformers—with Jane Addams, Lillian Wald, and Grace and Edith Abbott among the most famous—advocated humanitarian concerns and paternalist measures that became more politically palatable when focused on children. The child in this sense "united the campaigns for health, education, and a richer city environment; and he dominated much of the interest in labor legislation."[18] Similarly, the child served as a symbol of the human who could be redeemed or changed, and who then could help change society.[19]

Notions of the child as a creature different from adults occupied the inventors of the juvenile court as well, but the child's differences, according to those reformers, ranged from the child's innocence and impressionability to the child's dangerousness to society. Thus, alongside an environmental analysis that attributed children's crimes in the 1890's to their inhumane treatment by parents and society, arose a Freudian theory about the child who seethed with tensions and impulses, and lacked moral sensibility.[20] Environmental and psychological theories supported excuses for a child's deviant conduct and promoted social service programs to assist both child and family. Such developments, along with the social rules excluding children from adult activities, made ambiguous what exactly children were to be held accountable for, and what enforceable duties children should have.

2. Independence movement   The Progressive legal reforms offered a world of separate protections for children—and that very separation struck later observers as discriminatory and likely to expose children to adult indifference or abuse. Social critics starting in the mid-1950's attacked the creation of adolescence in particular for stigmatizing and excluding young people from adult worlds and responsibilities.[21] Thus, these recent reformers urged recognition of children's sameness or similarity to adults, rather than emphasizing children's differences. Like the civil rights movements extending rights to Blacks and women, children's rights advocates pushed to expand the definition of who is a self-determining person, who can make claims recognized by law, and who can assert entitlements to change how he or she otherwise would be treated. These movements of the mid-twentieth century proceeded on a conception of each individual's right to be treated the same as other individuals, and to be protected against unwarranted intrusions by the state.[22]

Notable decisions in the field of children's rights can be fitted within such a narrative. Perhaps the starting point for this story is its convergence with the movement for racial justice: *Brown* v. *Board of Education*[23] accorded equal treatment to children regardless of race, and in so doing, granted children the status of rights-bearing individuals. Next, in 1967, came the landmark juvenile justice case, *In re Gault,*[24] which required that delinquency proceedings use certain procedural protections much as adult criminal courts do—notably, procedural rights to a hearing, cross-examination, and access to legal counsel. Beyond specifically requiring these procedures, the decision announced children's entitlement to be treated as rights-bearing persons rather than subjects of paternalism. Because an institution ostensibly devoted to children's best interests could hurt them, the Supreme Court concluded that children need and deserve the kinds of rights against the exercise of state power that adults enjoy.

Similarly, the Court's decisions in *Tinker* v. *Des Moines Independent Community School District*[25] and *Planned Parenthood of Central Missouri* v. *Danforth*[26] recognized rights for children that approximated the rights of adults. In *Tinker,* the Court declared unconstitutional a school rule that prevented children from expressing their political views at school by wearing black armbands. Although the Court ruled that students' free speech rights are limited—their exercise cannot disrupt the school's daily operations—the Court announced that children enjoy rights and do not lose them when they enter the schoolhouse gate. In *Danforth,* the Court rejected a statute requiring parental consent to a minor's abortion. The Court ruled that the minor has a right, just as an adult woman does, to determine in consultation with medical personnel whether to terminate her pregnancy, and this right permits autonomy from both state intervention and the intervention by other persons—including parents.[27]

3. Counter-principles   These cases suggest a legal march away from the conception of the child as a dependent person, toward the view of the child's independent enjoyment of legal rights. Pushed as much by practical assessments of the abusive institutions and unrealistic hopes for parental authority as by theories of individual competency, advocates for these kinds of children's rights have transformed the legal landscape. Yet understanding this historical narrative as simply the march toward children's independence ignores some of the most recent legal developments that in fact curtail the rights of children and subordinate them to adults.

A Supreme Court decision in 1971, four years after *Gault,* denied children in juvenile court the same right to trial by jury assured to adults.[28] In 1984, the Court decided that a state can authorize detention for juveniles who pose a serious risk of committing a crime, because "juveniles, unlike adults, are always in some form of custody."[29] Accordingly, the Court reasoned that the state may subordinate whatever interests a child has in liberty to actions made in the name of the child's interests. Precisely opposite to the dominant reasoning in *Gault,* the Court revived a notion of custody, rather than liberty, as children's due and thereby legally enforced a difference between children and adults.

These are not simply two aberrant decisions. The Court has also ruled that unlike adults, children are not entitled to an adversarial hearing when they face commitment to an institution for the mentally ill.[30] Instead, the Court concluded that parents can be trusted to act in their child's interest when they seek such commitment decisions, and any doubt about this can be resolved by the admitting medical personnel, rather than by a legal proceeding.[31] The Court also countered an initial declaration of children's rights to hearings before facing school suspensions with a subsequent ruling that children have no right to a prior hearing when threatened with corporal punishment in the school setting.[32] Again, pitted against the rights theory is a view of children's essential difference from adults. Their liberty interests are made subordinate to their dependence on adults.

These counter-principles of child dependency and custody animate legislative as well as judicial action. Several states have enacted laws requiring minors who seek abortions to notify their parents, and the Supreme Court has approved at least one of these statutes.[33] Although this is not a reversal of the *Danforth* decision, which struck down a consent requirement for minors seeking abortions, it is a resurgence at least in part of a legal use of children's custodial relationships with parents as a curb on children's independent rights. In another trend, many states recently have raised the legal age for drinking or driving, or both, to combat the high risks of drunk driving among teenagers.[34]

4. Competing notions in public discourse   In each of these developments, state and parental interests in controlling and guiding children counter or constrict notions of individual rights for children. The legal treatment of children from this perspective expresses the results of a contest between two competing principles: the principle of individual rights, and the principle that the care and custody of children by adults serves the interests of both. This second principle—shared interests—indeed suggests that individual rights are not just unnecessary, but may actually damage the relationships between parent and child, teacher and child, and even judge and child, because children need authority, not rights. There is a real risk that this asserted identity of interests between children and adults will cancel out the intended effect of the public focus on children—and yet again subordinate children's interests to those of the adult society.

Contributing to the confusion in public debate over children's rights is the availability of rights rhetoric to both those who would preserve the Progressive Era reforms and those who challenge them. "Rights" may be claimed to underscore children's similarity to adults—but rights may also be invoked to call attention to children's differences. The notion of "Children's Rights" could—and has—been seized by advocates of both separate, protective treatment and identical, equal treatment for children and adults. This confusion bears a striking parallel to the special versus equal treatment debate about women's legal rights.[35] For women, too, a legacy of legal protections—and restraints—encounters challenges in the names of rights and autonomy. Arguments about the enduring value of special protections, however, complicate the meaning and shape of rights sought by advocates for women.[36]

Like the contest between special and equal treatment claims for women, the contest between rights and custody as principles for children's legal treatment hints at a choice between seeing the child as basically the same as or basically different from adults. Moreover, the debate about children contrasts a view of the child as independent of adults with a view of the child as totally dependent. Both of these choices obscure the child's relationship with the state under either principle. These choices also ignore the real possibility that the same child may need custody and care for one purpose, and rights of autonomy or self-determination for another. The next Section seeks to create a framework large enough to expose the significant features of relationships embedded in contrasting notions of children's rights.

II. Rights in Relationships

Part I suggested that underlying some of the inconsistencies and confusion about legal treatment of children is the significance, too often ignored, of children's relationships with adults and with the state. In this Section, I will suggest that accounting for these relationships among child, parent, and state not only challenges simplistic conceptions of rights, but also offers an avenue for developing richer notions of rights. I first look at how integrating children's relationships into a theory of children's rights draws support from a particular understanding of adult's rights; then I will view children's rights through the relational frame. I offer one instance—through the example of juvenile court history—of what an application of this relational conception of rights would look like, given existing institutional arrangements. My analysis is informed by three feminist concerns: appreciation of relationships, a commitment to a vision of the self forged in connection with—not just through separation from—others, and a preference for glimpses of complexity, contextual detail, and continuing conversation.[37]

A. The Concept of Rights as Problematic

The rhetoric of rights dominant in legal discourse poses a choice between persons under the law being treated either as separate, autonomous, and responsible individuals entitled to exercise rights and obliged to bear liabilities for their actions, or else as dependent, incompetent, and irresponsible individuals denied rights, removed from liabilities, and subjected to the care and protection of a guardian—or the state. In a sense, these two tracks of legal treatment for persons could themselves be located in different historical points of origin.[38] The modern, post-feudal state challenged traditional notions of a social organism that submerged each individual in the community and required obedience by each individual to the authority of the religious and political authorities. The modern state, at least according to some accounts, introduced ideas of the consent of the governed, and therefore, the autonomy of individuals to grant or withhold consent. This new set of ideas thus created an opening wedge for what has become the dominant set of conceptions about the relationship between the individual and the society: notions according rights to autonomous individuals against a state and notions imposing responsibilities on individuals for their willed actions. As applied to children, this simplistic view of rights would envision a program of drawing an exact line between incompetence and competence, childhood and adulthood.

These ideas co-exist, however, with earlier and persistent uses of law to facilitate interpersonal relationships. Feudal relationships themselves embodied a contractual dimension, a notion of chosen affiliation, permitted and enforced by law. Liberal freedoms in some measure retained the purpose of enabling affiliations between people. Freedom of association, freedom of religion, rights to marry, rights to procreate, and rights to preserve contact with family members are all current versions of this kind of rights conception—one at odds with the claim that rights protect autonomy rather than human relationships or connections.

Of course, for some individuals and some circumstances, the earlier feudal notions of status-based relationships and mutual obligation endured. Especially for people who continued to occupy special statuses even under the liberal order—persons like children, women, and the mentally incompetent—the dependency track of legal treatment remained in force. It is possible to see these people in special statuses as solely the exceptions to the liberal legal order. Yet it is also possible to see them as people for whom legal rules foster relationships: relationships of care, protection, and perhaps, at times, chosen affiliation. The tensions between rights to autonomy and rights to connection may seem most vivid and poignant with people like children, but these tensions arise for adults as well.[39]

Such tensions are evident in issues concerning women in the workplace. Should a woman be free to choose whether to work in a workplace hazardous to any child she might conceive and bear? Should a woman's pregnancy entitle her to special work-leave benefits unavailable to a man—or should a workplace designed without pregnancy in mind disadvantage her when she chooses to bear a child? A woman's relationships, or potential relationships, with her children challenge the premise that she is a separate, autonomous person; and yet treating her as connected to others could disadvantage her in the workplace or seem to justify restrictions on her own choices. Is the woman to be treated "the same" as a male employee—with no attention to her private relationships?

Or is the woman entitled to special treatment—potentially curbing her choices and her success in a work world that uses the autonomous person as the model?

Behind these doctrinal issues are deeper ones: Who is responsible to care for this woman in the workplace—to restructure the workplace if necessary to alleviate the tensions between her connections to her family and her own individual chances for success and self-determination? What collection of rights can be designed to permit her exercise of choices in favor of connections to her family as well as choices advancing her job success? It may be that the adult woman's interest in relationships arises most vividly when pertaining to children, yet relationships between adults pose similar complications for rights premised on autonomy.

These questions challenge a conception of rights that fits people into a slot labelled, "the individual," on a game board with the state as the only other player. These questions also implicitly reject the view that rights necessarily run only between an individual and the state, and that rights only mark and preserve distances between people. Instead, rights could be part of legal arrangements that permit, not to mention promote, relationships for adults—while also combatting hierarchy and fixed assignments of status. This conception remains problematic given a regime of rights that emphasizes individual autonomy to the exclusion of duty and interpersonal connection. These problems with traditional rights for adults mirror, but also compound, the difficulties in devising rights for children that can promote relationships while protecting autonomy.

B. Conceptions of Children's Rights

To the extent that the dominant conception of rights presumes both autonomy and a direct relationship between the individual and the state, rights for children are even more problematic than rights for adults. Conceptually and practically, children in our society are not autonomous persons but instead dependents who are linked legally and daily to adults entrusted with their care.[40] Children are doubly dependent. Their dependency is constructed by legal rules and also is in their lives as lived. This double dependency situates children outside the sphere of rights-bearing persons in a system that makes independence a premise for the grant of rights. Children's dependencies specifically situate them within the sphere of the private family, where parents stand between children and the state.

Yet a choice between rights of self-determination on the one-hand, and custody on the other, is too simplistic to capture the relationships among children, parents, and the state as embodied in legal rules and rights. Given the critical role of relationships with adults in children's lives, rights for children could take several forms, First, children's rights could represent efforts by the state to protect children from the neglect or abuse by the adults entrusted with their care. Perhaps better named "child protections," such rights appear in state statutes defining child abuse and authorizing state proceedings to evaluate, help, or punish parents on this basis. Child protective rights also arise in rules restricting child labor, and even rules restricting drinking and driving by children. Such rules cut in the opposite direction of adult rights that enable individuals to exercise autonomous choices. Yet the rhetoric of rights can, and has, been applied to child protection: these instances of state action penetrate the traditionally private sphere of the family and construct a direct relationship between child and state. The state thereby has obligations that can be invoked by or in the name of the child.

Alternatively, rights for children could protect children from state power but do so in a way that reinforces the privacy of the family, and indeed, the authority of the parents. A hint of this possibility appears in *Gault,* where the Court articulated the child's right to consult legal counsel in the context of juvenile court proceedings as a right of the child and parents, together.[41] The conception of the child's right here joins the child with the parent rather than either stationing the state with the child against the parent or offering the child state assistance to pole-vault over parental authority.

A more direct example of this form of children's rights appears in *Wisconsin v. Yoder,*[42] where the Supreme Court allowed Amish children to avoid the compulsory schooling requirement due to its asserted infringements on their religious beliefs and way of life. There, too, the Court's grant of protection to children from a state requirement strengthened parental authority, for it was parents who asserted the children's claims. Indeed, it was parents who faced sanctions for failing to assure their children's attendance at the public high school. This form of legal rule could be called "family protection," but family protection itself is a particular conception of the best way to advance the rights of children.[43]

Justice Douglas's dissenting opinion in *Yoder* formulated a contrasting, third form of children's rights by arguing that the children themselves should be allowed to voice their views about attending the public high schools.[44] In this form, children's rights involve the state in suspending its usual reinforcement of parental power. Indeed, this form of children's rights involves the state in lifting children from their usual dependence on and subjection to parental authority. Thus, under *Danforth,* the state gives minors the right to consent to their own abortions and thereby rejects parental demands to have their power reinforced by the state. The grant of the right also draws the state into authorizing doctors and other medical personnel to enter into treatment directly with the minor, without the parental consent customarily required. Further, the state's curtailment of paternalism entails a self-restraint: the state empowers adolescents to consent to their own abortions even where that decision departs from a judge's assessment of the minor's best interests.

These possible permutations of children's rights offer some analytic clarity. They may also shed light on why the same "Children's Rights" banner can be raised by sharp opponents over the role of the child's own voice, the parents' authority, and the responsibilities of the state. Consider, for example, a case where parents oppose medical treatment for their child. A state agency may bring suit to order such treatment over the parents' objections, and do so in the name of the child's rights. Yet a lawyer for the child, perhaps hired by the parents, may assert that the child has a right to determine whether she, herself, wants the medical treatment.[45] All sides have a fair claim to the assertion of "rights" for the child, because rights represent the coinage of opposition to two kinds of power: the power of the parents and the power of the state. Freedom from parental power could be achieved in some measure if the state asserted power over the child, but a very different sort of freedom would arise if the state accorded the child freedom to choose for herself. Even this latter form of freedom requires state involvement and state enforcement; and freedom for the child's own choice-making may be unimaginable or impossible in many situations facing children. Still, the double layers of parental and state control supply the bases for rights arguments on behalf of children that point in opposite, or contrasting directions.

C. The Dilemma for Juvenile Court

The juvenile court offers a vivid instance of the problems presented by these complex notions of rights for children. Not until 1899 did this country offer any special legal institution for adjudicating criminal charges against children; by the 1960's, however, the sprawling courts, social service agencies, and corrections facilities comprising the juvenile justice treatment institutions came under attack for unfairness and for exposing the minors under their supervision to abuse. The history of the rise and fall of the juvenile court could be understood as an experiment in restricting the liberal rights tradition and reviving the dependency and care track for juveniles. In this light, it was an experiment tried and rejected.

The initial effort called for carving out legal territory to remove juveniles from the realm of rights and responsibilities. The explicit rationale for this experiment drew from claims of children's incompetence and actual dependency, as well as from optimistic predictions about their ability to learn and grow into responsible, autonomous persons if helped toward that end. Creating a set of institutions that looked to the juvenile's needs entailed denying juveniles rights accorded to those already autonomous and responsible. Instead, the juvenile would enter into a dependency relationship with the state, much like the feudal orders of guardian and ward, and other hierarchical relationships.

Absent the disciplining focus of individual rights rhetoric and procedures to enforce it, the needs of society and bureaucracy rather than the needs or obligations of the individual took precedence. Without ascertainable rights to autonomy and liberty—not to mention rights to counsel, rights against self-incrimination, and other protections accorded *adult* criminal defendants—minors in juvenile court risked long detentions in hostile or abusive institutions.[46] The disillusionment with such results invited an obvious cure, the same cure developed for the defects of feudalism more generally: liberal rights to autonomy. Thus, *Gault* and subsequent developments prescribed rights for juveniles, in part to constrain the power of the state, and in part to fulfill the very educational function animating the initial juvenile court experiment. This time, juveniles were to learn the norms of a liberal order that metes out justice through the interplay of rights and restraints on governmental power. As a result, the differences in treatment of children have diminished somewhat in the criminal justice context.[47] Juveniles may now be tried in adult courts under some circumstances, and may receive adult punishments for crimes committed as juveniles.[48]

There is, however, a serious shortcoming in this rendition of the juvenile court as a failed attempt to revive the dependency and care track for juveniles. This analysis obscures the degree to which the juvenile court experiment borrowed only some features of the rights to care, connection, and indeed custody. The juvenile court does recognize some of these rights: it originally offered rights in the form of child protection against parents, in situations such as charges of abuse; it currently offers some forms of family protection against state power; and at times it affords juveniles power to assert their own wishes. Nevertheless, the court has not taken as its task the articulation or promotion of rights of care and connection or rights to affiliative relationships—or the preconditions for such relationships.

This omission would have been cured in part had the juvenile court spelled out not just rights, but duties—including both the duties of adults upon whom the juvenile is dependent, and duties of the juvenile to those entrusted with his or her care, as well as to the state and the larger community.[49] The notion of duty begins to introduce a bilateral dimension to rights that gives them content. Under this approach, difficulties in articulating the duties of parents, children, and state officials would certainly arise, but at least the task of formulating these duties would direct people's attention to aspects of rights committed to facilitating interpersonal connections. In this sense, rights would represent not only a social commitment to preserve individual freedom from the injuries and intrusions of others, but also individual freedom to form relationships with others.

This rhetoric of duty is only a first step, though. The critical need for the juvenile court, and other institutions addressing children's rights, is to focus on the preconditions for relationships. Treating children as though they already had working relationships with parents or other adults, and as though enforcing rights and duties alone would fix the problems brought to the court, could miss what those problems are truly about. What legal rules governing child custody, education, and child support would promote settings where children thrive? Similarly, what rules would promote adults' abilities to create these settings? To pose such questions and provide working answers to them, the juvenile court should be authorized to commandeer resources such as public support benefits, homemaker assistance, day-care volunteers, and job-training for both youths and their care-takers. Although it would be difficult theoretically, practically, and politically to empower the juvenile court to promote the preconditions for relationships in these ways, I suggest that pursuing this line of inquiry holds promise of breaking out of patterns of disillusionment. Reforms in the past at first treated children differently from adults, then treated them like adults, and in each instance, built bureaucratic institutions and a public sense of futility. The goal for the future is to devise reforms that help people help themselves—reforms that acknowledge the public as well as private influences on and preconditions for human relationships.

III. A New Generation of Rights and a Concluding Hope for Children

Children lack the autonomy presumed under one version of what rights mean. But so do adults. Children need environments where they can learn what is just, learn what it means to have their needs met, and learn what it means to have and fulfill obligations and to meet the needs of others. Adults need this too—from other adults, and from children as well. Debating whether children should be treated like adults for one purpose but not for another misses these points. So does debating whether children are entitled to liberty or custody, although both of these norms contain hints of an important line of inquiry. That inquiry addresses the interrelationships and tensions between rights for children that constrain abuses of power by their parents and by the state, and rights for children that promote their abilities to form relationships of trust, meaning, and affection with people in their daily lives and their broader communities.[50]

My hope is that efforts to bring the talk about children's rights in greater accord with the facts of children's double dependency on parents and on the state could begin to build a jurisprudence of children's rights of some use in current debate. Further, I believe that there remains a role for an institution, perhaps still called a juvenile court, that engages in efforts to educate parents, children, and the broader community about their interdependent needs, duties, and yes, rights. Someday, such a court could serve as a mender of a social fabric in which it is safe for children and adults to craft trusting relationships. Meanwhile, a richer debate over the rights for children—a debate joining goals of autonomy and goals of affiliation—would challenge social patterns that permit public neglect, assign private responsibility for children, and also perpetuate public failures to develop the preconditions for that private responsibility. Through that debate, people may exert pressure for autonomy—but the debate may also demonstrate how public and private realms, and indeed, children and adults, are potentially part of one another.

Notes

1. Wallace Stevens, "The Course of a Particular," in *The Harvard Book of Contemporary American Poetry*, 39 (H. Vendler ed. 1985).

2. See e.g., R. Mnookin, *Child, Family, and State: Problems and Materials on Children and the Law* (1978): W. Wadlington, C. Whitebread, & S. Davis, *Children in the Legal System: Cases and Materials* (1983).

3. See Minow, "'Forming Underneath Everything That Grows': Toward a New History of Family Law," *Wis. L. Rev.* (1985) 819–98.

4. See Gaylin. "Competence: No Longer All or None," in *Who Speaks for the Child: The Problems of Proxy Consent* (W. Gaylin & R. Macklin, eds. 1982).

5. See, e.g., Recent Development. "The Insurance Crisis: Who's Looking After Day Care?," 9 *Harv. Women's L.J.* 199 (1986) (discussing magnitude of response to child abuse in day-care centers).

6. Children's Defense Fund. *A Children's Defense Budget: An Analysis of the President's FY 1986 Budget and Children* 4 (1985) [hereinafter cited as *Children's Defense Budget*].

7. *Children's Defense Budget,* supra note 6, at 18.

8. My calculations from *Children's Defense Budget,* supra note 6, at 33, make it approximately 37.8% (13.3 out of 35.2).

9. *Better Health for Children: Action for the Eighties* 76 (S. Buka, M. Peck & J. Gardner eds. 1982) (proceedings of a conference sponsored by the Student Comm. Dept. of Maternal and Child Health and Aging, Harvard School of Public Health, April 17, 1982) [hereinafter cited as *Better Health for Children*]. The *Children's Defense Budget,* supra note 6, at 38, says 1.5 million.

10. Massachusetts Advocacy Center, Massachusetts: *The State of the Child* 82 (E. Vorenberg ed. 1982).

11. S. Levitan & R. Belows, *What's Happening to the American Family?* 73 (1981).

12. U.S. Commission on Civil Rights. *Disadvantaged Women & Their Children* 13 (1983) (32,000 pre-schoolers caring for themselves. 2 million between ages of 7 and 13 unsupervised).

13. *Better Health for Children,* supra note 9, at 75.

14. Id. at 76.

15. From another vantage point, however, the state is always "intervening" in the sense that its noninvolvement in family matters expresses its approval, or at least its lack of disapproval, of what goes on in the private realm. Further, public norms governing compulsory schooling, child employment, and indeed marriage, child support, and child abuse establish governmental rules about what children need and deserve. See Minow, "Beyond State Intervention in the Family: For Baby Jane Doe," 18 *Mich. J.L. Reform* 933, 951–53 (1985); Olsen, "The Myth of State Intervention in the Family," 18 *Mich. J.L. Reform* 835, 836–37, 855–58 (1985).

16. Even these turn-of-the-century rules for children trace back to earlier innovations, according to historians who claim that childhood was created by late Medieval society, and adolescence by industrial society. See P. Aries, *Centuries of Childhood: A Social History of Family Life* (R. Baldick trans. 1962); J. Demos, *A Little Commonwealth: Family Life in Plymouth Colony* (1970); J. Kett, *Rites of Passage: Adolescence in America—1790 to the Present* (1977).

17. See V. Zelizer, "Pricing the Priceless Child: The Changing Social Value of Children," 56–137 (1985) (attitudes about work and education figure in transformation of conceptions of child's worth).

18. R. Wiebe, *The Search for Order* 169 (1967).

19. See B. Wishy, *The Child and the Republic* (1968). See also Skolnick, "The Limits of Childhood: Conceptions of Child Development and Social Context," 39 *Law & Contemp. Prob.* 38 (1975) (contrasting ideas of child as innocent and child as evil). See generally E. Ryerson, *The Best-Laid Plans: America's Juvenile Court Experiment* (1978) (rationales for juvenile court).

20. See Skolnick, supra note 19.

21. See R. Farson, *Birthrights* (1974); E. Friedenberg, *The Dignity of Youth & Other Atavisms* (1965); P. Goodman, *Growing Up Absurd* (1956). See generally B. Greenleaf, *Children Through the Ages: A History of Childhood* (1978) (summarizing research on history of childhood).

22. One conception of the history of Western civilization locates these civil rights movements in the deeper context of the liberal tradition. Under this conception, liberal ideology challenged feudal hierarchies that established fixed patterns of social obligations and dependence and introduced notions of individual autonomy, freedom, and equality through the vehicle of individual rights. See Kennedy, "The Structure of Blackstone's Commentaries," 28 *Buffalo L. Rev.* 209 (1979). The French and American Revolutions adopted such notions as their watchwords, but this historical narrative could locate the liberal transformation even earlier. See S. Seidman, *Liberalism & the Origins of European Social Theory* (1983) (assessment of Enlightenment's consequences for liberalism).

23. 347 *U.S.* 483 (1954).

24. 387 *U.S.* 1 (1967). The reasoning in the decision has little to do with any assessment of juveniles' actual competence. Rather, it grew from a critique of the kind of institution that the juvenile court had become, an institution marked by abusive discretion. Justice Fortas concluded that "the condition of being a boy does not justify a kangaroo court." Id. at 28. *Gault* itself contains an undertow of commitment to children's custody and control by parents. See infra text accompanying note 41.

25. 393 *U.S.* 503 (1969).

26. 428 *U.S.* 52 (1976).

27. This right may have some basis in an asserted competence of the child: the Court suggested that any girl old enough to get pregnant is old enough to decide whether or not

to continue the pregnancy. Id. at 75. Yet the basis for the minor's right has as much to do with a pragmatic view that the minor is in fact a separate person, and the state cannot expect to force the child's submission. The Court reasoned that "where the minor and the unconsenting parent are so fundamentally in conflict and the very existence of the pregnancy already has fractured the family structure," then the "veto power [would not] enhance parental authority or control." Id.

28. *McKeiver* v. *Pennsylvania*, 403 *U.S.* 528 (1971).

29. *Schall* v. *Martin*, 467 *U.S.* 253, 265 (1984).

30. *Parham* v. *J.R.*, 442 *U.S.* 584 (1979).

31. Id. at 604.

32. Compare *Goss* v. *Lopez*, 419 *U.S.* 565 (1975) with *Ingraham* v. *Wright*, 430 *U.S.* 651 (1977).

33. *H.L.* v. *Matheson*, 450 *U.S.* 398 (1981) (rejecting challenge by unemancipated minor to Utah statute requiring parental notification before the minor could obtain an abortion).

34. See "Drinking Limit—State Impact," *U.S. News & World Rep.*, July 9, 1984, at 14; "Ahead: Minimum Drinking Age of 21," *U.S. News & World Rep.*, June 25, 1984, at 8.

35. See Foster & Freed, "A Bill of Rights for Children," 6 *Fam. L.Q.* 343, 343 (1972) (arguments for children's rights resemble arguments over slavery and over women's emancipation).

36. See Williams, "Equality's Riddle: Pregnancy and the Equal Treatment/Special Treatment Debate," 13 *N.Y.U. Rev. L. & Soc. Change* 325 (1984–85).

37. For illuminating discussions of emerging feminist concerns and methodologies. see C. Gilligan, *In a Different Voice: Psychological Theory in Women's Development* (1981); N. Noddings, *Caring: A Feminine Approach to Ethics & Moral Education* (1984); M. Frug, "Re-reading Contracts: A Feminist Analysis of a Contracts Casebook," 34 *Am. U.L. Rev.* 1065 (1986): Scales. "The Emergence of Feminist Jurisprudence: An Essay," *Yale L.J.* (1986) vol. 95, Je 86, 1313–403. "The 1984 James McCormick Mitchell Lecture: Feminist Discourse, Moral Values and the Law—A Conversation," 34 *Buffalo L. Rev.* 11 (1985); Schneider. Rights and Politics, (unpublished manuscript) (on file at *Harv. Women's L.J.*).

38. Though my rendition is in no way a comprehensive account of these sources, my thinking about this history has been influenced by, among others, M. Gilmore, "Individualism in Renaissance Historians," in *Humanists and Jurists: Six Studies in the Renaissance* 38 (1963); M. Glendon, *The New Family and the New Property* (1981); P. Laslett, *The World We Have Lost* (3d ed. 1984); W. Seidman, supra note 22; W. Ullmann, *The Individual and Society in the Middle Ages* (1966); R. Unger, *Knowledge and Politics* (1975); R. Unger, *Law in Modern Society: Toward a Criticism of Social Theory* (1976); Kennedy, supra note 22; Strayer & Coulborn, "The Idea of Feudalism," in *Feudalism in History* 3 (R. Coulborn ed. 1956).

39. This may be why the legal framework often seems inadequate for dealing with questions of inclusion and exclusion in group membership. The problem of inclusion and exclusion has come before the Supreme Court recently, see *Roberts* v. *U.S. Jaycees*, 468 *U.S.* 609 (1984), but it has not reached a stable resolution.

40. For a thoughtful sketch of this problem, see Rodham. "Children Under the Law," 43 *Harv. Educ. Rev*, 487 (1973).

41. 387 *U.S.* 1, 41 ("the child and his parents must be notified of the child's right to be represented by counsel retained by them, or if they are unable to afford counsel, that counsel will be appointed to represent the child"). The *Gault* Court also rejected the claim that neither the juvenile nor his parents should be advised of the juvenile's right to remain silent. Id. at 51. Here, though, the Court acknowledged potential conflicts between parents who might urge confession, and children who might react with hostility if punished after confessing. Id. at 52.

42. 406 *U.S.* 205 (1972).

43. Another example of this form of children's rights is the standard law of child support that entrusts a custodial parent or guardian with the power to assert the child's right to support, whether or not such assertion is what the child wants, or is even fully in the child's interest. See Sugarmen, "*Roe* v. *Norton:* Coerced Maternal Cooperation," in *In the Interests of Children: Advocacy, Law Reform, and Public Policy* 366–447 (R. Mnookin ed. 1985) (examining litigation challenge to such a rule).

44. 406 *U.S.* 205, 241 (1972) (Douglas. J., dissenting).

45. See *In re Green*, 448 Pa. 338, 292 A.2d 387 (1972).

46. See K. Wooden, *Weeping in the Playtime of Others* (1976). The Supreme Court in *Gault* reviewed the original justifications for, and ensuing disillusionments with, the juvenile court, 387 *U.S.* 1, 14-31.

47. Many differences remain to distinguish the juvenile justice process from criminal law for adults. Fourth amendment protections, for example, have not been granted to minors in the same form or degree as those accorded to adults. See *New Jersey* v. *T.L.O.*, 105 S. Ct. 733 (1985).

48. See "Killing Young Killers," *N.Y. Times,* Jan. 9, 1986, at A22, col. 1; "South Carolina Executes Killer: Age Stirs Protest," *N.Y. Times,* Jan 11, 1986, § 1, at 6, col. 1 (South Carolina case imposing capital punishment for crimes committed while defendant was a juvenile).

49. To some extent, the general substantive law defining offenses for which a juvenile could be punished defines such duties, but its terms are too general and courts usually lack the ability to make real for the adolescent the mutual social pact. That pact maintains that if the individual obeys the law, the individual will be accepted by the society, yet no such acceptance has been guaranteed for poor, minority youth.

50. See Schneider, supra note 37 (describing dialectical development of women's rights through theory and practice and through communal activity).

Suggested Readings

Aviram, Aharon. "The Subjection of Children," *Journal of Philosophy of Education,* Vol. 24, No. 2, 1990, pp. 213–234.

Kim, Ki Su. "J. S. Mill's Concept of Maturity as the Criterion in Determining Children's Eligibility for Rights," *Journal of Philosophy of Education,* Vol. 24, No. 2, 1990, pp. 235–243.

Mahowald, Mary. "Possibilities for Moral Agency in Children," in Creighton Peden and James Sterba, ed., *Freedom, Equality, and Social Change* (New York: Mellen, 1989).

Montague, Phillip. "A Child's Right to Privacy," *Public Affairs Quarterly,* Vol. 2, No. 1, January 1988, pp. 17–32.

Olsen, Frances. "Children's Rights: Some Feminist Approaches to the United Nations Convention on the Rights of the Child," *International Journal of Law and the Family* 6, 1992, pp. 192–220.

Schoeman, Ferdinand. "Rights of Children, Rights of Parents, and the Moral Basis of the Family," *Ethics,* 91, October 1980.

Weinstein, Mark. "Reason and the Child," *Proceedings of the Philosophy of Education,* Annual Meeting, 1990, pp. 159–171.

Children and Families

Cases for Discussion

Child Divorces Parents

In September 1992, 12-year-old Gregory Kingsley made the headlines by becoming the first child allowed to "divorce" his parents. Gregory wanted to be adopted by the foster parents with whom he had been living. While courts often hold custody hearings to decide where a child should live and have the power to terminate parental rights, this was the first time that a child initiated the legal action and had a lawyer who represented only his interests. The action involved Gregory vs. his parents rather than two adult parties against one another, with the child being "awarded to" the winner.

Gregory claimed that he had in fact been abandoned by his mother when she voluntarily put him into foster care and did not visit, call, or write to him for two years. While his father did not protest the divorce, Gregory's mother, with whom he had lived for only 7 months of the past 8 years, vigorously and emotionally fought to keep her rights as parent.

Gregory won his case, and this court decision is one blow in favor of those who want to liberate children from having all decisions made for them by adults.

Still, some see children and adults as having very different moral status. "Are you saying that the child has the same right as an adult?" asked Chief Judge Charles M. Harris. That is, indeed, the central philosophical question, and a case needs to be made for or against equal rights for children.

It is only as children become recognized as persons in their own right, with interests, needs, and wishes that may differ from or even conflict with those of their parents, that precedents like the Kingsley case become possible. Historically, one view, though often unstated, has been that children "belong to" their parents, and remnants of that view are expressed in the presumption typically made by the courts that children should be kept with or returned to biological parents whenever possible.

Abusive Parents

In 1984, Joann Rossi pleaded guilty to manslaughter in the death of her 4-year-old son, Stephen. She gave up rights to her three other children, and they were adopted when she went to prison. She served a little more than 3 years of a 12-year sentence and then was paroled. She married and had another child, and in 1993 she was arrested for alleged abuse of that child, Gian Carlo, then 4 years old. She also had a 2-year-old daughter and a month-old son, who were placed in foster homes at the time of her second arrest.

Should parents convicted of abuse of one child be allowed to raise their other children? When should the state intervene in families?

Traditionally, the home has been considered a sanctuary, a private place where people may live their lives as they want without interference or scrutiny from the general public. However, the state has a legitimate interest in the well-being of children. Indeed, it is thought to function as *parens patriae,* that is, guardian of all children. Since it is clearly naive to think that parents are always loving, that children's and parents' interests always coincide, and that the home is always safe from violence, there seems to be a need for some state supervision and at times intervention in families.

If society had unlimited resources and each child could be given the "best possible" family and home, there might be a case for separating a great many children from their parents. However, the state can only try to ensure "good enough" homes for children, which often means leaving them in less than ideal situations. Given the difficulty of predicting which parents will become abusive or neglectful and given the principle of privacy for families, the state tries to keep intervention to a minimum.

The Issues

1. It is generally assumed that parents are the appropriate persons to make decisions for children. Why is this? What is the moral basis of the authority that parents have over children?

2. The role of the state in relation to children and families needs to be clarified. What justifies state intervention into the privacy of the family? What limits should there be?

3. Until recently, children were seen simply as part of a family, with little opportunity to make their own voices heard independent of their parents. No one talked much about children as individuals with interests and rights. But cases like the Kingsley and Rossi cases have begun to focus attention on the question of whether or not children have rights as children. Are there certain things children are entitled to even though they are only children? Can they make moral claims, or have other adults make moral claims for them, against members of their own family? Should they be allowed to choose where to live, with whom to live, and who their legal parents will be?

The Arguments

For Parental Authority

Philosophers have offered various reasons why parents should have authority over children. A theory that is commonly held, but rarely defended by philosophers, is that children "belong to" parents simply by virtue of the fact that the children grew from genetic material contributed by their biological parents. Under Roman law, for instance, fathers had life and death power over their children. Sometimes this view is embellished by the assumption that because of their biological ties, parents have a natural affection for as well as a better understanding of their own children than anyone else can, and thus they will make the best decisions for them.

The weakness of this view becomes clear when the concept of family is refined. There are many different kinds of families: biological or adopted; nuclear, that is, parents and children, or extended, including aunts, uncles, grandparents, or other relatives; two-parent, one-parent, or communal; separated or blended, including step-parents and their children; and heterosexual or gay/lesbian. The so-called Cornflake family—mom, dad, and the kids—represents the norm for less than half of American children today.

At minimum, a family is made up of one adult and one child, where the adult takes responsibility for caring for the child. That adult becomes the "psychological parent" of that child. It is important that children have good psychological parents, but there is no evidence that only biological parents can be good psychological parents.

The philosopher John Locke (1632–1704) has an interesting explanation of parents' authority over children. Parents have duties to children, he says, such as the duty to educate them, but in order to fulfill their duties, parents must have authority over them and children must obey. Thus there is good reason for parents to have authority over children. According to Locke, there is a limit to parental authority, however, for the goal of good parents is to raise their children to adulthood, giving them increasingly greater authority over themselves until they are mature enough to obey the dictates of reason directly and no longer need parental guidance and authority.

For State Intervention

At an opposite extreme from the view that parents have primary responsibility for children and authority over them is the view that the state has this responsibility. Plato (428–348 B.C.), the best-known advocate of this view, placed the goals and values of the state above those of the individual and thought that having parents raise children in families would detract from the loyalty both should have to the state. In the *Crito,* Plato refers to the state as parent of all its citizens. In the place of families, he envisioned a system of communal child rearing, where children would live, play, and be educated in groups, and where all aspects of children's upbringing would be determined directly by the state.

Although some modern societies, such as Israel and the Soviet Union, have embraced some form of communal child rearing, it has generally been modified by democratic societies which place a high value on individualism. They see that differences in upbringing lead to differences in experience and opinion, which contribute to the open debate that is the strength of democratic institutions.

Yet, even though our society rejects a whole system of state-run child rearing and in general defends parents' authority over children, there is a legitimate role for the state to oversee children's welfare. The state has an interest in having citizens who are healthy and educated, and so it has a role in limiting parental discretion. The state may require families to provide certain things for children, such as education and basic health care, and it may set limits on what families may do. For example, the state defines certain practices as physical or mental abuse, and in Sweden, the state has ruled that parents may not spank their children.

One important argument for the state's role in children's lives is an argument about justice. Children are born into families, as it were, by a natural lottery—some into loving, stable families, some into families ill-suited by temperament, ill health, or extreme youth to raise children. There are great disparities in emotional resources, education, and economic resources. Because of this, children start out with unequal opportunities. This basic injustice could be eliminated by having all children raised by the state, as Plato advocates. But, short of this radical solution, the injustice can be remedied by having the state set basic requirements for and limitations on how families raise their children. The state has the authority to require that a basic minimal standard is met for all children, for example, that all 5-year-olds be vaccinated, that all children attend school until age 16, and that children not be beaten or sexually abused.

To some degree, the state already regulates who may raise children: It is possible to terminate parental rights when abuse is proven, and prospective adoptive parents or foster parents are screened and tested. A more extreme proposal has been advanced by at least one contemporary philosopher, Hugh LaFollette. Just as there are tests and licenses for driving a car because of the potential harm they can cause, there should be tests and licenses for future parents. If this were extended to those who want to bear children, as well as to those who want to raise them, it would constitute an ultimate degree of intrusion into the family by the state, but it could possibly be defended on the grounds of providing better families for children than the present biological lottery.

For Children's Rights

A different kind of challenge to parental authority over children comes from children themselves or from those adults who would grant children the moral and legal right to choose for themselves, at least in some circumstances. A very influential advocate of this view is John Holt, whose 1974 book, *Escape from Childhood,* proposes giving children all the rights that adults have, which implies their being free of parental authority at whatever age the child can assert those rights.

Less radical views stop short of giving children equal rights but argue that it is time to rethink the nature of the family. Family relationships should be structured to show respect for all members, to empower the powerless, and to avoid domination of some members by others. Children are protected within the family if they are accorded rights, which are claims they can make against parents when interests conflict, as in the Kingsley case, or which can be claimed on their behalf by the state, as in the Rossi case.

There is resistance to the idea of according legal rights to children, or even recognizing moral rights that place restrictions on parents. The arguments against children's rights include (a) the belief that parents know best, that is, they are the best decision makers for their children, (b) the widespread belief that children are incompetent to know what is in their best interest, and (c) the fact that if children have rights, then the state has the duty to enforce them, and this would constitute unwarranted invasion into the privacy and intimacy of the family. The arguments for and against children's rights plays out in the arena of education and health care as well as in the family, and the proper balance of parent, state, and child in decision making is the central focus of many controversies, both philosophical and practical.

The Readings

"The Right to Found a Family," John Harris, Professor of Applied Philosophy at the Centre for Social Ethics and Policy, University of Manchester, England.

Harris raises a provocative question in the light of cases of child abuse and the issue of the rights children may have against their own families. He asks if it is everyone's right to bear or raise children, or if some prospective parents have a moral duty not to parent children. His position is that this should be answered only by considering the fate of the children.

"Equal Opportunity and the Family," Peter Vallentyne, Professor of Philosophy, Virginia Commonwealth University and Morry Lipson, Professor of Philosophy, Reed College.

Vallentyne and Lipson discuss the issue of state intervention into the family and propose an argument to defend it. Those who subscribe to Mill's liberalism should reject autonomy for the family, they claim, because children with equivalent capacities should have equal expectations of developing valued life skills, but this will not occur unless the state interferes in families to ensure equal opportunity for all children.

"Does a Child Have a Right to a Certain Identity?" Anita L. Allen, Philosopher and Professor of Law, Georgetown Law Center.

Allen considers a special case of the issue of whether or not children have independent interests and rights. She discusses arguments for and against transracial adoption and argues that it should be permitted because children do not have a right to any particular racial identity.

"Child Abuse: Parental Rights and the Interests of the Child," David Archard, Senior Lecturer in Philosophy, University of Ulster at Jordanstown.

Archard addresses the issue of whether or not parents are always the best decision makers for their children and the issue of the limits of family privacy. He questions the presumption often made in favor of family privacy and autonomy, for these are the conditions that allow child abuse to be hidden.

"Rights-talk Will Not Sort Out Child-abuse: Comment on Archard," Mary Midgeley, Professor of Philosophy, Newcastle, England.

Midgeley writes from a feminist perspective, moving questions away from the language of rights. She criticizes Archard for focusing narrowly on parents' rights instead of the broader practical context in which questions about child abuse arise.

The Right to Found a Family*

John Harris

The right or freedom to found a family expresses something so basic and deep-rooted in human psychology and social practice that it seems hardly worthy of special attention. And yet it is problematic in the extreme. Since it is, in a way, more fundamental than even the right to life, it is important to be clear about just what might be involved in sustaining or denying claims about the right to found a family and about the legitimacy of interfering with this supposed right or circumscribing it in various ways.

I must make clear that by talking of the *right* to found a family I do not of course mean to be metaphysically tendentious about the existence of rights, in the manner, for example, of Robert Nozick, who asserts on the first page of *Anarchy, State, and Utopia* that "[i]ndividuals have rights . . .," "things" that are in some sense self-evidently possessed by people and which, by their very nature, are overriding and operate to "trump" conflicting non-rights claims.[1] I mean merely that when we talk about rights, we do so to signal that we are talking about claims to the freedom to do certain things that we take very seriously indeed. This means that where a right to do something is recognised, it is implied that it would be wrong to interfere with a person's exercise of that right and that, if such interference were to be justified, quite extraordinarily strong reasons would have to be produced to justify it. And, perhaps equally important, that these extraordinarily strong reasons are weighty enough for us to regard the interests of the person whose rights are defended as sufficiently important for holding that others have an obligation to respect those interests.

So, is there a right to found a family? The European Convention on Human Rights[2] has seen fit to recognise and protect such a right and its authority has been much invoked of late in arguments about what aid might be called on in the legitimate exercise of that right. The occasion for this interest has been the debates surrounding the use of new techniques in medicine, particularly in human embryology, and the consequent reawakening of old debates about surrogate parents.[3]

For the record, this right, while very briefly and succinctly stated as Article 12 of the Convention is, in the Convention's formulation, profoundly ambiguous. Article 12 reads as follows:

> **Men and women of marriageable age have the right to marry and to found a family according to the national laws governing the exercise of this right.**

---

* I am much indebted to Geoffrey Scarre for his very patient and insightful editing of this piece and for many helpful suggestions.

It will be obvious that this article is almost totally opaque. How is it to be interpreted? Do men and women have the right to found a family independently, or only if married? Must they be of marriageable age to found a family or only of marriageable age to marry? Can national laws take away these rights or only regulate them? Is marriageable age defined by law, custom, or biology?

Clearly the European Convention on Human Rights is of little help if we wish to understand just what might be involved in respecting or even comprehending the right to found a family. What I want to do is examine the moral constraints that ought to govern the foundation of a family and in the light of these, consider the fundamental question of what rights or freedoms may appropriately be spoken of in this context. I shall assume that marriage is morally as well as biologically irrelevant to claims that may legitimately be made about the foundation of a family and I shall ignore this institution except in so far as it figures in the articulation of prejudices that should be dismissed.

My strategy will be to start by assuming that we would wish to respect the right to found a family and by reviewing the many problems involved in understanding what such a right might amount to. This will reveal a number of important moral issues that must be resolved before a coherent view of the rights and wrongs of having children can be arrived at. From this, a view about the morality of founding families will emerge.

I. The Right to Found a Family

1. What Is the Point of the Right to Found a Family?

When we wish to understand whether or not we might be justified in respecting a particular right we need to know something about its point, about what interests or values it is supposed to protect.[4] There are a number of perspectives from which we might wish to defend the right to found a family, and although they overlap at many points and even collapse on occasion one into another, if we start at least with a sense of how they differ this will help us to be clear about one dimension of the issues involved. I want to start by distinguishing what we might call "society-centred," "adult-centred," and "child-centred" views of family foundation.

a. Society-centred views These regard the family as a "fundamental unit of society"[5] and see the right to found a family in terms of the perpetuation and protection of one of society's basic units. The point of such a right from this perspective is to serve the needs of a particular conception of society and to do so by protecting a particular conception of the family as a social unit. More loosely, society's interest might simply be served by measures which help to ensure that there *will* be a next generation, or a sufficiently populous one, by facilitating the production of children. This may also, of course, be part of an adult-centred view. And in so far as there might be a "society view" about the sorts of children it would be socially desirable to produce, such a view might well set limitations on the right to produce, say, severely handicapped children.

b. Adult-centred views   Such views would see the right to found a family as perhaps simply a dimension of human freedom, or, more specifically, the right might be seen as protecting adult desires for the satisfactions of procreation—child-bearing and birth or child-rearing. Relatedly the importance of founding a family might be viewed in terms of the desirability of securing succession or inheritance, or as attaching to the prestige of founding or heading a family, or in terms of the need to secure the protection of a family to provide for a secure old age. In all of these cases and others we might imagine the right claimed is for the protection of the various interests of would-be founders of families. These may not be adults in the legal sense, nor indeed in the biological sense (if there is one). They will at any event be existing individuals with views about having or looking after children.

c. Child-centred views   The child-centred view would regard the right to found a family as securing the interests of the next generation. As with society-centred views, this conception of family foundation might well involve constraints on the sorts of people judged fit to produce and rear children as well as on the sorts of children it is judged right to bring into or allow to continue in existence. It might, for example, be thought wrong to inflict on children certain sorts of disadvantage whether these stem from the context in which they are to be reared, the people who are to look after them, or from handicaps it is known or can be predicted they will possess.

Understanding just what the point of a right to found a family might be will tell us about what might be involved in granting the protection of such a right to various classes of individuals. Of course the legitimacy of each of these views might well be challenged, as might the morality of enforcing them. This is another issue and one to which we will return.

In addition to understanding the point of a right to have children we might need to know about what might be called the ambit of such a right. Against whom might it be enforced or claimed and how are conflicts of rights to be resolved?

2. What Is the Ambit of the Right?

Founding a family involves much more, and perhaps also much less, than simply doing what comes naturally and hoping for the best. Perhaps it is time to say something about just what might be meant by "founding a family." I've persevered with this rather quaint phrase used by the European Convention on Human Rights because it is usefully ambiguous. However, it is time to be clear about what we mean when talking of founding a family.

a. What is a family?   I'm not interested here in producing a definition of the family or indeed in producing any watertight definition at all, but merely in making plain what for the moment I mean by "founding a family." I shall take "founding a family" to mean something as broad as the acquisition by a person or persons of one or more children, where "acquisition" involves taking those children into the person's home as full members of the household and where those acquiring the children take on the obligation to afford them care and protection and are consequently entitled to regard those children as in some sense "their own."

Now the paradigm, if not any longer the established way to found a family, is for a man and a woman to marry and then lie back and think of their native land. This is probably what the European Convention envisages, and its Article 12 is designed to prevent states from putting impediments in the way of marriage or procreation by consenting couples. However, most of the rights we know of are rights possessed by individuals, and so we must ask what sort of people can claim and maybe enforce such rights, against whom or what can they do so, and in what circumstances?

b. Rights against individuals   If we imagine what might be involved in the enforcing of the right to found a family by one individual against another we can see immediately how this right would have to be limited by other individuals' competing rights to self determination and freedom from assault. Clearly any man, for example, wishing to claim his right to found a family in the absence of a consenting partner, either in the form of a woman willing to bear or try to bear his children, or in the absence of a willing egg or embryo donor and a suitable surrogate mother, would be demanding the right to perform rape or its moral equivalent. If individuals have rights to found families which might be enforceable against other individuals this, clearly, can only mean that they have the right to attempt to found families with consenting partners of various sorts which must give way to equal competing rights of the other individuals. However, it might involve the claim that third parties should not impede legitimate attempts to found a family by, say, legislating against the use of consenting surrogates by individuals unable to have children without their assistance or by putting obstacles in the way of individuals who wish to obtain medical assistance with procreation. Or, what amounts to the same thing, by declining to provide medical assistance with procreation to some where such assistance is available to others (married couples, say) without restriction.

c. Rights against corporations   Although the choice of a sexual and hence sometimes a procreational partner is usually regarded as a matter of individual choice, there may be many circumstances in which we might envisage rights being claimed by couples against the state or other agencies for assistance of various kinds in the foundation of a family. We are familiar with the claims that are already standard for neonatal and postnatal care and for particular types of assistance at birth as well as with "family planning," which is not always a euphemism for attempts to avoid the foundation of a family.

Less familiar are the claims made for assistance with infertility. These may now involve the need for Artificial Insemination by Donor (AID) or In Vitro Fertilization (IVF), and women who cannot themselves carry or give birth to a child may need the help of a surrogate mother. Some of these techniques are very costly and often require the aid not only of health care professionals of various sorts but also of amateur or professional third parties, who may be

needed for the donation of sperm or eggs or even embryos, and for the lease
or loan of that most valuable piece of gynaecological real estate, the womb.

Thus, claims for assistance with the foundation of a family may be very
costly to satisfy and may involve the co-operation of many people and institutions. This is of course true of many of the rights claimed in complex societies.
Think, for example, of the right to due process of law. This is immensely
costly and demands, *inter alia,* the forced attendance of many innocent third
parties as witnesses, as members of juries, or to give "expert" opinion, as well
as the co-operation of numerous professionals.

A further set of problems raised by considering the ambit of this supposed
right concern precisely who can claim it.

d. Who has the right to found a family?   In addition to married couples and
heterosexual couples in what are sometimes referred to as "stable continuing
relationships," homosexual or gay couples may also wish to found families, as
may single people of either gender or any sexual orientation. These may even
be quite young people. The recent House of Lords' judgement in *Gillick* v.
*West Norfolk and Wisbech Area Health Authority and the Department of Health
and Social Security* (All England Reports, 1985) established that the courts were
not compelled to "hold that a girl under sixteen lacked the legal capacity to
consent to contraceptive advice" and that in certain circumstances that advice
could be given without her parents' knowledge or consent. Of course young
girls can and frequently do have children even though they are not "legally"
able to consent to sexual relations. Interestingly, this case seems to have
established that whereas girls under sixteen cannot in law consent to sexual
relations, they may give valid consent to medical treatment, which may of
course involve much more complex considerations and the effects of which
may be more far reaching. Such treatment could presumably include both AID
and IVF followed by embryo transfer (the fertilization of their own eggs
externally followed by the transfer of the fertilised egg to their own uterus).
This judgement thus seems to establish that while it is illegal for a girl under
sixteen to consent to become pregnant in the usual way via sexual intercourse,
she may legally consent to become pregnant via various forms of medical
intervention in a much more complex way. Thus, young girls may consent to
being made pregnant by doctors but not by their lovers.

We may expect young people of both genders to begin to claim *de jure,* as
well as *de facto,* "rights" to found families on an increasing scale.

The last case we must mention briefly for the sake of completeness is that
of posthumous parenting. Here, frozen eggs and sperm or frozen embryos
might be left behind by men or women with a view to their being fertilised
and/or implanted after the death of either or both genetic parents. Indeed, a
will might request the posthumous foundation of a family and provide funds
to secure it.

II. Controlling Reproduction

We must now consider what legitimate reasons there might be for imposing
controls or restraints upon the freedom to have children or found families.

Before doing so we should remind ourselves of the claims made about having children, both in the sense of being entitled to bring them into the world and also of ensuring that they be well and properly looked after once they are here. The right to have children or found families is claimed for a number of reasons: because people badly want to have children; because it is important to individuals, to society, and to the children that they do have them; and perhaps not least because people see having children as part of the purpose and indeed the meaning of life. The claim to the freedom to have children is a very strong one, which of course is partly why it is expressed in the language of rights. Arguments as to why people should not have or should not be permitted to have children must clearly be even stronger. It will be convenient to review the arguments that are often produced in support of controlling reproduction under the three headings we have already considered (considered this time, for variety, in reverse order).

We must also be clear what might be meant by "controls and restraints" in this context.

Controls and Restraints

It will be useful to distinguish between attempts to control reproduction or parenting—in the sense of absolute prohibitions on reproduction or of depriving parents of the custody of their children—on the one hand, and attempts simply to hinder reproduction or parenting on the other.

It might appear that attempts to control reproduction via legislation are doomed to failure—for how could they be enforced? But even if any purported legislation stopped short of compulsory sterilisation, or even compulsory abortion, it might none the less be effective. Making it illegal for certain people or types of people to reproduce and attaching financial penalties if they defied the legislation, coupled with deprivation of the custody of any resulting children, might be highly effective. But even if we rule out of court any such draconian measures, the judicious placing of various obstacles and hindrances in the way of reproduction might be equally effective in fact. These are common enough already, for many individuals need help with reproduction, and if medical services refuse their assistance to certain individuals or types of people then they may effectively be prevented from reproducing themselves or gaining the custody of their children. We will return to these possibilities as we consider particular cases.

a. Child-centred arguments   A classic formulation of the strongest argument against the freedom to reproduce is perhaps still that of John Stuart Mill in his essay *On Liberty:*

> It still remains unrecognised, that to bring a child into existence, without a fair prospect of being able, not only to provide food for its body, but instruction and training for its mind, is a moral crime, both against the unfortunate offspring and against society.[6]

Now of course the crimes that Mill adverts to are relatively easily remedied as Mill is himself aware, for he continues:

> if the parent does not fulfil this obligation, the State ought to see it fulfilled, at the charge, as far as possible, of the parent.[7]

Thus, we need not prevent people from reproducing themselves but should merely ensure that their children are properly educated and cared for. However, the powerful argument that Mill introduces involves the idea that one can harm people by bringing them into existence under adverse conditions. The question arises as to how adverse the conditions must be before this becomes true.

Clearly we must distinguish between adverse conditions that are remediable and those which are not, and we must also distinguish between conditions which, while technically remediable, are in fact either unlikely to be remedied or unlikely to be remedied in time to make a difference to the child or children in question. Equally clearly, the severity of the adverse conditions the children will have to face is also crucial.

It is likely to prove impossible to be at all precise on the question of just how adverse the conditions must be before bringing a child into the world will be properly regarded as criminal. Probably there will be considerable agreement at the extremes and a very large grey area in which we are unsure just what to think. We will be looking into this grey area in due course, but for the moment we need to clear up another troublesome issue. It is the problem of just when what we do about the creation of children counts as affecting them adversely.

It is sometimes argued that one cannot affect others adversely unless they are there to be adversely affected, in short, unless they exist. If this is right, it is clearly impossible to affect adversely children who have yet to be conceived. This seems so obviously true as to require no further discussion, and yet a simple but important argument advanced by Derek Parfit shows that this is not so. He invites us to consider the actions of two different women:

> The first is one month pregnant and is told by her doctor that, unless she takes a simple treatment, the child she is carrying will develop a certain handicap. We suppose again that life with this handicap would probably be worth living, but less so than a normal life. It would obviously be wrong for the mother not to take the treatment, for this will handicap her child. . . .
> We next suppose that there is a second woman, who is about to stop taking contraceptive pills so that she can have another child. She is told that she has a temporary condition such that any child she conceives now will have the same handicap; but that if she waits three months she will then conceive a normal child. And it seems (at least to me) clear that this would be just as wrong as it would for the first woman to deliberately handicap her child.[8]

It is clear from this example that our responsibility for what happens to our children extends to what we knowingly do to affect how their lives will be, whether or not those lives are in being at the time we make relevant decisions. This is an important conclusion with ramifications far beyond our present concerns.[9] However, it also highlights a disturbing problem about just how bad the conditions adversely affecting our children must be before we are morally obliged to refrain from inflicting those conditions on them.

Suppose, along the lines of the above example, a woman learns that if she conceives a child this month it will have a minor handicap but that if she waits for three months she can conceive a perfectly healthy child. We would all judge that she should wait the three months rather than have a handicapped child. We should notice a very important feature of this case. It is that if the woman decides not to wait she will have a child that while handicapped, will have a life that is still well worth living. We can imagine that the handicap in question will be, say, the absence of one hand. Now, to be born thus handicapped is that child's only chance of being born at all—that is, it is that child's only chance of life. For the child that will be conceived three months hence, coming as it will from a different egg (let alone different sperm) will be a *different child*—not the same child minus the handicap. So, if she doesn't wait, it would be difficult to suggest that the child who results, handicapped as she will be, has been wronged by her mother, for that child will still have a life worth living and has the chance of a life thus handicapped or no life at all. So if we judge, as surely we must, that the mother in this example ought to wait, it is not because if she fails to do so she will have wronged her child but rather, that she will have done wrong. What then is the wrong she will have done? It seems that this must be understood in terms of the wrongness of bringing needless, avoidable suffering into the world, suffering that would be avoided if the woman waited for three months.

We clearly need to modify Mill's argument, for consideration of the present example makes it clear that our responsibility with regard to having children is not the responsibility to avoid harming people by bringing them into existence under adverse conditions, but the responsibility not to cause needless avoidable suffering by bringing into existence, when we need not do so, individuals who we know will suffer.

But this clarification brings a further problem in its wake. It seems clear that a mother faced with the dilemma we have been considering should not go ahead and conceive a handicapped child when she can wait and conceive a child who will be normal. But what if waiting will make no difference? What should a mother do when faced with the choice of having a handicapped child or no child (or no further child) at all?

We are surely far less confident that a woman faced with that dilemma should decide to have no children rather than have a child with a significant but still relatively minor handicap. When and why do the good reasons a woman has to postpone pregnancy to avoid bringing into the world a child who will inevitably suffer, cease to have effect? It looks as though the answer is that they cease to have effect at the point at which she can no longer regard her prospective child as replaceable. But why should this be? If she is right in thinking it wrong to add to the suffering of the world when she can avoid doing so by, in this case, postponing pregnancy and having a normal child later, why does it not remain wrong for this woman to add to the suffering of the world when the only alternative is to avoid absolutely having a child (or another child)? If she is wrong to have a handicapped child when she can *replace* it with a normal one, why does it seem less wrong, or not wrong at all, when that child is not replaceable?

It would be simple (though not easy) to say that it would be just as wrong for the mother in our present example who can have only handicapped children to go ahead and have them—and maybe this is what we should say, although we must be clear as to what *else* we would be saying if we did say so. One of the other things we would be saying, and perhaps this is partly why we hesitate here, is that certain people or certain sorts of people may not reproduce themselves. For, given the strong desire and strong interest people seem to have in having children, to prevent those who can only have handicapped children from reproducing themselves is to deny those people an important opportunity; and to deny their children the chance to exist at all.

But perhaps an easier answer is available. It is simply that, so long as the handicapped children will none the less have lives that are on balance worth living, the parents would be contributing more happiness than misery to the world by producing such children.

So, in addition to weighing the avoidable suffering that would be brought into the world by the birth of these handicapped children, we have to count in the happiness of such children also, and we have to consider the avoidable suffering to the parents who want offspring but can only produce progeny with some handicap. Faced with the prospect of the frustration of their desire to reproduce, and also with the attack upon their equal status as citizens, which would be involved in denying them an opportunity that others can freely exercise, such individuals would certainly suffer and would feel rightly that they had been victimized. And since their children, though handicapped, would still be glad to be alive, their case looks a strong one.

We can see, then, that a balance has to be struck between the suffering of those who are born handicapped on the one hand and, on the other, the harm which may be done to individuals or classes of people by preventing them from founding families. In conceding this we can see why our intuitions are different in each case we have been considering. We can understand why the person who by postponing conception can avoid the infliction of handicap on her child should do so. We can also understand that, where an individual's only chance to have a child is to have one with a certain degree of handicap, the wrong of creating unavoidable suffering must be balanced against the wrong that would be done in denying people the chance to have the children they desire; children, moreover, who despite a certain degree of handicap will have lives that are worth living.[10]

b. Adult-centred arguments   We have already reviewed some of the adult-centred reasons for founding a family and I will not go further into most of these. One of the most significant adult-centred claims about family foundation concerns more particularly the decision *not to found a family*, and centres on what have come to be thought of as *feminist* claims concerning "a woman's right to choose." Now, this slogan covers a large number of separate claims about a woman's control, not only over her own body, but also over the fate and sometimes the very existence of other individuals. The nature and variety of the claims that are made under this umbrella are of the first importance and it is well worth rehearsing some of the main ones. Before we do so, however, one claim that is sometimes made about the legitimacy of arguments about women's rights needs to be considered. It is the idea, often introduced by feminists, that only women are eligible to debate these issues.

Women Only!   It is perhaps paradoxical that the advent of feminism, which is in essence a movement for equality, has evolved a separatist strand which not only excludes men from gatherings of feminist women—a not unreasonable and perhaps even an essential measure—but, more significantly, denies the eligibility of men to talk of, or judge, matters regarded as strictly the business of women. The main idea is, I suppose, that one is only qualified to speak of or judge what one knows, and men cannot possibly have the requisite knowledge or experience. They cannot, so the argument goes, know what it is like to be a woman—particularly, what it is like to be a woman oppressed by men. This essential lack of basic data makes men ineligible to contribute to the debate and also of course disqualifies the present author. My own special interest in rebutting this view will be obvious, but even interested parties can be right, and in this case the suggestion that men are ineligible to speak about a range of feminist issues—including those we are now addressing—is either tautological or false. False because, as Wittgenstein has shown,[11] most of the claims to knowledge that we can make, and most indeed of what passes for knowledge in education, is communicated by language rather than by personal and private experience. And anything communicated in language is in principle understandable by competent language users. If the feminists were right, then their own entitlement to speak about most things would be undermined, for most of the issues about what they (or anyone) would wish to speak require knowledge based on other than personal experience.

There is also a rather suspicious elitism about this position. If it were correct, it would deny any excluded minority from talking or making judgements about the domain from which they had been excluded, thereby disqualifying them from a valid critique of their oppressors.

Control of Reproduction   We must now take up again the question of the validity of feminist claims about "a woman's right to choose." Many of these claims have to do with what is often called a woman's "reproductive destiny": whether or not to have sexual relations at all, choice of partners, decisions about whether or not to take contraceptive precautions and choice of method, decisions about whether or not to have—or try to have—children, and decisions about whether or not to have abortions. All of these claims are contested by some people and are regarded as controversial.

There are of course disputes about the age at which women may legitimately be free to have sexual relations with others, and there are also legal constraints on such matters. In marriage there are disputes about whether a woman is free to decline sexual intercourse and hence as to whether rape within marriage is legally possible. Many people besides parents may attempt to influence the choice of sexual or marriage partners and there may be cultural and racial (or racist) influences here also. The now notorious "Gillick" case, the bare bones of which were mentioned earlier, has highlighted attempts to influence or circumscribe a young girl's ability to take contraceptive measures on her own responsibility as well as her ability to choose whether or not to have an abortion.

A woman's right to choose abortion, for example, depends not simply on establishing her competence to make autonomous choices for herself, but also on what might be termed the moral status of the foetus. And her right to choose to have children if she wants them will depend on the justifiability of bringing children into the world in circumstances that could for some reason be morally questionable.

These dimensions of the problem of understanding the morality of choosing to found a family—or of choosing not to do so—are apt to be lost in the fog of political rhetoric and religious humbug that so often surrounds discussion of these issues. For example, those feminists who are inclined to say that "no true state of equality can exist for women in a society that denies them freedom and privacy in respect of fertility control"[12] must be entitled to claim that women would be justified in purchasing their equality, or that society is entitled to establish such equality, at the cost of the lives of the many foetuses that must be sacrificed to the establishment of such a right.[13] Equally, those who regard the life of the foetus as *sacred* must be satisfied that there are good reasons for supposing that the life of the foetus is not only valuable, but that it has a value comparable with that of the adults whose freedom and political rights its protection may threaten.

If it could be shown that the life of the foetus is sacred or that unborn children are entitled to the same protections as are afforded to adults, then a woman's right to choose would have to be balanced against the competing rights of the foetus to exist, or at least its right not to have its existence terminated at the wish of its mother. But the foetus does not possess those capacities that make its life valuable, that render it capable of valuing its own existence and hence make it wrong to deprive that individual of something that it values.[14] "A woman's right to choose" does not then have to compete with the right of the foetus to exist, and one very powerful set of arguments against the freedom of choice for women concerning the foundation of families disappears.

Two challenges to a woman's right to opt for abortion if she wants it are often produced at this point and it would be as well, while we are on the subject, to give them the brief attention that they deserve. The two challenges usually appear in the form of demands that either the father's interests in founding a family or (usually if she is young) the girl's parents' preferences about these matters are to be given due weight. Certainly they should be given due weight, but the weight due to them is far from massive, for if the woman whose pregnancy is at issue does not want the pregnancy to continue, then to give the sort of weight that might tip the scales to the preferences of either the father of the foetus or its maternal grandparents (whatever their parental authority) would be to conclude that any of these third parties might be entitled to subject the woman most concerned to the risks and pains of continued pregnancy and childbirth against her will. It is one thing for women to run these risks and endure these pains voluntarily, but to be effectively forced to do so by the weight given to the preferences of her lover, husband, or parents would be to legalise assault, battery, and imprisonment to a quite unprecedented extent.

The justification for permitting the preferences of others to force these things upon a woman in the absence of arguments that refer to the need to protect the foetus seems entirely absent. We have seen then, that women capable of autonomous choice, whether or not they are of "legal" age, may elect not to found families if that is their choice and may take whatever steps they please to this end including, if necessary, aborting the unwanted foetus. I say "if necessary," for no rational women would regard abortion, with its attendant dangers and unpleasantnesses, as a first-line method of contraception.

If, however, a woman decides that she would like to have children, are there any moral considerations that would prove stronger than her own preferences and which should incline us to conclude that she may not in fact be entitled to do so?

Unfit Parents   There are a number of circumstances in which it is claimed that certain individuals or certain types of people might be unfit for parenthood. Some of these considerations might with equal appropriateness have been considered under the heading "Child-centred arguments," for they depend on the supposition that these adults are "unfit" to have children because of disastrous consequences for the children. Before moving to a consideration of these cases, we must look quickly at some circumstances in which the alleged unfitness has nothing or little to do with the consequences for the child.

1. *Harm to the Parents.* Some parents might be thought unsuitable candidates for parenthood because of the consequent risk to themselves. The clearest case is where it is known that a mother would risk her own life or risk severe damage to her own health if she were to become pregnant or continue her pregnancy, and where the child would be normal and could probably be born alive, perhaps by post mortem Caesarian section. This is not the place to examine the question of suicide nor indeed the question of autonomy. If we assume that autonomous individuals may choose even to harm themselves or even their own lives it would be hard to think that they are not entitled to do so in circumstances in which they would thereby give life to others. To conclude otherwise would also, incidentally, rule out those acts of heroism, quite unconnected with childbirth, in which someone rescues another at the cost of her own life.

    Children may also threaten their parents where the disability of the potential addition to the family would strain the health and resources of the parents. Here again this seems clearly a matter for parental choice.

2. *Harm to the Other Children of the Family.* There are, however, some circumstances in which particularly demanding additional members of a family may damage the other siblings or other children in the family. Should parents knowing that this is likely to be the case go ahead and have, say, a child

they know will be handicapped and thus likely to damage other children by its demands—or, for that matter, a specially gifted child who, they know, would be likely to have the same effect?

Such circumstances may constitute good reasons for parents to decide not to have any more children, and good reasons for anyone to conclude that perhaps they ought not to have any more. But the question for us is whether, if the parents decide that it is worth the risk or the certainty of some damage, they should be permitted or helped to go ahead. Do they have the right to have children in such circumstances?

This is perhaps no great problem; the damage we are talking about is likely to be at best speculative and at worst far from serious. It would be hard to conclude that children are entitled to be protected from such damage at the cost of draconian penalties against their parents of the sort that would have to be imposed in an attempt to prevent them from adding to their families, or indeed at the cost of consigning such children to the—under the circumstances—gratuitous fate of being brought up as "orphans."

c. Society-centred arguments   Under this heading we must look again at those whose fitness to become parents is challenged on the grounds of some alleged defect. One group of people who are increasingly "up front" about their desire for, and intention to, have children, are homosexuals of either gender. Of course, gay women have always been able to have children in the normal way by finding a willing male to oblige, but with the advent of artificial insemination and *in vitro* fertilisation, it has been possible for lesbians to have children without compromising their sexuality. But the necessity of their availing themselves, to a greater or lesser extent, of technical and medical assistance with fertilisation has raised the possibility of the denial of that assistance. And indeed it is still rare for single women, let alone those who are openly lesbian, to be offered the assistance of health professionals in their endeavours to become pregnant.

It is important to be clear that when a particular and identifiable group of people are denied the opportunity to have the children they want, or are denied the assistance in that endeavour which is standardly provided for the generality of women, they are wronged in three important and separate ways.

First, and obviously, they are denied the chance to have their own child in the way that they want, something universally regarded as a benefit both to themselves and to society, and one so great that it is often cited not only as among the most worthwhile experiences and important benefits of life, but as one that gives point and meaning to existence. To be denied this benefit, which is available to others, is certainly to be wronged.

Second, such people are wronged if they are treated in a way which is tantamount to singling them out as second-class individuals, deemed unfit for parenthood and unsafe to be offered the care of children. To treat them so is to stigmatise such individuals and to offer them a public insult from which they are unable to defend themselves and to which it is difficult to reply. This happens also when information about, and discussion of, their way of life is excluded from school education on the grounds that it is offensive or unsuitable for consideration in that context.

Finally, where against all the odds such women do manage to succeed in becoming pregnant, they are further stigmatised by being made the subjects of especially stringent scrutiny and suspicion. They—and others—notice that they are singled out from the generality of mothers-to-be, and this again does them a separate and not insignificant wrong.[15]

The justifications for imposing these disadvantages on individuals and for insulting them and stigmatising the group with which they identify would have to be strong indeed, and we will consider these supposed justifications while examining the case of those who would acquire families by methods other than those of genetic reproduction.

III. Controlling Family Acquisition

Genetic reproduction is obviously not the only way of founding families. Families are also founded when people acquire the custody of children whom they treat in some sense as their own. Adoption, fostering, and surrogacy agreements are all methods by which people may absorb children into their family who are not, or are not entirely, genetically related to the "parents." In our society, and in most industrialised societies, it has been customary to screen adoptive and foster parents and, lately, those entering into surrogacy agreements as to their suitability for the role and responsibility of parenting. This is somewhat odd, for it implies that we think it matters that people establish that they are fit and proper potential parents before we permit them the custody of children; it implies that we care about the sort of people who propose to have children. But we do not. Anyone who doubts this has only to think of the cavalier way in which society allows any Thomasina, Dorothea, or Harriet to go out and have children without so much as a "by your leave." We must remember that adoptive, foster, and surrogate parenting is a tiny proportion of the total parent population, so that the percentage of parents that we bother to scrutinise for their adequacy in the role is a negligible proportion of the whole.

The alternatives seem to be these: Either it matters that people demonstrate their adequacy as parents or it does not. If it matters, then it matters not only that adoptive and foster parents do so but that all children get whatever protection it is that screening might afford. If it doesn't matter, or if we believe that screening is useless or otherwise unacceptable, then why subject adoptive and other non-genetic parents to such a process?

It may be thought that these alternatives as stated are misleading, for might it not be argued that we cannot regulate sexual behaviour or stop people from having children if they so choose, and therefore have no alternative but to allow the current unbridled procreation? But where existing children are for some reason left without natural parents willing or able to assume the role, then we have some responsibility to be careful about whom we allow to have care of them.

But this way of stating things is not quite right either. For, as we have suggested, it *would* be possible to regulate even sexual procreation by attaching various disincentives and mandatorily depriving unlicensed parents of the custody of their children—at least until they had been screened like any adoptive parents. The reason we don't do so is not because we cannot, but because we don't want to. And we don't want to for very good reasons. These reasons have to do with the importance we attach to having children and being parents—an importance already more than once spelled out in detail. They also have to do with our reluctance to place so much power in the hands of any government: a power not only to regulate the population, but an immense one of general interference. This power would enable governments not only to interfere with what is acknowledged as one of the most important human freedoms, but also would give them the ability to use that power selectively or arbitrarily to intimidate or punish individuals or sections of the population for other and ulterior reasons unconnected with the desirability of protecting children. The power would have to be quite extraordinarily comprehensive, for it is difficult to imagine what areas of life would not be relevant to forming a view about an individual's suitability for parenthood. There would be no limit to the ambit of those officials charged with screening potential parents, and so no limit to a government's power to delve into the private affairs of citizens.

Moreover, these powers would be unnecessary, for we are able to protect candidates for adoption or fostering in the same way as we do all other children—by removing from the custody of their parents any children who have been palpably ill-treated or placed in danger and by disqualifying any potential parents who have proved their unfitness by a history of damaging or ill-treating children.

There is another and very important reason why we do not screen all potential parents. It is that we haven't the first idea of what makes someone a bad parent *in advance of their actually being one.*

Nor for that matter and equally importantly, do we have the first idea of what it is for someone to be a good parent.

What I mean to imply is that we do not have the first idea of how to characterise a "good parent" and so do not know what the description of a "bad parent" would be, *except* in the sense that a parent who neglects, batters, or who sexually assaults her child is unfit to have the care of children. But we have no reliable way of predicting in advance of seeing the bruises, so to speak, just who these child batterers will be. Moreover, the injustice of attempting to find people "guilty" in advance of the offence seems no less applicable to cases such as these than it does in any other areas of human affairs.

There is absolutely no evidence that homosexuals of either gender make bad parents, nor for that matter do we have any hard information as to the adverse effects on children of being brought up in single-parent families. In the absence of such information it is hard to imagine what justifications there might be for stigmatising homosexuals or single people as somehow unfit for parenting, or the justifications for placing obstacles in the way of their becoming parents or for not affording them the help of any social or medical services that they may need to call in aid in order to found families.

IV. Conclusion: Decontrolling Family Foundation

The conclusion that we have reached seems to be the following: The desire to found a family—whether by procreation, adoption, fostering, or surrogacy—is constrained only by consideration for the fate of the children who will constitute that family.

Where the children are or will be severely handicapped, there may be an obligation not to bring them into or allow them to continue in a world where their existence will be genuinely terrible. Where the handicap is something less than this—that is, where the children will have a reasonable if restricted life, and are likely to prefer that life to non-existence—then, if the parents can have their own children without inflicting even that handicap, say by having healthy children later, they should do so. Where there is no alternative for particular parents but to have handicapped children, then so long as bringing those children into existence would not constitute cruelty to them, the parents may reasonably choose so to do.

People who wish to found families where the question of handicap does not arise are entitled to do so and are entitled to all normally available assistance unless it can be palpably shown that they are unfit to be parents. And this unfitness must be palpable and demonstrable, not statistical, speculative, or based on sheer prejudice.

Notes

1. Robert Nozick. *Anarchy, State, & Utopia* (Oxford: Basil Blackwell, 1974), p. ix. See also Ronald Dworkin, *Taking Rights Seriously* (London: Duckworth, 1977).
2. For what it's worth! The European Convention on Human Rights can be found in Brownlie (see note 5).
3. Going back at least to Abraham, or to whoever set down the story of Abraham, whichever has the greater historicity.
4. See my *Violence & Responsibility* (London: Routledge & Kegan Paul, 1980), Chapter 2, and my "The Morality of Terrorism" in *Radical Philosophy*, Spring 1983, for the elaboration of this point.
5. See *inter alia* European Social Charter 1961, Part I, Sec. 17, in *Basic Documents on Human Rights*, ed. Ian Brownlie (Oxford: Oxford University Press, 1971).
6. John Stuart Mill, *On Liberty*, Chapter 5, in *Utilitarianism*, ed. Mary Warnock (London: Fontana, 1972), p. 239.
7. Ibid.
8. Derek Parfit, "Rights, Interests and Possible People," in *Moral Problems in Medicine*, ed. S. Gorovitz (Englewood Cliffs, N.J.: Prentice-Hall, 1976).
9. See my *Violence and Responsibility* (London: RKP, 1980).
10. See Peter Singer, *Practical Ethics* (Cambridge: Cambridge University Press, 1979) for a related discussion, particularly Chapters 1 and 2.
11. Wittgenstein's famous private language argument establishes this. I cannot hope to summarise it here. It is to be found in his *Philosophical Investigations* (Oxford: Basil Blackwell, 1953), Part I, para 243 ff.
12. See Madelaine Simms, quoted by Elizabeth Kingdom in her "Legal recognition of a woman's right to choose," in *Women in Law*, ed. J. Brophy and C. Smart (London: Routledge & Kegan Paul, 1985).
13. 150,000 abortions are performed annually in the United Kingdom and there would perhaps be even more if abortion on demand were legalised.
14. See my *The Value of Life: An Introduction to Medical Ethics* (London: RKP, 1985), Chapter 1.
15. The argument here follows the same lines as that developed in my *The Value of Life*. See note 14.

Equal Opportunity and the Family

Peter Vallentyne and Morry Lipson

Introduction

Liberals cherish the right of individuals to pursue their conception of the good—subject, of course, to the constraint that doing so does not harm others. Having and raising children is part of many people's conception of the good life, and for that reason liberals have defended a significant degree of autonomy for parents in deciding how to raise their children. In this paper we shall argue that *on good liberal principles* liberals must reject this claim of parental autonomy. And we shall suggest that it is very likely that this will require significant changes in the role of the state in raising children.

We build upon some work of James Fishkin. In his book, *Justice, Equal Opportunity, and the Family*[1] he has clearly laid out the incompatibility of effective equal opportunity and the autonomy of the family.[2] Quite simply put: if effective equality of opportunity is to be enjoyed by all, the family must lose some of its traditional decisionmaking powers for children. More specifically, Fishkin shows (pp. 35–36) that the following three principles are not jointly satisfiable:

Merit: Positions should be allocated on the basis of qualifications.[3]

Life Chances (Equal Life Chances): Children with equivalent capacities (i.e., who have the same potential for qualifications) should have the same prospects for eventual positions in society.

Family Autonomy: Consensual relations within a given family governing the development of its children should not be coercively interfered with except to ensure for children the essential prerequisites for adult participation in society.

We follow Fishkin in understanding these essential prerequisites to be fairly minimal relative to current North American standards. Very roughly the essential prerequisites are basic physical health, some minimal level of psychological health, and some minimal level of cognitive skills. On the intended reading, then, most current North American families seek to ensure (as a matter of contingent fact) that their children have the essential prerequisites.

Fishkin's argument that these three principles are not jointly satisfiable rests on the following empirical assumption (which Fishkin does not state as explicitly as we do):

Family Influence (Familial Influence on the Development of Skills): If consensual relations within a given family governing

---

From *Public Affairs Quarterly*, vol. 3, no. 4, Oct. 1989. 27–45. Copyright 1989. Reprinted by permission of *Public Affairs Quarterly*.

the development of its children are not coercively interfered with except to ensure for children the essential prerequisites for adult participation in society, *then* in general children with equivalent capacities will not have the same prospects for qualifications.

Given this empirical assumption, the three principles are not jointly satisfiable. For given this assumption, if Family Autonomy is satisfied, then children with equivalent capacities will not have the same prospects of developing qualifications. And if positions are allocated on the basis of qualifications (as required by Merit), then children of equivalent capacities will not have the same chances of being assigned the various positions, thus violating Life Chances.[4]

To illustrate the incompatibility, consider two identical twins that are adopted by different families, one family being well-educated, economically well-off, stable, and loving, and the other family having none of those characteristics. Since they are identical twins, they have equivalent capacities. But given the differences between the families, and the significant impact of the familial environment (assuming Family Autonomy and Family Influence) the twins will not normally develop qualifications equally. Indeed, the twin in the less advantaged family will normally develop fewer qualifications (e.g., mathematical skills and verbal skills) than the twin in the more advantaged family. Consequently, if, as required by Merit, adult positions are fairly allocated on the basis of qualifications, the twin from the less advantaged family will have less of a chance than her sibling of being allocated one of the more skilled positions (since she will have fewer qualifications). But that violates Life Chances (which requires that they have the same chance), since the two have equivalent capacities.

Of course, if Family Influence does not hold, the three principles can be satisfied. Parents could be given their traditional control over their children (thereby satisfying Family Autonomy) since such control would have no serious effect on the development of their children's eventual qualifications. Non-familial social institutions could be arranged so that children of equivalent capacities develop the same qualifications and positions could be allocated on the basis of qualifications (thereby satisfying both Merit and Life Chances). Family influence, however, is a very plausible assumption. Studies show, and common sense concurs, that the impact of the family is profound, and that the familial advantages/disadvantages for the development of qualifications can only be partially offset by social institutions that do not interfere with family life.[5] So rejecting Family Influence is not a tenable way of denying the incompatibility.

Note that even given Family Influence any two of the principles are compatible. Merit and Family Autonomy can be satisfied if one gives up Life Chances (as illustrated above). Merit and Life Chances can be satisfied if Family Autonomy is given up—for example, if jobs are allocated on the basis of qualifications and children are raised in state foster homes of uniform quality. And Life Chances and Family Autonomy can be satisfied if Merit is given up—for example, if parents are allowed to influence the development of their children's qualifications, but positions are randomly allocated (thereby giving all an equal chance).

Given Family Influence the three principles are incompatible. Which principle should be given up? Fishkin's view is that all three of the principles should be given up as *absolute* principles, but that all three are valid as *prima facie* principles. Interpreted as *prima facie* principles there is, of course, no incompatibility between the three principles.

We regard this resolution as unacceptable. The commitment among most liberals to some form of equality of opportunity is stronger than a (weak) *prima facie* commitment. Perhaps liberals need not be committed to Merit and Life Chances, but they are surely committed absolutely to some minimal form of equality of opportunity. (They are absolutely opposed to laws that prohibit blacks from voting, for example.) The issue, we submit, is whether liberals can weaken their (absolute) commitment to equality of opportunity so as to avoid the incompatibility with Family Autonomy without giving up entirely the spirit of liberalism.

In what follows we show that there is a principle much weaker than the conjunction of Merit and Life Chances, that is incompatible on its own with the traditional autonomy of the family. Although it may be open to liberals to reject Merit or to reject Life Chances, it is not open to them, as we shall argue below, to reject this much weaker principle. Consequently, we conclude that liberals must reject the traditional autonomy of the family (since it is incompatible with this weak, and very plausible, principle). Unlike Fishkin, then, our aim is not merely to show an incompatibility between a certain equality of opportunity requirement and the traditional autonomy of the family; it is to argue that liberals should accept the former requirement, and reject the latter.

Strengthening the Argument:
The Equal Life Skills Principle

Fishkin's incompatibility result rests on understanding effective equality of opportunity as requiring both (1) that all allocations of positions be made on the basis of qualifications (Merit), and (2) that children of equivalent innate capacities have roughly equal chances of obtaining the various positions (Life Chances). But many will hold that this result is uninteresting because this notion of equality of opportunity is too strong. Some, for example, hold that it is permissible for private employers to hire on whatever basis they want. If they want to hire a less qualified person over a more qualified person, that, they claim, is the employer's personal business. On the other hand, there are those who advocate strong forms of affirmative action. They hold that preferential treatment should be given to individuals that are members of groups that have been systematically wronged in the past. At least sometimes, they claim, members of such targeted groups should be allocated positions for which they are not the most qualified.

The merit principle, then, is not uncontroversial. Many would thus resolve the incompatibility of the three principles simply by rejecting Merit, thereby seeming to leave Family Autonomy intact. But Family Autonomy cannot be protected that easily—at least not if one accepts the plausible empirical assumption that qualifications generally are a factor (no matter how weak) in the allocation of positions. This assumption is plausible, since even if positions are allocated primarily on the basis of sex, race, and religion, for example, it is plausible that qualifications will (as a matter of fact) at least sometimes be used as a tie-breaker (for example, between two white males).

Given this empirical assumption and Family Influence, Life Chances is incompatible with Family Autonomy—even without Merit. For given Family Influence, satisfying Family Autonomy has the result that children with equivalent capacities, but in different families, will in general have different prospects concerning the development of qualifications. And given the assumption that qualifications are a factor in the allocation of positions, it follows that such children will not in general have equal chances for positions—thereby violating Life Chances.

So giving up Merit does not suffice to avoid a conflict with Family Autonomy. In order to maintain Family Autonomy, Life Chances must be given up as well. Liberals cannot, however, simply drop Life Chances without replacing it with some similar principle. To do so would be to abandon liberalism. Merely insisting on Merit, for example, is compatible with social arrangements in which only boys (or whites) are educated and trained, and hence (given Merit) in which only boys (or whites) end up with the desirable social positions. But such arrangements are patently illiberal.

What these considerations show is that liberals cannot protect Family Autonomy simply by (1) rejecting Merit, or (2) by rejecting Life Chances without replacing it with some sort of similar (although perhaps weaker) requirement. In order to maintain Family Autonomy, then, liberals must replace Life Chances with a similar principle that preserves the spirit of liberalism, but that does not conflict with Family Autonomy. We shall now argue that this is not possible. For liberals are deeply committed to a principle that, although much weaker (and therefore more plausible) than the conjunction of Life Chances and Merit, is incompatible on its own (given Family Influence) with Family Autonomy.

To help motivate this new principle, note that in the presence of Merit, Life Chances' requirement is equivalent to the requirement that children with equivalent capacities have the same expectations concerning eventual qualifications for positions. For, if (as Merit requires) positions are allocated on the basis of qualifications, then two children of equivalent innate capacities will have equal chances of being allocated any given position (equal life chances) if and only if they have the same expectations concerning qualifications. That is, if positions are allocated on the basis of qualifications, then life chances and chances of developing qualifications coincide.

Call the skills deemed relevant for the various positions *life skills*[6] and call a specification, for each of the life skills, of a child's expected skill level upon the attainment of adulthood his/her *life skill expectations*. In the presence of Merit, then, Life Chances requires that children with equivalent capacities (i.e., the same potential for developing the various life skills) have the same life skill expectations. That is roughly our new principle (although in the next section we shall modify it in several ways). Consider then:

Life Skills (Equal Life Skills Expectations): **Children with equivalent innate capacities should have identical life skill expectations.**

In the presence of Merit, Life Skills and Life Chances are effectively equivalent. So anyone who finds both Merit and Life Chances plausible will also find Life Skills plausible.

On its own, however, Life Skills neither entails, nor is entailed by, Life Chances. For, if positions are not allocated on the basis of skill, there need be no connection between life skills and life chances. For example, if all children are given equal opportunities to develop, but all the desirable positions are allocated to men, a boy and a girl of equivalent innate capacities would have equal life skill expectations, but not have equal life chances. Likewise, if girls are given much less opportunities to develop, but all adult positions are allocated on the basis of an appropriate lottery, then a boy and a girl of equivalent innate capacities would have equal life chances, but not equal life skill expectations.

Life Skills is a relatively weak principle. It leaves open how adult positions are to be allocated. Both invidious discrimination and strong forms of affirmative action (for positions) satisfy it. And it allows, but does not require, children with greater innate capacities to have greater life skill expectations. It only rules out people having greater life skill expectations solely because of more favorable childhood environments.

Life Skills is so weak that (after a few modifications we shall make below) liberals cannot reasonably reject it. For, as we shall argue below, it is implied by a principle that lies at the core of liberal thought, *viz.* that the state should treat everyone with equal concern and respect. If we are right about this, then, liberals are committed to (a modified version of) Life Skills.

Of course, many will object that Life Skills is too weak, but that would miss one of the main points of this paper. Life Skills is clearly incomplete as a characterization of liberalism, since, as we have just noted, it is compatible with all sorts of illiberal arrangements. It is compatible, for example, with: (1) invidious discrimination in the allocation of positions; and (2) with the systematic suppression, or even elimination, of an entire group of children with equivalent innate capacities (the principle only requires that they all be treated the same). A full statement of liberal principles would require Life Skills to be supplemented in a wide variety of ways. It might, for example, require supplementation by (1) adding Merit; (2a) adding a principle that says: a child with *greater* capacities than a second should have life skill expectations that are greater than those of the second child; or alternatively, (2b) adding a principle that requires all children—regardless of their capacities—to have equal life skill expectations; or (3) adding a principle that all children's skills are to be developed above some minimal level.

For our purposes, however, we do not need a complete statement of liberal principles. We only need a partial statement. In fact, in the present context, the weakness of Life Skills is an asset rather than a liability. For if liberalism entails Life Skills, and if Life Skills is incompatible with Family Autonomy, then liberalism is incompatible with Family Autonomy.

Now, although Life Skills is considerably weaker than the conjunction of Merit and Life Chances, it is still incompatible with Family Autonomy. For, as we have seen, the traditional autonomy of the family has the effect that children with equivalent innate capacities (for example, identical twins adopted by different families) do not in general have the same life skill expectations. Thus, granting the traditional parental autonomy violates the equal life skills expectations principle. In the last section of the paper we shall highlight the ways in which the life skills principle requires that parental autonomy be restricted.

Given that Family Autonomy is incompatible (given Family Influence) with Life Skills, one of the principles must be rejected. In the next section we acknowledge that Life Skills, as formulated above, is subject to several powerful objections. These objections, however, do not undermine the spirit of Life Skills; they merely show that it needs to be qualified in various ways. We therefore modify Life Skills so as to make it immune to these objections. In the section after next we argue that liberalism is committed to the modified principle.

Modifications and Clarifications

1. Life Skills

In order to preserve a parallel with Fishkin's discussion, we have so far construed life skills to be whatever skills are deemed relevant for the effective performance of the duties of positions. So understood, life skills include the highly specific skills that are relevant for certain positions (e.g., for being a surgeon, being a sculptor, etc.). Based on this notion of life skills, Life Skills requires that children with equivalent capacities have the same chance of developing these highly specialized, job-specific skills.

This makes Life Skills a highly demanding requirement, since it requires equal expectations—not only for broadly useful skills, but also—for highly specific skills. But one might reasonably object that liberalism is not committed to the equalization of expectations concerning such highly job-specific skills.

We find this objection plausible, and we shall therefore modify the construal of life skills. As a first try, instead of understanding life skills as job-related skills, understand them as widely valued skills, i.e., as skills that a significant portion (e.g., at least 50%) of the population ranks highly (e.g., in the top 50%) when they rank the various skills in terms of their desirability. Life Skills on this new interpretation is likely to be much less demanding than on the original interpretation. It does not require children with equivalent capacities (i.e., capacities that are equally conducive to the development of the various life skills) to have the same expectation of developing the skills of a surgeon (for example), but only that they have the same expectation of developing the same mathematical and verbal skills (for example) up to the point that they are widely valued. This weakening makes Life Skills significantly more plausible.

A problem remains, however. For the skills that are widely valued in society need not be skills that *every* child is likely to value highly upon the attainment of adulthood. It therefore seems unfair to require of children that (for whatever reasons) are likely to value few of the widely valued skills that they develop those skills. This is unfair, because (due to the finite resources, for example) developing widely valued skills will often have the effect of reducing the development of skills that they are likely to value highly.

This problem can be illustrated by considering children in relatively isolated communities that have radically different values than the larger society of which they are a part. It seems unacceptable from a liberal perspective, for example, to require a child in a traditional rural Amish community to develop all the skills that are widely valued in the larger modern, urban society (e.g., computer skills), if she is unlikely to value those skills.

The point is not that there shouldn't be any minimal requirements on what skills are developed in isolated communities, but rather that the requirement proposed above—that children with equivalent capacities have the same expectations concerning those skills *that are widely valued in society* is too strong. It is not sufficiently sensitive to the differences among communities within society concerning what skills are likely to be valued highly.

One way of overcoming this problem would be to relativize the equal life skill principle to communities. The principle would require only that two children with the same community have the same expectations concerning the widely valued skills of their community (not society at large). Relativizing to communities would eliminate much of the objectionable value imperialism. It wouldn't, for example, require Amish parents in a rural Pennsylvania Amish community to supply their children with basic computer skills simply because such skills are widely valued in the United States. The modified principle would only require that children *within* the Amish community have the same (perhaps very low) expectations concerning the development of basic computer skills.

Unfortunately, even with this modification the life skills principle still seems too imperialistic. Consider, for example, a family that does not share the values of the fairly homogeneous community of which it is a part. Suppose that the family favors an extremely austere life-style, and is suspicious of the western acquisitive and competitive ways of the community at large. Suppose further that the parents are quite likely to transmit their values to their children, and that the skills that would be useful relative to the values their children will acquire are actually incompatible with those that are widely valued by the community at large. The community-relative version of the life skills principle would nonetheless require that the children of the family have the same expectations as other children concerning the widely valued skills—even though such expectations would interfere with the development of the skills that the children of the given family are likely to highly value. It could thus plausibly be held by liberals that even the community-relative version of the life skills principle is too imperialistic. It is not sufficiently sensitive to the skills that children are expected to value.

Perhaps, the residual imperialism in the community-relative life skill principle can be eliminated by a suitable understanding of communityhood. Rather than pursue this line, however, we shall drop the community relativization, and take a more direct approach. For what the above discussion suggests is that the liberal interest is to prepare children to pursue the life their values dictate—hence, to develop whatever skills would be useful to them in the pursuit of their goals, whatever they turn out to be.

The idea is this: At conception there are a wide variety of ways that a child might turn out upon the attainment of adulthood. Corresponding to each of these ways that the child might turn out there is a set of skills that the child upon the attainment of adulthood values highly (e.g., in the top 50% of the skills when ranked). Some skills (such as being able to read) will be highly valued in almost all scenarios, whereas others (such as being able to deal with computers) will be highly valued only in a few scenarios. The idea is to have the principle consider, for a given child, only those skills that the child is highly likely (e.g., more than 50%) to highly value (e.g., in the top 50%). The new principle, then, says: Society should be arranged so that for any skill, if two children with equivalent capacities are both highly likely to highly value that skill upon attainment of adulthood, then they have the same expectation concerning the development of that skill upon the attainment of adulthood.

This revised principle does not necessarily require that society be structured so that, for example, children of a traditional Amish community be raised so that they have the same life skill expectations as children with equivalent capacities in modern urban environments. If the Amish children are unlikely to highly value computer skills, then they need not have the same computer skill expectations as the urban children who are highly likely to value the skill. On the other hand, if the Amish children *are highly likely to value* computer (geography, history, etc.) skills—perhaps because of a breakdown of traditional Amish society—then the principle requires that society be structured so as to ensure that they have equal expectations with their urban counterparts. The revised principle seeks to ensure that children are not disadvantaged in terms of the skills that *they* are likely to end up wishing they had. Consequently, the principle is sensitive to issues of community autonomy—but only up to the point that the children are likely to end up adopting their community's values.[7]

For brevity, we shall ignore the modification just introduced in the next subsection. Ultimately, after another modification has been made, we shall, however, reformulate the resulting principle.

2. The Problems of Unlimited Costs and Intrusiveness

Another objecton to Life Skills is that it requires something that is impossible. The amount of time, effort, and other resources required to achieve the appropriate equality of life skill expectations exceeds, it might be argued, the amount available. It is empirically impossible to achieve the requisite equality. We doubt that this is so, but in any case the principle should be reformulated so as to avoid the possibility of requiring the impossible. The principle should require only that life skill expectations for children of equivalent capacities be *as equal as possible.*

A related, and considerably more forceful, objection is that the cost of ensuring equal life skill expectations for children having equivalent capacities would be enormous—even if strictly speaking they do not exceed the resources available to society. Indeed, the costs might be so great that all social structures that ensure equal life skill expectations make *everyone* worse off[8] than some social structure that yields unequal life skill expectations. But surely, the objection continues, justice does not require making everyone worse off in order to ensure equal life skill expectations.

We agree that this is an objectionable feature of Life Skills, but it is one that can be avoided by modification. The requirement of equal life skill expectations should, we propose, be understood as setting a *minimum* welfare level. Everyone should be at least as well off as they would be if equal life skills expectations were ensured. So interpreted the principle does not require the adoption of a structure that yields equal life skill expectations. It allows the adoption of a structure that yields unequal life skill expectation, if (and only if) it makes everyone at least as well off as all structures yielding equal life skill expectations.[9] So interpreted the principle is not subject to the objection that it might require the adoption of social structures that *no one* wants.[10]

3. Summary

In this section we have introduced two modifications to Life Skills. The modified principle is now:

> **Modified Life Skills (*Modified Equal Life Skills Expectations*):** Society should be arranged so that everyone is expected to be at least as well off as he/she would be if society were suitably arranged[11] so that any two children having equivalent capacities have—to the extent that it is possible—equal expectations concerning those skills that both are highly likely to highly value upon the attainment of adulthood.[12]

This modified principle is *not* incompatible with Family Autonomy—even given Family Influence. For suppose that the *only* way to ensure equal life skill expectations is to raise children in state group homes (which makes Family Influence true) but that, although children develop equally in such an environment, they all develop less well and/or are less well-adjusted than they would be if they were brought up by their parents in the traditional manner. In such a case bringing up children in the traditional manner would satisfy both Family Autonomy and Modified Life Skills (since the children would all be at least as well off as they would if equal life skill expectations were ensured).

Thus, we do not yet have an incompatibility with Family Autonomy. One is close at hand, however. For the family influence assumption can be strengthened and still remain highly plausible. In particular, it is plausible that the traditional autonomy of the family always makes at least some children less well off than if equal life skill expectations were ensured. Gifted children in severely impoverished families, for example, are less well off than they would be if they received the same opportunity to develop as other children having equivalent capacities.

Accordingly, we propose to strengthen Family Influence to:

Strong Family Influence (*Strong Influence of the Family on the Development of Qualifications*): If consensual relations within a given family governing the development of its children are not coercively interfered with except to ensure for the children the essential prerequisites (on the minimal construal outlined in the introduction) for adult participation in society, then at least some children will be less well off than they would be if society were suitably arranged so that children having equivalent capacities have equal expectations concerning skills that are both highly likely to highly value.

Given Strong Family Influence, Family Autonomy is incompatible with Modified Life Skills. Because Strong Family Influence is relatively uncontroversial, liberals must reject either Family Autonomy or Modified Life Skills. Liberalism, we shall now argue, is more deeply committed to Modified Life Skills than it is to Family Autonomy. Consequently, liberals must reject Family Autonomy.

Rejecting Family Autonomy

Let us be clear from the outset that we are here construing liberalism in the narrow sense that excludes hard core libertarianism. Dworkin and Rawls are liberals in this sense, but Nozick is not. Although it may be possible to give a plausible argument that a sophisticated form of libertarianism is also deeply committed to Modified Life Skills, we shall attempt only the less ambitious task of arguing that "welfare" liberals are so committed.

Admittedly, it is not very clear what the core idea of liberalism is. A common characterization of the core idea is that the state should be neutral between competing conceptions of the good life. Ronald Dworkin has argued persuasively, however, that, although liberalism is committed to such neutrality, it is because of a deeper commitment to the view that the state should treat everyone with equal concern and respect.[13] Only the latter understanding of liberalism, he argues, can adequately justify liberalism's commitment to effective equality of opportunity.

We shall assume that Dworkin's characterization of liberalism is correct. More specifically, we shall assume that liberalism requires the state not only to protect, but also to promote, the interests of its citizens. Although these assumptions are not uncontroversial, it is clear that a wide range of liberals hold them. We argue now that such liberals are deeply committed to something like Modified Life Skills.[14] To establish this conclusion we need to contrast the implications of the equal concern and respect principle when applied to adults with its implications when applied to children.

Start, then, by considering what equal concern and respect requires of the state *vis-à-vis* adults. Plausibly, it requires that the state leave adults relatively free to live their lives as they choose (as long as they don't harm others). This is because most adults are fully developed autonomous agents: they have relatively stable and informed beliefs, they have relatively stable and informed conceptions of the good, and they are fairly good at choosing options that they believe best promote their conception of the good. Equal concern and respect (we are assuming) requires the state to promote and protect the interests of all. For autonomous adults the best way to promote and protect their conception of the good is to leave them free to make their own choices.

Children, on the other hand, are not fully autonomous agents. They are not very well informed. They do not have a stable conception of the good: it is in the process of being developed. And they are not very good at choosing options that they believe best promote their current conception of the good. What, then, does equal concern and respect require with respect to children?

It does *not* require that children be given as much liberty to control their lives as adults are. Leaving young children to live their lives as they choose is not—as it is in general for adults—an effective way of promoting and protecting their interests. Young children just aren't very good at looking after their true long run interests. Consequently, equal concern and respect for children does not require that the state leave children as much freedom as adults. Rather, it requires that the state take an active role in promoting and protecting their developing conceptions of the good.[15]

But what aspect of these developing conceptions of the good is the state to promote and respect? Children, we have said, do not have a stable conception of the good. This is not, however, to say that no part of their conception of the good is stable. In addition to the obvious first order interests in food, love, etc., they also have a second order interest in having whatever skills are highly useful for promoting whatever conception of the good they end up having. They have an interest, that is, in there being a fit between their values and their skills. The interest in having whatever skills are useful for pursuing one's conception of the good is, of course, a second order value that everyone has. It is thus reasonable to think that it is exactly the sort of interest that equal concern and respect as applied to children would require the state to promote and protect.

Giving equal respect and concern to children plausibly requires, then, that children have an effectively equal opportunity to develop the skills they are likely to value, and that requires that two children with equivalent innate capacities have an equal chance of developing any skill that they are both highly likely to highly value. But that is just to require Modified Life Skills. So liberalism is committed to Modified Life Skills.

Of course, liberalism may be committed to the equalization of life skills only because they are *instrumentally* valuable. Liberals may deem life skills valuable, that is, only because they serve persons in pursuing their life plans, whatever they happen to be. Liberalism may not be committed to Modified Life Skills no matter what the world is like. In a world in which how one fares is totally unrelated to the exercise of one's skills (e.g., where goods fall from the sky like manna) liberals might very well not insist on the equalization of life skill expectations. However, in worlds (such as the actual world) in which life skills are instrumentally valuable liberalism is committed to this equalization. Liberalism as it applies to this world then, carries an absolute commitment to Modified Life Skills.

These considerations indicate that liberalism is not deeply committed to Family Autonomy. For once children are recognized as falling under the scope of the equal respect and concern, Family Autonomy is seen to be at best a contingently derivative liberal principle. For, just as the requirements of equal concern and respect for (say) blacks override the interests of racists in treating blacks as they see fit, the requirements of equal concern and respect for children override the interests of parents in raising their children as they see fit.

Why, then, have liberals accepted Family Autonomy? Perhaps at some earlier time some liberals implicitly assumed that children are their parent's property, or, more weakly, that children are part of some "private" realm in which the state has no role. But no reflective liberal today holds that the state has no business in how parents raise their children. The state must protect the basic interests of children (for example, it must ensure that they are not being systematically physically and mentally abused). So, if there is a conflict between treating children with equal concern and respect and the interests of parents in raising their children as they see fit, liberalism will sacrifice the latter. Since equal concern and respect requires Modified Life Skills, and it conflicts with Family Autonomy, liberalism must reject Family Autonomy.

Liberalism is thus not deeply committed to Family Autonomy. It is only contingently and derivatively committed to it. In general it has been assumed that the interests of children are best protected by leaving almost all decision-making powers about the raising of children with their parents. We have argued, however, that this is not so. Consequently, liberals will have to give up Family Autonomy.

Conclusion

Family Autonomy allows *some* state intervention in family life. It allows such intervention when—and only when—it is necessary to ensure that children obtain the essential prerequisites for adult society. Following Fishkin we have understood the essential prerequisites to be rather minimal: roughly, minimal food, shelter, education, and freedom from extreme physical and psychological abuse. Modified Life Skills requires state intervention even when these minimal prerequisites are being provided. Consequently, because liberalism is committed to Modified Life Skills, it must reject Family Autonomy.

One could, of course, weaken the family autonomy principle, by invoking a more demanding conception of the essential prerequisites for adult society. One could, for example, understand essential prerequisites as including the equal opportunity to develop highly valued skills. If one weakens the family autonomy principle by allowing state intervention to ensure that these more demanding prerequisites are obtained, there is no incompatibility between Modified Life Skills and the weakened version of Family Autonomy. The former requires, and the latter allows, intervention to ensure such "essential prerequisites."

Liberals can, and probably should, defend such a weaker form of family autonomy. By endorsing the weak—but not the strong—form of family autonomy, they can avoid inconsistency. The move from strong to weak family autonomy is not, however, a minor revision of received liberal doctrine. It has the potential of legitimizing very significant state intrusion into family life. Many liberals have already recognized this fact. But many have not. It is therefore worth considering some of the arrangements that Modified Life Skills might force liberals to accept.[16]

The satisfaction of Modified Life Skills probably would require that a wide range of high quality, state funded developmental programs be available to all children. This would probably include programs of the following sorts: programs of nourishment to pregnant mothers, counseling and training for parents, programs to ensure that all children are adequately nourished (e.g., by providing meals in day care centers and in schools), education programs (perhaps including university programs for those qualified), and extracurricular programs. Admittedly, some (but certainly not all) such programs are already in place (e.g., schools); but it hardly needs arguing that many of them vary considerably in quality depending upon the average income of the members of the community in which they are run. The upgrading and expansion of programs likely required by Modified Life Skills would certainly be a good deal more expensive than our present programs are. Further, in order to ensure that accessibility to these programs does not depend on the resources of the family, they would need to be *state funded* (at least in cases where the family does not have the means to pay). Thus, some citizens (e.g., the well off; or perhaps, more narrowly, well off parents) would be required to share significantly the cost of such programs for other people's children. Thus, to the extent that parents are required to spend their money (via taxes) on other people's children, their freedom to spend that money on their own children is restricted.

Increased taxes to fund the upbringing of other people's children is, of course, an implication that most liberals already accept, but it is only the beginning. More dramatically, there may well also be restrictions on who is allowed to raise children. People who do not have certain minimal qualifications for raising children might, for example, be legally prohibited from doing so.[17]

Furthermore, even those parents judged suitable to be parents may be restricted in what they can require or prohibit their children from doing. It may be legally forbidden, not only for parents to prevent their children from attending school, but also for parents to prevent their children from participating in various skill developing extra-curricular activities (e.g., sports, music, etc.). Parents may not have the legal option of not sending their children to such programs. These would be very direct restrictions of traditional parental autonomy.

More problematic yet is the possibility that Modified Life Skills might (given Family Influence) also require that parents be prohibited from raising their children *too well*. For, if Modified Life Skills requires equal life skill expectations for equal capacities, well off parents would need, it seems, to be prohibited from sending their children to private schools of above average quality, of providing extra lessons (in music, sports, mathematics, etc.) that are not available to everyone, etc. For if this special attention is not prohibited, children from privileged families will have greater life skill expectations than their counterparts in less privileged families.

It is even possible that Modified Life Skills might require, not only severe restrictions on parental decision-making powers, but the total abolition of the family. If familial influence on the development of life skill is extremely strong, Modified Life Skills might require that all children be raised in state funded group homes with the natural parents having no special access to their children.

We doubt that Modified Life Skills requires the abolition of the family. For the institution of the family (with a small number of children being raised by a small number of adults) has all sorts of benefits. The love and intimacy, for example, that usually occurs in a family context, would not be present to a significant degree in state homes. And love, intimacy, and the like are important for children's sense of self-worth, for example, which in turn is essential for the development of their capacities. So, raising all children in state homes would likely make many, if not most, children worse off than they would be if they were raised under some form of familial system. Thus, it is unlikely that Modified Life Skills would require the abolition of the family.

If, however, the family does not provide the above sorts of benefits to enough children, then it is plausible that Modified Life Skills would require its abolition. But in such a case, the family is a pernicious institution (providing little benefit to children, and having a significantly adverse affect on many). And so, it seems appropriate that Modified Life Skills requires its abolition in such a case.

These, then, are some of the potentially radical implications of accepting Modified Life Skills and abandoning Family Autonomy. Many liberals, however, have been reluctant to abandon Family Autonomy. Although many liberals accept that they have a very significant financial responsibility for other people's children (and therefore less autonomy on how they spend their money on their own children), not all liberals recognize how great that responsibility is. Furthermore, most liberals are reluctant to accept the legitimacy of more than minimal state intrusion into family life. But liberals must accept Modified Life Skills, and that very probably endorses such intrusion as legitimate.

Liberals have been reluctant to abandon Family Autonomy because of a profound commitment to the freedom of individuals to pursue their conceptions of the good. Liberals have generally supposed that such freedom extends into their own homes—and in particular into how they raise their children. What they have not seen very clearly, however, is that the right to an equal opportunity to pursue one's conception of the good is a right to which children will lay claim when they become adults. Liberals must therefore ensure that children have an equal opportunity to develop the skills that are likely to be useful in pursuing their conception of the good. And since that conflicts with the traditional autonomy of the family, liberals must reject the strong form of family autonomy.[18]

Notes

1. James Fishkin, *Justice, Equal Opportunity, and the Family* (New Haven: Yale University Press, 1983).

2. The conflict between some form of effective equality of opportunity and the traditional autonomy of the family is also discussed by: Jeffrey Blustein *Parents and Children* (New York: Oxford Univ. Press, 1982); John Charvet, "The Idea of Equality as a Substantive Principle of Society," *Political Studies,* vol. 17 (1969), pp. 1–13; Joel Feinberg "The Child's Right to an Open Future," in William Aiken and Hugh LaFollette *Whose Child?* (Totowa: Littlefield, Adams & Co., 1980); Amy Gutmann "Children, Paternalism, and Education: A Liberal Argument," *Philosophy and Public Affairs,* vol. 9 (1980), pp. 338–58; Amy Gutmann *Democratic Education* (Princeton: Princeton Univ. Press, 1987); Laurence Houlgate *Family and State* (Totowa: Rowman & Littlefield, 1988); Kai Nielsen, *Equality and Liberty: A Defense of Radical Egalitarianism* (Totowa: Rowman & Allanheld, 1985), ch. 8; and David A.J. Richards, "The Individual, the Family, and the Constitution," *New York University Law Review,* vol. 55 (1980), pp. 1–62.

3. Fishkin's official statement of the merit principle is: "There should be widespread procedural fairness in the evaluation of qualifications for positions," (p. 22), but his discussion makes it clear that the main thrust of this requirement is that positions be allocated on the basis of (relevant) qualifications.

4. The incompatibility relies on the uncontroversial, but hidden, assumption that there are children with equivalent capacities. For if no two children have equivalent capacities, Life Chances is vacuously satisfied.

5. See, for example, Samuel Bowles and Herbert Gintis, *Schooling in Capitalist America* (New York: Basic Books, 1976); James S. Coleman et al., *Equality of Educational Opportunity* (Washington: Government Printing Office, 1966); Christopher Jencks et al., *Inequality* (New York: Basic Books, 1972); and Christopher Jencks et al., *Who Gets Ahead?* (New York: Basic Books, 1979).

6. Here and below, we use 'skill' in a broad sense that includes not only physical and intellectual skills in the narrow sense, but also "non-cognitive skills" such as discipline, patience, initiative, etc.

7. To see that even this relativized version of the life skills principle has bite, consider, for example, a child, of a *very* traditional immigrant family, that watches "mainstream" television, goes to public school, etc. In contemporary America such a child is very likely to end up adopting many "mainstream" values and rejecting many of her parents' values. The relativized principle requires roughly that society be so arranged so that such a child has the same opportunity to develop those "mainstream" skills that she is highly likely to value as other children who are highly likely to value those skills. Since there are lots of skills that children from different community backgrounds are likely to highly value, the relativized principle still has significant implications.

8. We leave open here what the relevant notion of well-being is (e.g., material well-being, or desire satisfaction).

9. We think it plausible to further strengthen the principle so as to *prohibit* the adoption of a social structure that yields equal life skill expectations if it makes everyone worse off than some other adoptable structure. For the purposes of our argument against Family Autonomy, however, we want to keep the equal life skill expectations principle as weak as possible, and so we shall not incorporate this strengthening. For further discussion of how rights considerations can be incorporated into a welfaristic theory, see Peter Vallentyne, "Rights Based Paretianism," *Canadian Journal of Philosophy,* vol. 18 (1988), pp. 527–544.

10. Note, however, that, unlike Rawls' difference principle, our Modified Life Skills principle does not require—indeed, it may forbid—maximizing the net benefit to the worst off members of society. For our principle will prohibit doing so when doing so would require that some (non-worst off) child be made less well off than he/she would be were equal skill expectations ensured.

11. Since in general there are many arrangements that would ensure equal life skill expectations (e.g., one in which all children are treated poorly, another in which they are all treated well, etc.), we say that society should be arranged so that everyone is at least as well off as they would be if society were "suitably" arranged to ensure equal life skill expectations. An arrangement is suitable (in our intended sense) just in case it satisfies all other principles that one might want to impose (but we leave unspecified).

12. There is at least one further possible weakening of Life Skills. As it stands, it prohibits abortion except when all fetuses having the same capacities are also aborted. For if one fetus

is to be aborted and another having the same capacities is not, then the not-to-be-aborted one has greater life skill expectations than the to-be-aborted one. To avoid this implication Life Skills could be weakened in some appropriate manner. For brevity, we ignore this modification in the text.

13. Ronald Dworkin, "Liberalism," in Stuart Hampshire, ed., *Public and Private Morality* (Cambridge: Cambridge Univ. Press, 1978), pp. 113–43, and "Neutrality, Equality, and Liberalism," in Douglas MacLean and Claudia Mills, eds., *Liberalism Reconsidered* (Rowman & Allanheld, 1983). Fishkin endorses this view (on p. 158). See also Bruce Ackerman *Social Justice in the Liberal State* (New Haven: Yale Univ. Press, 1980), p. 11.

14. In "Libertarianism, Autonomy, and Children," *Public Affairs Quarterly,* 5 (1991); 333–52, we argue that *all* liberals—even libertarians—are committed, at least with respect to children, to the view that the state should *promote,* as well as protect, interests. Hence, given the argument that follows in the text, all liberals are committed to Modified Life Skills.

15. We do not mean to deny that children should (as argued by children's rights activists) be given more control over their lives. We mean only to claim that at least with respect to very young children some sort of paternalism is required by the principle of equal concern and respect.

16. Most of these implications are mentioned, and often discussed, by Fishkin.

17. One may have to obtain a *license* to raise children, just as one currently has to obtain a license to drive a car, or to practice medicine. This view is defended by Hugh LaFollette in "Licensing Parents," *Philosophy and Public Affairs,* vol. 9 (1980), pp. 182–97.

18. We have benefited from the critical comments of Jeffrey Blustein, James Fishkin, Shelly Kagan, Will Kymlicka, Heidi Malm, Geoff Sayre-McCord, and Karen Wendling.

Does a Child Have a Right to a Certain Identity?

Anita L. Allen

I.

Adults who regard themselves as morally responsible for the upbringing of children commonly view themselves as having an obligation—at minimum—to feed, clothe and educate. Such adults also view themselves as having an obligation to ensure that their children, or their families', friends' or communities' children, have suitable identities.

What is thought to constitute a "suitable" or appropriate identity for a child? Perhaps the clearest example is gender identity. Most parents assume that male children ought to be brought up to think of themselves as men rather than as women. Many parents teach masculine gender identification through frequent overt references to "my little boy," to "boy's clothes," to "what boys like" and to "taking it like a man." However, male gender identification can be and probably is taught through more subtle social practices as well, such as half-consciously encouraging sons to emulate their fathers and forming gender-segregated play groups for very small children.

I make these general empirical observations toward suggesting another, namely that the common understanding in most Western societies is that children ought to be brought up in such a way that they will have, not only *an* identity but a *certain* identity. Thus it is supposed that a male child should come into the identity of a male and not a female; and that a female child should come into the identity of a female and not a male. A parent or guardian or public school official who permitted or encouraged a male child to view himself as a female, or a female child to view herself as a male, would be regarded with disdain as negligent or even malicious and abusive.

Gender identification, the disposition to view oneself as male or female, and to display appropriately gendered affects, is only one type of identification with which responsible adults typically concern themselves. There is similar concern for ethnic, racial, national and religious identification. In terms comfortable to those whose political outlook is liberal, children are presumed to have a moral and political right to a certain identity or a certain set of identities: the identity or identities that reflect what they really are. In terms that may be preferred by the international human rights community, children are thought to need, and therefore to have as a human right that civilized nations are bound to respect, a certain identity or set of identities.

From *Law, Justice, and the State*, ed. Mikael Karlsson et al. *Rechtstheorie, Beiheft* 15, 1993, 109–119. Reprinted by permission of the author.

On this pervasive view about children's rights and needs, a male of African-American descent born and living in the United States, is owed the identity of a male and a black. To rear him in a way that permitted him to have the self-identity of a white female would be condemned widely as cruel and immoral. And in some quarters, to rear him in a way that permitted him to have the self-identity of a white male would garner similar condemnation.

Yet, in the minds of some, the norms that prescribe that children be brought up to have the identities suitable to them do not regard race and gender identities as equally essential. One can imagine someone making the argument that it is imperative that a black male child be educated to think of himself as male because "maleness" is a factual biological category; but it is less imperative, if imperative at all, that a black male be educated to think of himself as a "black" or an "African-American." The ground of the distinction is the belief that gender is a fact of nature but race a mere social construction—with a pernicious history at that. On this view, a human, male identity is enough, regardless of skin color and family history.

Yet even assuming that one wants to apply consistently the idea that there is something, in a physical or metaphysical sense, that a person is and that he or she therefore ought to identify as, it is not clear why physical traits (vagina, penis) and biological capacities (pregnancy, impregnation) are more basic to what one really is than social traits (born to a Catholic). Society could treat the penis/vagina difference the way it treats the tall stature/short stature or the red hair/brown hair differences.

Concerns about children "having" certain identities are ambiguous. The concerns have at least two aspects relevant to my analysis. First, they have what I will call an *internal* or *private* aspect. Adults believe that children should come to think themselves (privately, internally, in their own thoughts) through the appropriate, factually accurate ontological categories of self-description. Again, a person who is a male should think of himself as a male. A person who is a female, an Irish, and a Catholic should come to think of herself as a female, an Irish, and a Catholic. To do otherwise is to be uneducated, and worse. It is to be at risk for social dislocation and psychological malaise.

The second aspect of concern over personal identity I will call an *external* or *public* aspect. Adults believe that children should manifest to others in the community traits generally regarded as definitive of persons belonging to the groups to which the children in fact belong. A boy who fails to manifest publicly a sufficient number of (or to a sufficient degree) the traits associated with maleness is labelled "effeminate." The label indicates that the speaker believes the boy is not quite as he ought to be, without regard to whether he in fact has a strong internal, private masculine self-concept. We adults take external appearances as signs, if not proof, of internal realities.

Thus, affluent African-American parents worry that their highly assimilated children with the tastes, speech and mannerisms of the mainstream white-dominated culture also internally think of themselves as white. Why the worry? What difference does it make? Virtually all parents want their children to be informed, proud and accepting. And for some people of color, accepting oneself as "different" and belonging to a particular race with a particular history is part of what it means to be informed, proud and accepting. A black parent who suspects that her child "thinks she's white" (as the expression goes) fears that the child is not well-informed about her race, not proud of her race, and not accepting of the fact that she is a member of her racial group. The parent may also fear that the child will not fit into the extended family or the black sub-culture.

Importantly, parents may view the external signs of white identity in their black children as warnings that the children have rejected, or will reject, the parents. This rejection by the next generation is felt as a major assault on the parents' own identities. I want to suggest that typical parents—and indeed all adults who take responsibility for children in typical western societies—want their children either (1) to share much of their identities or, failing that, (2) to have an insider's appreciation for their identities. This is true, I would also suggest, even when the parents' identities include the scars of a bitter history of personal or group hardship, such as slavery or Nazi genocide; and, even when associated with dysfunctional or disapproved traits and behavioral dispositions, such as sexism or alcoholism.

It is worth noting that, although I am focussing on the adult/child relationship, a similar desire for shared identity and appreciation arguably affects same-generation peer relations. On U.S. college and university campuses in the 1970's and 1980's youths of African and Asian ancestry were labelled "Oreos" and "Twinkies"—two popular commercially produced sweets that are black or yellow on the outside and white on the inside.

II.

The idea that children have a right to a certain identity that reflects who and what they really are is reflected in the tenor of major international human rights documents promulgated by the United Nations and endorsed by many western countries. These suggest that children have a right to *their* parents, *their* nationalities and *their* religions.

The popular idea that a child has a right to a certain identity is more problematic than is generally recognized. I therefore propose to examine this assumption more closely, tracing its contours and implications for how we view the justice of social practices—including legal autonomy for families and trans-racial adoption—that affect how children are likely to come to think of themselves and to present themselves to others.

I am skeptical of the assumption that children have a right, or morally important need, to a certain identity simply because of their ontological reality. It seems to me that the popular assumption that a child is owed a specific identity reveals as much or more about the needs and privileges of adults than about the needs, rights or ontological reality of human young. In particular, this assumption reflects adults' own socially created needs for contexts that do not deeply threaten their own wishes for communities of like-minded persons who can share and appreciate their identities.

That adults have such needs may be something more than a contingent fact of human history. But whether the need for the sharing and appreciation of identity is mainly nature or mainly nurture, it seems clear upon reflection that any plausible explanation for why the needs take the particular forms they take in modern life includes the social fact that we adults tend both to impute *and* to transfer similar needs to our young.

None of this points toward an argument against rearing and educating children about what society will call their "their" genders, races, religions, etc. The adult world is structured so that social life can be full of peril for someone who fails on the internal and/or external level to be what he or she is supposed to be. It is social, rather than ontological, reality that is most importantly behind any practical duties adults have to ensure that the children for which they are responsible have certain identities.

Yet some of what we do in the name of prudentially or morally assuring that children will have certain identities is foolish. It may do individual children more harm than good. In the United States, it appears, for example, that the political power struggles between both blacks and whites and Native Americans and whites are being fought, inhumanely, over the backs of little children whose childhoods are all but ruined by well-intended adult efforts to place them in homes where their cultural and racial identities are most likely to be preserved.

III.

Apart from the question of moral entitlement to gender identification, the concerns of this paper may seem rather remote to anyone whose country is largely without heterogeneity of, for example, race, culture or religion. They will strike residents of the United States and Canada as, quite literally, closer to home, for ours are countries populated by peoples who speak different languages, observe different rituals and are assigned different races by custom and law.

As a resident and citizen of the United States I am struck by how much of our social practice assumes that a child has a right (or need) to grow up, not only medically healthy and literate, but with an identity reflecting what he or she "really" is in some amalgam of genetic, cultural and historical senses: African-American, Jewish-American, Irish-Catholic, Navaho, Latino, Caucasian etc. The imperative to teach identity persists, despite the significant, genetic, historical, and cultural overlapping that actually and potentially blur the lines of demarcation between and among various groups. In terms of genetic ancestry, most blacks in the United States are partly white; many whites partly black. Many blacks and whites are partly Native American; many Native Americans are partly white and/or black. There is a decided political component to the group affiliation and hence the appropriate "identity" assigned to an American child.

Recently in the United States, the belief that adults are obligated, based on children's rights or needs, to bring up the young as certain kinds of persons has been associated with the social ideal of "diversity." Only by cultivating ethnic identity can the rich array of culturally plural groups in the country be preserved, it is said. But it would be a mistake to view the idea of the young having a right to a certain identity as essentially egalitarian. Racism and xenophobia can underlie the moralistic demand for group identification.

Thus, long before the egalitarian "diversity" movement, many people believed in the separation of "whites" and "negroes" on the grounds that it would be morally undesirable for white children to acquire the (putatively vulgar, degraded) cultural traits of negroes or for negroes to acquire the (putatively cultivated, proud) traits of whites. Recall the flap caused by the infatuation of southern white teenagers with black music in the 1950's and 1960's. Officially, the ideal of "integration" replaced the ideal of "segregation" in the U.S., but the ideal of diversity replaced them both, I believe, because it became apparent that the ethical demand that the young be treated both as equals and as what they "really" are could not find full expression under the assimilationist model of integration.

IV.

Children can fail to have "appropriate" identities for any number of reasons. One reason is that they are reared by persons who lack "appropriate" identities. Such a fate can be the result of the whims of a dictator or the popular laws of a liberal democracy.

Suppose an anti-Catholic, totalitarian dictator decreed that his Department of Child Welfare and Public Morality forcibly and permanently remove newborn babies from the arms of Catholic mothers and see to it that they are raised by good Protestant families. Part of what is inhumane about the tyrant's act seems to be that the children are deprived of their "real" identities. But is it?

Suppose now that under the law of the United States, an adoption agency places a newborn (who was voluntarily surrendered by its Roman Catholic parents) with a loving Protestant family. Few (even few Catholics) would regard the adoption as inhumane. Yet the child who lacks Catholic identity because of America's liberal abortion policies suffers from the same disability as the child who lacks a Catholic identity because of a totalitarian dictator. It appears that what is inhumane in the first case is the lack of voluntarism on the part of the genetic parents, combined with the prejudiced principle used by the oppressive regime to allocate parental privileges: religion.

It is doubtful that an adoption agency in the U.S. today would view it as inhumane to permit loving, well-heeled Protestants to adopt a child of Catholic ancestry without promises of rearing the child as a Catholic. The intuition here seems to be that when it comes to Protestants and Catholics, the difference of religion is not very important. For in the U.S., whether the child is a Catholic or Protestant will generally not much affect her life prospects. (However, there are significant income and educational differences between Catholics and Protestants in some American communities.) By contrast, whether a child is male- or female-identified affects life prospects a great deal. A person with a penis who regards himself as a woman is subject to ridicule and discrimination not suffered by persons with penises who regard themselves as men.

Adoption is governed by state (rather than federal) law in the U.S. Under American state law, no representation is required of adopting parents that the child be reared in keeping with its own religious or cultural ancestry. (Though some native American tribes officially limit extra-tribal adoptions.) So-called international adoption has become increasingly popular in the United States. However, it is the exception rather than the rule that Caucasian-American families who adopt children from South America or Asia seriously attempt to expose the children to their foreign cultural heritages. On the contrary, one of the perquisites of adoption, American style is that adoptive parents may mold the child they adopt in their own image. The curious governmental practice of issuing the adopted child a birth certificate bearing the adoptive parents' names makes it possible to conceal the fact of adoption from just about everyone, including the child. Viewed in this light, U.S. state adoption laws and adoption practices do not presuppose a right to a certain identity linked to who or what one "really" is.

But aspects of adoption practices in the U.S. nonetheless very much presuppose the imperative to cultivate a suitable gender, racial, cultural and religious identity. A prospective adoptive parent who openly expressed a desire to rear a female child as a male would be disqualified. (Indeed, some of the opposition to permitting gays and lesbians to adopt stems from the implausible belief that homosexuality is essentially a gender-identity confusion, and that persons suffering from such a disorder might transfer it to their children.) I would also expect the effective disqualification of black parents or brown parents who said they wanted to adopt a healthy white male child. By contemporary American standards, there is something peculiar about wanting to rear a boy as a girl, or wanting to parent a white child if one is not white.

The practice of matching race and religion is commonplace in the adoption world. There are even some private adoption agencies that specialize in attempting to match children with persons of the same race or religion. In Washington, D.C., an agency called "Homes for Black Children" attempts to find black families to adopt black children. An organization called Catholic Charities places an emphasis on finding Catholic homes for unwanted children. Certain professional groups openly advocate same-race adoption. The largest association of African-American social workers opposes placing black children with white families, even if long-term foster care is the only alternative.

V.

Trans-racial adoption in the United States is one context in which to think about the complex imperative to bring children up to have the appropriate identities, and in which to see its problematic character. In the United States some categories of identification are treated as essential (e.g., gender), while others are treated as not essential (e.g., religion). Officially, under progressive "color blind" civil rights laws, race is supposed to be treated like religion—a weak factor to consider in matching children to families. In practice, according to Harvard Law School Professor Elizabeth Bartholet, race is treated as being nearly as important as gender; that is, non-whites virtually never adopt whites, and whites adopt non-whites with difficulty, mainly in response to scarcity. (There are currently very few American-born healthy white infants available for adoption.)

Trans-racial adoption is much more controversial than trans-religious adoption. (But religion is sometimes an explosive issue in divorce/child custody cases. From time to time it emerges as an issue for the criminal law, as it did in February of 1993, when a member of a strict Jewish sect was arrested in New York after kidnapping a child he believed would not be reared in the customs of his faith.)

One curiosity of the trans-racial adoption controversy is that many of the "black" children who are adopted by "white" families are in fact bi-racial or racially mixed. The segregationist rule of the Old South that "one drop" of "black blood" makes a person black has given rise to an ultimately arbitrary labeling system that potentially makes opposition to the placement of racially mixed children with whites look silly. Yet the experts agonize over the placement of black-ancestry children for good reason. Even for blacks (defined by the "one drop" rule) who look white, the fact of African ancestry, if disclosed, can negatively affect social and economic prospects. For all blacks, of all hues and social classes, there are special problems and concerns for which white parents may be less able than black parents to prepare their children, less able to explain, and less able to endure. This has led to the "transmission of survival skills" argument for preferring black parents for black children. Among the survival skills are comprehending discrimination in historic terms and knowing enough about black social rituals to fit in. The latter may include manifesting certain external, public indicia of identity in the senses outlined earlier. Whites may be unable to see to it that their black children have the public traits that lead other blacks to conclude that they share or at least appreciate others' internal, private black identities. To fit into the black community, and to become one of its respected leaders, a black person may need an identity whites cannot provide.

Closely related to the "transmission of survival skills" argument against trans-racial adoption is the "cultural genocide" argument, according to which the distinctiveness of black culture will be lost if blacks are adopted by whites; and there is also the "community self-determination" argument, which says that the aggregate of blacks—not whites—should be permitted to take responsibility for the welfare of blacks orphaned by poverty, drug abuse, or death. Arguments analogous to these are heard in battles over the fates of children in other settings: would it not be the end of culturally distinct, self-determining French Quebec if children were not compelled to learn the French language?

The aforementioned arguments against trans-racial adoption are too strong when marshalled to explain why a few black children each year should not be permitted white parents. The truth of the matter is that the demand for black children by whites is too low to pose a significant threat to black community self-determination and cultural survival.

The "survival skills" argument requires separate comment. One wants children to have "survival skills." It is true that blacks reared by whites, however kindly brought up and well-schooled, may fail to fit into traditional African-American culture. Blacks' ability to be a part of black culture may be impaired by a "white" upbringing. (I will ignore the fact that it can also be impaired by living with black parents in a majority-white neighborhood and going to a majority-white school.)

If one believed that a black child had a right to a black identity one might have to oppose trans-racial adoption on the ground that whites may be unable to see to it that their black children have a black identity in either the internal or the external senses. One might prefer foster care, or group homes among blacks, to adoption by whites. Yet, in the abstract, it seems indefensible to conclude, as very many people do, that a black child will be, along every relevant educational, psychological and social dimension, all things considered, automatically better off if he or she is not reared by whites. A white family may be better in particular instances than foster care, group homes, and adoption by available blacks, despite the consequences for identity formation. (And some white children might be better off reared in black families than in the best available white families.)

I contend that having a family of one's own is more important to a child than having any particular racial identity. In making this assertion, the clear implication is that I reject the idea of children having a strong right to form a certain racial identity. I reject the idea because I think it is largely a surrogate for another idea, one I find more plausible—that adults have a right to respect for their identities.

Respecting a group's identity means tolerating and appreciating (as Professor Michael Sandel now stresses) key linguistic, religious and other cultural practices that comprise its identity. The adoption laws and practices that allow black children to be placed with white families wound blacks who see in the laws a paternalistic lack of regard for the ability of blacks to help themselves and one another, and a step into a slippery slope toward black cultural genocide. Allowing whites to adopt black children can make black adults feel superfluous; it seems to narrow blacks' sphere of influence and our ability to create and sustain a world in which blacks are accepted by our families and fellow citizens for what we are.

I would regard it as relevant to legal policy-making in the adoption field that black adults consciously or unconsciously feel as I have just described. For example, appealing to the identity needs of black adults and also to their civil rights, I would oppose proposed legislation categorically disqualifying low-income blacks from adopting. But since children need families of their own, among their other important needs, and since permitting some blacks to be reared by whites does not significantly erode black culture in fact, neither the identity needs of black adults nor the identity needs of black children warrant opposition to trans-racial adoption.

In conclusion, my discussion of trans-racial adoption in the U.S. is but an example. I suspect that behind many other important applications of [the] idea that children have a right to a certain identity are concerns about adult identity, and how law and social practice can be better molded to accommodate it.

References

Bartholet, E. (1991), "Where do Black Children Belong? The Politics of Race Matching in Adoption," *University of Pennsylvania Law Review,* Vol 139.

Bartlett, K. (1984), "Rethinking Parenthood as an Exclusive Status: The Need for Legal Alternatives When the Premise of the Nuclear Family Has Failed," *Virginia Law Review,* 1, Vol. 70.

Hafen, B. (1983), "The Constitutional Status of Marriage, Kinship, and Sexual Privacy—Balancing the Individual and Social Interests," *Michigan Law Review,* Vol. 81.

Howard, M. (1984), "Transracial Adoption: Analysis of the Best Interests Standard," *Notre Dame Law Review,* Vol. 59.

Karst, K. L. (1986), "Paths to Belonging: The Constitution and Cultural Identity," *North Carolina Law Review,* Vol. 64.

Kymlicka, W. (1992), "The Right of Minority Cultures: Reply to Kukathas," *Political Theory,* Vol. 20.

———— (1991), "Liberalism and the Politicization of Ethnicity," *The Canadian Journal of Law and Jurisprudence,* Vol. 4.

Lupu, I. (1987), "Home Education, Religious Liberty, and the Separation of Powers," *Boston University Law Review,* Vol. 64.

Minow, M. (1991), "The Free Exercise of Families," *University of Illinois Law Review.*

———— (1986), "Rights for the Next Generation: A Feminist Approach to Children's Rights," *Harvard Women's Law Journal,* Vol. 9.

Perry, T. (1990–91), "Race and Child Placement: The Best Interests Test and the Cost of Discretion," *Journal of Family Law,* Vol. 29.

Raz, J., and Margalit, A. (1990), "National Self-Determination," *Journal of Philosophy,* Vol. 87.

Scott, E., Reppucci, N., and Aber, M. (1992), "Children's Preference in Adjudicated Custody Decisions," *Georgia Law Review,* Vol. 33.

Woodhouse, B. (1992), "'Who Owns the Child?' Meyer and Pierce and the Child as Property," *William and Mary Law Review,* Vol. 33.

Child Abuse: Parental Rights and the Interests of the Child

David Archard

ABSTRACT   I criticise the 'liberal' view of the proper relationship between the family and State, namely that, although the interests of the child should be paramount, parents are entitled to rights of both privacy and autonomy which should be abrogated only when the child suffers a specifiable harm. I argue that the right to bear children is not absolute, and that it only grounds a right to rear upon an objectionable proprietarian picture of the child as owned by its producer. If natural parents have any rights to rear they derive from duties to bring their children into rational maturity where they can exercise rights for themselves. The presumption that natural parents are best suited to rear their own children should be discounted, as should the assumption that alternatives to natural parenting are unacceptably bad. I reject the suggestion that parents should be "licensed" but argue for a much closer monitoring of the family. Familial privacy, which such monitoring breaches, is shown to have a culturally specific and, given the facts of abuse, dubious value. In conclusion, I briefly specify the forms of monitoring I approve.

A familiar complaint of social workers is that they are, in their everyday work, impaled on the horns of a dilemma. Over-zealous intrusion into the lives of families whose behaviour does not in fact warrant such interference brings the charge that rights to privacy have been violated and innocents caused unnecessarily to suffer. On the other hand adequate failure to monitor the private activities of abusing parents has meant children being left to suffer lives which are, in every sense, "solitary, poor, nasty, brutish and short." This dilemma—protect children even at the cost of wrecked families or lose children out of respect for the sanctity of the family—sometimes finds expression as a question of balancing rights, those of the parent against those of the child.

I want to register scepticism about this balance. I want to do so by urging the view that insofar as the best interests of the child are of paramount importance the supposed rights of parents and of families should count for little or nothing. I think that talk of getting a balance right concedes a weight and significance to these latter rights which they should not be accorded.

From *Journal of Applied Philosophy*, vol. 7, no. 1, 1990, 183–194. Reprinted by permission of Blackwell Publishers.

The present debate in Britain about the abuse of children within the family has quite obviously found a focus in the events surrounding the Cleveland crisis, when, during a few months, many children in the Cleveland area of Northern England were diagnosed as having been sexually abused, and removed from the care of their parents. There are many reasons to regret this and to despair of the terms in which the issues have been discussed. The major problem of the Cleveland controversy has been the difficulty of keeping its various elements separate. One could easily talk at length about the diagnostic value of certain alleged means of detecting sexual abuse; about the role that each agency involved—police, social services, voluntary organisations, doctors—can and should play both individually and in concert with the others; about the proper use of the various statutory orders available to these agencies. Unfortunately, it would often seem as if there is only one motion to be debated with one's views on a range of questions following automatically from one's position on this main motion. It is even more unfortunate that the depressingly familiar British custom of personalising important issues should have meant that the main motion is currently worded in terms of unconditional support for (or repudiation of) Doctor X, Reverend Y, or the MP for Z.

Behind the arguments about particular personalities, events and decisions in Cleveland there is at stake the value of a certain widely accepted norm or ideal of child care policy. I should add that, as in so many matters theoretical, there is a considerable similarity between British and American approaches to the matter. It is this norm of family policy, recognisably liberal in character, which I want to lay bare and criticise. In simple terms, the ideal commends the minimum state and social intervention compatible with an adequate protection of the child's interests. Let me now spell out its elements.

First, there is a clear statement of the paramountcy of the best interests of the child. In the United Nations Declaration of the Rights of the Child, formally adopted in 1959, we find Principle 2 urging the child's protection by laws which will enable him or her to develop in a healthy and normal manner. It continues, "in the enactment of laws for this purpose the best interests of the child shall be the paramount consideration."[1] This sentiment has found continuous re-expression in legislation, agency reports and general statements of intent. A Bill currently being considered in the UK begins with a formulation of general principles, the very first of which is that when a court determines any question with respect to the upbringing of a child or the administration of its property "the child's welfare shall be the court's paramount consideration."[2]

The second element in the ideal under scrutiny is the rights of parents or guardians with respect to the children under their care. Parents are those individuals who, in the first instance, are accorded responsibility for the welfare of their children. This entitles them, subject as we shall see to standard conditions, to autonomy and privacy. Autonomy in this context means the freedom to bring up children, educate and rear them as is seen fit; privacy in this context means the absence of unconsented intrusion upon the family's domain. An admirably concise, and influential, statement of these rights was given by the United States Supreme Court in the case of *Prince* v. *Massachusetts, 1944*. The case arose out of the attempt by Massachusetts to use its child labour legislation to prevent a family of Jehovah's Witnesses sending its child out upon the streets to sell religious literature. The judge commented: "it is cardinal with us that the custody, care and nurture of the child reside first in the parents, whose primary function and freedom include preparation for obligations the state can neither supply nor hinder. And it is in recognition of this that [previous] decisions have respected the private realm of family life which the state cannot enter."[3]

The third and final element in the liberal ideal is a specification of the threshold of state intervention, that is a statement of those conditions satisfaction of which would warrant State agencies in breaching the rights to parental privacy and autonomy. These conditions can obviously vary but they nearly always require that the child should have been subjected to, or be in immediate and real danger of being subjected to actual and specific harms. By way of representative example, the present Children Bill states that a court may make care, supervision and emergency protection orders—all of which abrogate in different ways existing parental rights—only if satisfied that "the child concerned has suffered significant harm or is likely to suffer such harm." Significantly, the Bill adds that the harm, or likelihood of harm, should be attributable to "the standard of care given to the child . . . being below that which it would be reasonable to expect the parent of a similar child to give to him."[4] Evidence that a child is being harmed must also be evidence that a parent is neglecting or abusing the child.

The three elements of this ideal can be shown as mutually reinforcing one another in the following way: it is in the immediate best interests of any child to be reared by its parents as they deem appropriate and in a family context protected against intrusions upon its life; however, when the child is treated in certain deleterious ways by its parents, these parents must forego their erstwhile rights of autonomy and privacy, and the best interests of the child may now be served by its guardianship passing from parent to state.

Before I proceed to criticise this ideal, a brief word about the use of the adjective 'liberal' is in order. It seems clear to me that what the liberal prescribes as the proper relation between State and individual citizen is also viewed as most appropriate for the relation between State and family. Famously, J. S. Mill thought the individual should be guaranteed freedom from interference with his self-regarding action, that is accorded a private and protected domain of behaviour insofar as this does not adversely affect anyone else. Only when an individual's acts harmfully intrude upon others is the State permitted to intervene. Mill believed that such a guaranteed private space was necessary to the flourishing of individuality, and thereby to the improvement of society as a whole. Similarly, the liberal ideal of family policy guarantees a space for the life of an individual family within which what is done is both unsupervised by State and freely chosen. The flourishing of the family, and its members, is argued to be secured by such a guarantee of non-interference. Only when harms are directly occasioned to the child does the family become accountable to the State for its private behaviour.

The analogy between individual citizen and individual family has one important, and instructive, limitation. Autonomy and privacy are conceded to individual citizens and it is for their acts within the public domain that they are responsible to the State; in the case of the individual family, privacy is given to the family but autonomy to the parents, that is, to individuals *within* the family. And again it is for harms done *within* the private familial space by *some* members of the family to *other* members of the same family that the family as a whole loses its right to privacy. This important difference between the cases of the individual and of the family is obscured by writers who speak as if the rights to privacy and autonomy are both possessed by the family as a single unit. Thus, for example, in their influential text, *Before the Best Interests of the Child,* Goldstein *et al.* speak of the value of "family integrity" which encompasses both parental autonomy and privacy.[5] Their conflation of quite distinct rights can only spring from a tendency to view the separate interests of child and parents as unified into that of a single familial interest. This is a not uncommon tendency in liberal writing on the family.

What is to be said in favour of the liberal ideal of family policy? That it is both justified and obviously preferable to any other feasible alternative will be the likely response. I propose now to challenge this answer. Justifications of the liberal ideal seem to me to be of two broad kinds, which are mutually reinforcing rather than exclusive alternatives. The first kind of justification attempts to ground a right such as parental autonomy in some other prior right; the second kind of justification is teleological in character and appeals to the morally desirable ends which are served (and which can only or can best be served) by this ideal. I begin by examining the first kind of justification.

It may be argued that a human being has a right to have children. Indeed, some such right seems to be recognised and enshrined in various famous charters, such as the U.N. Declaration. Unfortunately, this is not an obvious or straightforward right. It comprises at least two rights: the right to *bear* children and the right to *rear* children. (It should be obvious that the right to have children cannot, as Hugh LaFollette points out, mean that the infertile should be given children.[6]) If there is a right to bear children—and, strictly speaking, only women could be possessors of such a right—it is clearly not absolute. There may be moral reasons for denying an individual her right to procreate. This seems to be the case if a new human being would by its existence threaten the lives or seriously worsen the welfare of other human beings already existing. Thus, a society might be justified in imposing birth control policies where unlimited population growth in a context of scarce resources jeopardised the well-being of its present and future citizenry (and where non-coercive policies will not or have already failed to work). More imaginatively, we could think of a woman whose highly dangerous and contagious illness is known to be automatically transmitted to the fetus.

Since one gives birth to another human being who presumably *also* has rights, chiefly of course rights to life and libety, a right to bear would have to be circumscribed by an obligation to ensure that the life of this new being is both secure and free. Thus, Onora O'Neill, for instance, thinks that the right to beget or bear "is not unrestricted but contingent upon begetters and bearers having or making some feasible plan for their child to be adequately reared by themselves or by willing others".[7]

Even conceding a limited right to bear children, what relation does this right have to one to rear children? On one account of parentage, the relation is direct and foundational. Those children I bear I may also rear, and do so *because* I bore them. This account is a proprietarian one. It reasons that whatever I produce I justifiably own. Such an account may employ a Lockean theory of property entitlements as grounded upon labour and ownership of one's own body (and rejoice in the felicitous association of the word 'labour' with childbirth). Whatever the theoretical foundations, it seems clear that in previous centuries at least the view of children has been as the property of their parents, or, more specifically within patriarchal societies, of the father. Thus, for instance, "under ancient Roman law the father had a power of life and death (*patria potestas*) over his children that extended into adulthood. He could kill, mutilate, sell, or offer his child in sacrifice."[8] In the *Nicomachean Ethics* Aristotle speaks of children as being a part of their parents—"for the product belongs to the producer (e.g. a tooth or hair or anything else to him whose it is)."[9]

Viewing any human being as the property of another is deeply, and rightly, repugnant to present Western culture. It is important to add that the proprietarian thesis is extremely hard to defend. If begetting did generate ownership, then it is hard to see why ownership should not be lifelong, how we would apportion property rights between mother and father, and how we might acknowledge the productive contributions of medical staff. I foreswear consideration of all the questions raised by donation of semen, *in vitro* fertilisation and surrogate motherhood. Again, it would be curious to argue that someone who is owned has legitimate claims against their owner in respect of their treatment. Yet not only do we accord children such claims against their parents, but also believe that as third parties we are justified in enforcing these claims.

Nevertheless, it is probably, if regrettably true that some shadow of the proprietarian thesis stalks even current thinking about the rights of parents to rear their own children. In the absence of a proprietarian justification, it is difficult to see how the bearing of a child would ground a right to rear it. The only justification I can see as remaining is that the best interests of the child are served by remaining with those who begat him. That is, it may be argued that ties of natural affection ensure that a child's best chance of developing and prospering lies in his staying with his biological parents. Or, at least, that this is the presumption we should act upon. I will return to this claim.

Before I do so, it should be noted that no-one can or will defend a right to rear *simpliciter*. Standardly, philosophers and lawyers writing on this subject speak of a right which is conditional upon the fulfilment by the rearers of duties and responsibilities in relation to the children. In other words parents may bring up a child only insofar as and to the extent that they provide those conditions necessary for the child to enjoy a normal physical and emotional development. Some indeed have argued that the relation between parents and their children should be thought of in fiduciary terms: the parents acting as trustees, the rights they exercise belonging not to them but to their children, this exercise of rights lasting only as long as the trust, namely up to that point where the trust's purpose has been accomplished and the children are able to exercise their own rights for themselves.[10]

I am very sympathetic to this view. I certainly believe that it gets the right way round the relationship between rights and duties. It is not that a right to rear pre-exists but is circumscribed by a duty to meet certain minimum conditions of upbringing. For one thing as I have tried to argue it is hard to see what that pre-existing right would be based upon. It is rather that given a general duty to ensure that children are given a normal and protected development into adulthood, those who undertake that duty in relation to a specific child thereby acquire certain rights to make decisions and choices for that child.

It may well seem that I have been too summary in my dismissal of a natural parent's right to rear his own children. So I shall try again. In general, an individual's right to something is based upon, and derives its value from the individual's having a strong interest in that thing. Joseph Raz, for instance, writes, "a law creates a right if it is based on and expresses the view that someone has an interest which is sufficient ground for holding another to be subject to a duty" and "to be a rule conferring a right it has to be motivated by a belief in the fact that someone's (the rightholder's) interest should be protected by the imposition of duties on others."[11] But, of course, for us to recognise a right it is further required both that the interest should be of value and that its protection does not interfere with the securing by other individuals of things they have a valuable and comparable interest in. We are right, so the argument runs, to have an interest in being as free as possible, and it is consequently evident that we may claim a right to the maximum liberty compatible with a like liberty for others.

How is it with parenthood? There are many possible reasons for a human being to have an interest in rearing children: to bring about a life that avoids the errors of its begetter, to create a companion and an assistant for one's dotage, to add another soldier to the army of the motherland or another true believer to the ranks of the faithful, to prove it can be done, to spite another adult. None of these interests in rearing a child are of self-evident value or obviously consonant with the interests of existent adults. An interest in having a child that we might recognise as of real value would be to bring into existence another human who could be the object of our disinterested love, concern and care. Such an interest would seem to merit the protection of a right to rear. But is this not the same in effect as arguing that such a right is generated by the adequate discharge of a certain responsibility owed the child?

To summarise: I have argued that the right to bear children is not absolute, and that it only grounds a right to rear upon an objectionable proprietarian picture of the child as owned by its producer. If there are any rights to rear they derive from duties to bring children into rational maturity where they can exercise rights for themselves. If then natural parents have a right to rear their own children it is because they are or may be presumed to be best at discharging the duty of upbringing in relation to these children.

This neatly brings us to teleological justifications of parental autonomy. Parents are justified in taking decisions about the upbringing of a child insofar as they thereby promote the best interests of the child. It follows that natural parents are justified in deciding for their offspring only if they are the best persons to care for the child. Our culture presumes that this is normally the case. It is a deep-rooted and understandable presumption. However, those who offer themselves as foster or adoptive parents must satisfy the State through its social service agencies that they can provide an adequate home background, within which the child will be given all reasonable opportunities to flourish. We do not ask natural parents to pass a similar test. If we do not—and discounting any unconscious resort to a proprietarian view—it can only be due to a belief on our part that biology alone equips a person to pass the test of adequate parenthood.

There are two things to be said about such a view. First, it is badly mistaken. Natural parents do abuse and neglect their children. They have done so throughout history and continue to do so today. They do so in such numbers that talk of rare exceptions to a general rule appears naive at best and dangerously misguided at worst. Secondly, the presumption of natural affection is counter-productive. It is often our very reluctance to believe that parents could ill-treat their own children which blinds us to the reality of what is actually happening. Our deep shock before the facts of incestuous sexual abuse remains as much *who* is doing it as *what* is done. But our unwillingness to accept that our neighbour is anything other than a loving father may very well inhibit our investigating further—even in cases where we might have initial suspicions.

My own view then is that we should discount any presumption of natural affection, and assess the capacities of natural parents to rear their children as we would any potential surrogate guardians. Two important disclaimers are in order. First, I do not ignore the importance to the child of a stable, permanent and affectionate home background. I say only that this may be provided by natural parents, foster or adoptive parents, or even within forms of community care. What I am concerned to deny is the assumption that, in advance of any other information, the best interests of children are served by their remaining with their natural parents.

The defender of the liberal ideal may nevertheless reply that the natural parents, for all their faults, represent "the least detrimental alternative" (the phrase is from Goldstein et al., and has been widely adopted). We should, so it is argued, recognise that even if natural parents are not the best for the child, they may be the "least worst." And for two reasons: the available options are unacceptably poorer than natural parentship, and the trauma of separation will involve harms for which a reallocation of guardianship cannot compensate.

The first claim if true is so only contingently. Institutional alternatives to the family can be and have been very poor, but this is for two reasons, a historical and an ideological one. Such alternatives owe their form to their historical roots—as custodial and preventative responses to juvenile delinquency and orphanhood. Ideologically, society remains unwilling seriously to support non-familial structures for the upbringing of children. Were society to be convinced that an alternative to the family is needed in the case of very many children who need not as a result be stigmatised as "misfits," then the first claim would fail to be persuasive. Moreover, such a conviction might draw strength precisely from a recognition that a child is not necessarily best served by remaining with its natural parents.

It is also worth adding that some studies cast direct doubt on the presumption that, in all cases, natural parenting does better for the child than any alternative. Barbara Tizard, for instance, has shown that within a group of initially institutionalised children, those adopted fared better than those who were returned to their natural parents.[12]

The second claim—that separating the child from its parents does irreparable harm—is an empirical, psychological one. It is thus no accident that the defenders of the liberal ideal rely heavily on psychoanalytic theories of the parent–child relation, such as those of John Bowlby and Anna Freud. They also, it must be added, make use of studies of institutionalised children where the institutions in question were those operating immediately after the Second World War in conditions of Dickensian austerity.[13] "Revisionist" child psychologists such as the Clarkes, Michael Rutter and Jerome Kagan are currently far more sanguine about the adaptability of children to changes in their environments. They have also argued against the alleged importance of the parent–child bonding to the long-term health and development of the child.[14]

At this point it is worth briefly responding to a possible double-edged criticism of my argument thus far. This is, first, that talk of parental and children's *rights* is not the only and is perhaps an overstrong way to understand the problem; and, secondly, that the relationship between natural parent and child displays an emotional reality which is very unlikely to be true of that between an unrelated guardian and child, this reality being misrepresented by talk either of ownership or of grounding rights to rear.

My use of the language of rights to the apparent exclusion of any other moral discourse should not be taken to imply an acceptance that the former represents the only legitimate means of representing the problem of familial privacy and child abuse. However, it remains a fact that it is in terms of parental and children's rights that the legal and social policy debate about families has been conducted. Moreover, it seems clear that the attribution of putative rights to parents and children is the strongest way in which to express and defend the moral concerns of these individuals. If only standard considerations of overall social welfare prevail then the case for children to stay with their natural parents may be a much weaker one. There is, after all, no right to rear which might trump these considerations.

Nevertheless, there may be reasons for children to remain with their natural parents which have not to do with any ownership of the former by the latter, and which do not ground parental rights. It will be said that parents are emotionally bound up with, involved with, and attached to their children in ways that are simply not true, or are very unlikely to be true of mere guardians. Parents *feel* for their own children. They need not view them as owned, nor does their feeling automatically give them rights over their own. However, to neglect this emotional reality would, it can be argued, be implausibly to conclude that natural parents and guardians do not differ in any interesting respects.

I suspect that this alludes to an important feature of human relationships which deserves a more careful and extended treatment than is possible here. For the purposes of my argument a terse, and probably unsatisfactory rejoinder is in order. Feeling bound up with another is no guarantee that one is the best person to promote that other's good. Parents may be more willing than others to tend their own, and be so on account of their parental feelings. But this fact, if it is a fact, does not acquit them from the responsibility of showing that they are good guardians, and better guardians than others who might be available. The ways in which foster and adoptive parents can care for children shows that the feeling of being bound up with another is not exclusive to blood ties. Indeed, the absence of blood ties may make for more sagacious and judicious parenting.

We should not be blind to the reality of parental love, but equally we should not be blinded by it. Social policy should not ignore feelings, but it should also learn to discriminate between feelings. The danger is that an ideology of blood love is self-confirming. Our unwillingness to explore and encourage feasible alternatives to the natural parent may rest on the mistaken belief that the love only a natural parent can feel for its own must be a necessary condition of a good upbringing. I cannot see that it is necessary, and my argument thus far is to the effect that it is certainly not sufficient.

To reiterate, my view is that the capacities of any natural parent to rear their children should be viewed neutrally, that is by discounting any presumption of their biologically grounded superiority as guardians. My second disclaimer, announced earlier, concerns the practical import of this view. One practical proposal would be that advocated by Hugh LaFollette in an admirably provocative article, namely the licensing of parents.[15] LaFollette defends the view that the rearing of children is an activity which, being potentially harmful to others and requiring demonstrated competence in its execution, demands regulation. Someone, LaFollette argues, should not be able to rear children unless they acquire a license to do so, and such a license should only be granted on evidence of the requisite ability safely to bring up a child.

Although LaFollette's point of attack is the right to rear, his argument could be extended to the right to bear children, and would thus appear to warrant a licensing of procreation. This would raise enormous difficulties. How, for instance, should an unlicensed recidivist begetter of children be treated? Compulsory abortion and/or sterilisation suggest themselves as obvious but extremely unpalatable solutions. It will be practically impossible to prevent all human beings who might be deemed unfit to bear children from having them. Or at least it will require a machinery for the detection and punishment of offenders that few would be prepared to countenance.

Any practical questions then concern what to do *after* children have been born. LaFollette would presumably re-allocate children from parents who are unlicensed to those who are. A criticism of LaFollette is that he, unreasonably, requires a person's future skills (as a parent) to be predicted, whereas licensing normally requires only that a person's present performance be assessed.[16] We cannot know how people may be as parents in the future. I would make a related but slightly different criticism. LaFollette concedes that we may neither agree what counts as nor be able successfully to predict who actually will be a "good parent." But, he says, his scheme "is designed to exclude only the very bad ones."[17] Now he also rightly suggests that we are gaining a better idea of the profile of the person who is likely to abuse their children. This means, in effect, that we know of some people that they will most probably be very bad parents, even if we may not know of any one of the others that they will not be a bad parent. Thus, licensing alone will not guarantee that all parents are adequate, and licensing of everyone is not needed to exclude in advance the palpably bad parents. The argument against licensing is completed by recognising its costs and outlining a more feasible alternative which serves the same ends just as well.

LaFollette's scheme requires that licenses be fairly and efficiently granted upon the basis of an agreed and workable criterion of "fitness to parent" which can cover all eventualities. There are obvious, and perhaps insuperable difficulties with such a proposal. However, my practical suggestion prevents those harms LaFollette wishes to see prevented by his scheme and does not involve the difficulties his does. Those who are brought to the attention of society as obviously bad prospective parents may be prevented from rearing their own or anybody else's children. Such persons fit either the profile for an abusing parent of which LaFollette speaks, or a more general profile such as would disqualify them as adequate parents. I am thinking here of something like a previous history of extremely violent behaviour.

For the rest, a child will remain with its parents, but only subject to an extensive and rigorous monitoring of their development after birth. Such monitoring is required by the logic of LaFollette's own argument. Any license may be revoked upon evidence of subsequent and seriously harmful incompetence in the activity for which the license was originally granted. Thus, LaFollette would have to be assured that even licensed parents were still fit to care for their children. My point is that, having already excluded those who can be confidently picked out as very bad prospective parents, monitoring alone does all the work that LaFollette's more cumbersome and impractical licensing scheme is designed to do.

Since such extensive monitoring clearly represents a direct challenge to the alleged familial right to privacy, I must now turn to consideration of the grounds for such a right. A familiar defence of the right to privacy in respect of individuals urged by people like Charles Fried is that it permits the intimacy which is essential to relationships of love and friendship.[18] Similarly, it has been argued that familial privacy is necessary for the healthy development of the normal, loving relationships between parent and parent, parent and child which characterise a healthy family.[19] It may further be argued that such familial bonds are "critical to every child's healthy growth and development."[20]

My reply is two-fold. First, the kind of privacy to which the twentieth century Western family feels entitled and which it has come to expect is historically and culturally very specific. It is worth emphasising the degree to which the private nuclear family, a self-contained household of kin only living within its own well-defined space, is a peculiarly late twentieth century Western phenomenon, a compound of various changes in society—the separation of home and work activities, a decline in the number of children born per family, an end to apprenticeship and the "putting out" of children, the demise of servants as household members, the emergence in various architectural forms of the family house, and the development of entertainments which are or can be home-based.[21]

Families in previous times and in other types of society have enjoyed a quite significantly smaller degree of privacy. Of course it can be shown that in all cultures and societies there is some line drawn to divide space, demarcate activities, specify roles in terms of a distinction between public and private. Thus, for example, a particular tribal culture may involve households comprising several kin groups preparing and eating food together, sleeping in the same unpartitioned building, but with some "private" spaces and times associated with sexual activity and enforced through rules of non-encroachment.[22]

However, it is only in this century in the West that the line between private and public has been so clearly and sharply drawn around the nuclear family in so many of its aspects. Importantly, there is little or no evidence that these significant differences in the scope of familial privacy are correlatable with equally significant differences in the degree to which children develop into normal healthy adults.

Secondly, whilst privacy may serve as the precondition for a healthy and loving intimacy, it can equally function as a cloak for abuse and neglect. The ill-treatment of children takes place in a "private" space, the family home, and to the very extent that it is a private space, it may continue undetected and unsuspected. In response to Richard Wasserstrom's views on privacy Lorenne Clark has written, "Wasserstrom points out . . . that 'we have accepted the idea that many things are shameful unless done in private.' The irony is that such shameful things go on just because they are left in private."[23] The "privacy" of the family protects the abuser in a number of ways. The abuse is literally unobserved, and whilst physical abuse may display itself through the consequent bruises and burns upon the child, sexual abuse has no obvious public face. Abused children may have no sense that what is "privately" happening to them is radically and terribly different from what would be "publicly" acceptable. So many victims of incest have subsequently reported that they did not think of their abuse as anything other than natural, as what happened within even "normal" families. Finally, the abused child within the "private" space of the family will probably be pressurised not to reveal the abuse, or to retract previous accusations of abuse. It is sometimes tragically ironic to read about accusations of social workers bullying confessions of abuse from children, when no mention is made at the same time of the brutal means by which abusing parents so frequently secure the silence of their victims.

All these are reasons why abused children will not—as our society sometimes seems to expect—step forward and publicly identify themselves as victims of abuse. They are also thus reasons why the disclosure of abuse will have to involve intrusions upon the privacy of the family prescribed by the liberal ideal. It is important—before I specify something of the intrusiveness upon the family which I favour—to emphasize the extent of the evil which it would help to prevent. The abuse of children—especially sexual abuse—ruins lives, and not just those of the victim. Abuse is deeply traumatising, and its scarring effects last well into, if not throughout adulthood. There is increasing evidence of a cycle of abuse—abusers being themselves very frequently the victims of previous abuse. There is also evidence linking subsequent criminality, alcoholism, drug addiction and violent behaviour to a history of childhood abuse.

So what intrusions upon family privacy would I favour? I would give those social workers who specialise and are trained in child abuse statutory powers of entry into family homes and access to children. It is of course significant that the biggest percentage of referrals to social services of suspected abuse in the United Kingdom comes from health workers who currently enjoy *de facto* rights of access into homes and to children. I would strive to redraw the line that separates the "private" family from the public domain by creating "spaces" in which the health of children can be reviewed and monitored with a view to possible abuse. By this, I mean that family doctors, consultants, emergency medical personnel, police and teachers—all those who for professional or statutory reasons may come into contact with children—must be specifically trained in the diagnosis of abuse, educated in the importance of detecting abuse and persuaded as to the need for their contact with the child to present opportunities for the diagnosis of possible abuse. The reporting of cases of suspected abuse to social services by such professionals must also be made mandatory.

It is clear that presently the vast majority of these professionals honour the liberal ideal for familial privacy, are loath to suspect parents of ill-doing, and favour interference only as a last resort. In their study of how the agencies concerned with child welfare operate within the UK, *The Protection of Children* (1983), Robert Dingwall *et al.* conclude: "We have clearly shown that, at each and every stage, the structures of the organisations involved and the practical reasoning of their members have the effect of creating a preference for the least stigmatising interpretation of available data and the least overtly coercive possible disposition. Officially-labelled cases of mistreatment are, quite literally, only those for which no excuse or justification can be found. Compulsory measures are employed only in those cases where parental recalcitrance or mental incompetence leave no room for voluntary action."[24]

Closely related to my preference for a greater intrusiveness upon the family is a dislike for the liberal ideal's threshold for statutory action: the occasioning or risk of specific harms to the child. The criterion is essentially "negative." Parents are given the benefit of the doubt, and the onus is upon the State to establish neglect and abuse of a concrete form. I would rather that the State established affirmative duties of care which guaranteed the best possible conditions for the development of the child. This ideal is enshrined within the ancient prerogative of *parens patriae* whereby the State may assume, in the last analysis and last resort, the protective role of parent to its infant citizens. In turn, this doctrine justifies the jurisdiction of High Courts over minors in cases of wardship. Wardship has been defined as "essentially a parental jurisdiction" wherein the "main consideration to be acted upon in its exercise is the benefit or welfare of the child . . . the Court must do what under the circumstances a wise parent acting for the true interest of the child would or ought to do."[25] My point might be expressed rather baldly as follows: the liberal ideal requires that parents be shown to be palpably bad before the State will intervene. I would rather that the State requires its parents to be good, and act accordingly when they are not.

There is much talk nowadays of the emergence of children's rights, and the correlated fragmentation or disappearance of parental rights.[26] As I have noted, the paramountcy of the child's best interests is, at least formally, insisted upon in the rhetoric of legal and social welfare provision. Interestingly, however the doctrines of paramountcy derives principally from custody cases, in which the family *has already broken down*. Similarly, the liberal ideal of family policy presumes the benevolence of existing parental control and intervenes only when there is proven familial failure. If we are to take seriously the notion of the child's best interests, and the reality of children's rights, then we cannot continue uncritically to speak of competing rights to family privacy and parental autonomy. On the contrary, respect for these latter rights serves only to perpetuate the very conditions under which children, out of sight and too often out of the "public" mind, suffer the "private" hell of preventable abuse. Despite all the obfuscations and distortions of the facts, I still hope that the events of Cleveland will help to teach us that invaluable lesson.[27]

Notes

1. U.N. Declaration of rights, in: O. O'Neill & W. Ruddick (Eds.) (1979). *Having Children: Philosophical and Legal Reflections on Parenthood* (Oxford, Oxford University Press), pp. 112–114.
2. *Children Bill* (1989), Part I, 1(1).
3. Quoted in: M. D. A. Freeman (1983) "Freedom and the welfare state: child-rearing, parental autonomy and state intervention," *Journal of Social Welfare Law*, p. 71.
4. *Children Bill* (1989), Part IV, 26(2).
5. Goldstein, A. Freud, & A. J. Solnit (1980). *Before the Best Interests of the Child* (London, Burnett Books), p. 5.
6. Hugh LaFollette (1980) "Licensing parents," *Philosophy & Public Affairs*, 9:2, pp. 186–187.
7. Onora O'Neill (1979) "Begetting, Bearing and Rearing," in: O. O'Neill & W. Ruddick (Eds.) (1979).
8. Mason Thomas (1972) "Child Abuse and Neglect. Part I: Historical Overview, Legal Matrix, and Social Perspectives," *North Carolina Law Review*, 50, p. 295.
9. Aristotle, *Nicomachean Ethics*, Book VIII.12, 20–25.
10. C. K. Beck, G. Glavis, S. A. Glover, S. A. Jenkins, & R. A. Nardi (1978) "The Rights of Children: A Trust Model," *Fordham Law Review*, XLVI:4, pp. 669–780.
11. J. Raz (1984) "Legal Rights," *Oxford Journal of Legal Studies*, 4:1, pp. 13–14.
12. Barbara Tizard (1977) *Adoption: A Second Chance* (London, Open Books).
13. J. Bowlby (1965) *Attachment and Loss. Vol. 1: Attachment* (London, Hogarth Press & Institute of Psycho-Analysis); J. Bowlby (1973) *Attachment and Loss. Vol. 2: Separation—Anxiety and Anger* (London, Hogarth Press & Institute of Psycho-Analysis); A. Freud & D. Burlingham (1944) *Young Children in War Time: A Year's Work in a Residential Nursery* (London, Allen & Unwin); A. Freud & D. Burlingham (1944) *Infants Without Families: The Case for and Against Residential Nurseries* (London, Allen & Unwin).
14. A. M. Clarke & A. C. B. Clarke (1976) *Early Experience: Myth and Evidence* (London, Open Books); M. Rutter (1972; 2nd ed. 1981) *Maternal Deprivation Reassessed* (Harmondsworth, Penguin Books); J. Kagan, R. B. Kearsley, & P. R. Zelazo (1978) *Infancy: Its Place in Human Development* (Cambridge, MA, Harvard University Press).
15. Hugh LaFollette (1980), pp. 182–197.
16. Lawrence Frisch (1981) "On Licentious Licensing: A Reply to Hugh LaFollette," *Philosophy & Public Affairs*, 11:2, pp. 173–183.
17. Hugh LaFollette (1980), p. 190.

18. Charles Fried (1970) *An Anatomy of Values* (Cambridge, MA, Harvard University Press), Ch. IX.

19. Francis Schrag (1976) "Justice and the Family," *Inquiry,* 19, pp. 193–208; Ferdinand Schoeman (1980) "Rights of Children, Rights of Parents and the Moral Basis of the Family," *Ethics,* 91, pp. 6–19; Iris Marion Young (1983) "Rights to Intimacy in a Complex Society," *Journal of Social Philosophy,* 14, pp. 47–52.

20. J. Goldstein, A. Freud, & A. J. Solnit (1980), p. 10.

21. Barbara Laslett (1973) "The Family As a Public and Private Institution: An Historical Perspective," *Journal of Marriage and the Family,* 35, pp. 480–492.

22. Irwin Altman (1977) "Privacy Regulation: Culturally Universal or Culturally Specific?", *Journal of Social Issues,* 33 : 3, pp. 66–84.

23. Lorenne Clark (1978) "Privacy, Property, Freedom and the Family," in: Richard Bronaugh (Ed.) *Philosophical Law* (Connecticut, Greenwood Press), p. 182.

24. Robert Dingwall, John Eekelaar, & Topsy Murray (1982) *The Protection of Children: State Intervention and Family Life* (Oxford, Basil Blackwell), p. 207.

25. Lord Justice Kay (1893) *Reg.* v. *Gyngall,* quoted in: S. M. Cretney (1984) *Principles of Family Law,* 4th ed. (London, Sweet & Maxwell), p. 326.

26. John Eekelaar (1973) "What Are Parental Rights?", *Law Quarterly Review,* 89, pp. 210–234; Susan Maidment (1981) "The Fragmentation of Children's Rights," *Cambridge Law Review,* 4 : 1, pp. 135–158; John Eekelaar (1986) "The Emergence of Children's Rights," *Oxford Journal of Legal Studies,* 6 : 2, pp. 161–182.

27. My grateful thanks to Bernarde Lynn, Jim Brown and the members of Bristol University Philosophy Society for comments on a previous draft of this article.

Rights-Talk Will Not Sort Out Child-Abuse: Comment on Archard on Parental Rights

Mary Midgley

ABSTRACT   Argument about Rights can be either purely formal or substantial—meant to affect conduct. These two functions, which need different kinds of support, often become confused. The source of much confusion is the idea that rights-language is an all-purpose "moral theory" which is in competition with others such as Utilitarianism. Since these are not really rivals but complementary aspects of moral thinking—parts of it, both of which need to be used along with many others—attempts to establish one of them as sole ruler are doomed to incoherence. The ambition to deploy an all-purpose thought-system is distinct from the moral motivation to change the world, and the two aims inevitably interfere with one another. Among these "moral theories," however, the language of rights is specially ill-suited for all-purpose use. This becomes plain when philosophers, taking its adequacy for granted, conduct moral argument in terms of it alone, as if it were obviously appropriate, without background discussion. Rights-language is of particularly limited use because it is simply the most competitive and litigious of such thought-systems. Its win-or-lose formula allows no more scope for doing justice to defeated claims than a lawcourt does. For the serious conflicts of value that underlie large moral problems, this is disastrous.

. . .

The Rights Habit

Preference for talking in terms of rights is, of course, not always marked by explicit converting zeal. It often seems to be more a matter of habit, as if the first thing to be asked in any moral dilemma were always "what rights are involved here?" No conceptual scheme ought, I think, to have this kind of automatic priority, but there is a special objection over rights. *This is simply the most competitive and litigious of moral concepts.* If rights appear to clash, then one of them must give way. The legal model, which is very close here, dictates a zero-sum solution. If I win, you lose. There is a conceptual deadlock; the losing party must simply leave the court.

Now no doubt there are indeed situations in life where this is what ought to happen, and careful reflection may convince us that we have reached one of them. But careful reflection is just what the rights schema leaves no room for. It contains no pathways for comparing the *nature* of different claims and

From *Journal of Applied Philosophy*, vol. 8, no. 1. 1991, 105–110. Reprinted by permission of Blackwell Publishers.

different ideals, nor for inventive compromise. Debates that have been handled in this way are thus notorious for producing sterile and unshiftable controversial blocks. Over abortion, the absolute right to life of the foetus confronts blankly the woman's absolute right over her own body. Over euthanasia, the absolute right to life confronts the right to control one's own destiny, or the right not to be forced to suffer. The only concept commonly brought in to break the deadlock is that of personhood, which is also used as a rigid yes-or-no concept. It is easy to argue for, or against, any one of these rights, or any particular definition of "person," if one avoids facing the fact of conflict—which is, of course, the real crux. We need to drop the obsession with the win-or-lose legal model and instead consider the various reasons for different courses open-mindedly, looking for new ways out.

The Problem: Child-Abuse

Meanwhile, the debates go on. In order to make clear what is wrong with an approach that has been so widely accepted, I must, I think, discuss an example in some depth. I hope there is nothing invidious about picking one from a recent issue of this journal, namely, David Archard's article "Child-Abuse: Parental Rights and the Interests of the Child" (*Journal of Applied Philosophy*, Vol. 7, no. 2, 1990). It is a good example because I am in strong sympathy with its central theme. Here is its abstract:

> I criticise the "liberal" view of the proper relationship be-tween the family and State, namely that, although the interests of the child should be paramount, parents are entitled to rights of both privacy and autonomy which should be abrogated only when the child suffers a specifiable harm. I argue that the right to bear children is not absolute, and that it only grounds a right to rear upon an objectionable proprietarian picture of the child as owned by its producer. If natural parents have any rights to rear they derive from duties to bring their children into rational maturity where they can exercise rights for themselves. The presumption that natural parents are best suited to rear their own children should be discounted, as should the assumption that alternatives to natural parenting are unacceptably bad. I reject the suggestion that parents should be "licensed" but argue for a much closer monitoring of the family. Familial privacy, which such monitoring breaches, is shown to have a culturally specific and, given the facts of abuse, dubious value. In conclu-sion, I briefly specify the forms of monitoring I approve.

Archard is surely right to call for changes in deeply established concepts to meet the frightening revelations that have surfaced about child-abuse, espe-cially in view of the strange incredulity which the public and many journalists still show towards the children's evidence. But what changes do we need? He approaches this question entirely as an advocate in an ongoing debate on rights, attacking a previous advocate's assertion of a strong parental "right to rear."

In what world does this debate arise? The reason why parents are taken to be normally the least bad available rearers for their children is not any belief about a particular right. It is widespread experience that other people are, almost always, much less willing even to try to do the job properly than the parents are. Of course there are many successful adoptions and fosterings. But attempts to provide adoptive or institutional or foster-care rely on finding people to give it who will provide the enormous devotion the job demands, *and who do not share the faults of the parents.* Since parents are not a peculiar group, how can we expect that, in a given society, average foster parents and house-parents will behave any better than average parents do?

As things are, child-abuse by these substitute parents is quite often reported—even today, when they are carefully selected, and when very few people are so employed, so that those employing them presumably have a wide pool of candidates to choose from. With the expansion of such care that Archard demands, where would the new mass of reliable, superior carers come from? (Which of us would, ourselves, actually be willing to take over the care of a deeply disturbed child, or could make a success of it if we did?)

What, then, about institutions? Archard is confident. Liberal theorists, he claims,:

> make use of studies of institutionalised children where the institutions in question were those operating immediately after the Second World War in conditions of Dickensian austerity.

But this is not a local difficulty. The care of orphans raises grave problems everywhere, at all epochs. Never mind Dickens, there have been, in the last two decades, a whole series of resounding scandals involving long-standing child-abuse in children's homes, as well as reports from former residents in them of this and other troubles. Foster-parents, step-parents and adoptive parents have also been involved in many cases of abuse. (Archard says that no society has ever put enough effort into the institutional option to give it fair trial. In Israel, however, immense devotion and resources were put into the Kibbutz nurseries. Certainly things do not seem to have gone badly there, and the parents were, of course still present. But the next generation has voted with its feet to go back to domestic parenting).

Archard seems to me not to have noticed the really frightening thing about recent revelations—namely, that this evil turns out so much more widespread than we thought. Though it is true that natural parents have been behaving far worse than was supposed, the record of other carers does not seem to be better. We can no longer think in terms of a vast, reliable majority of respectable citizens standing ready to rescue children from their parents. *The issue is not one of "liberalism" at all—not a conflict between awkward individuals and the State. It concerns the whole condition of our domestic life.*

Natural Bonding and the "Right to Rear"

I have turned first to the practical problem of "who will care for the children if the parents are removed?" because this seems to me the first question any responsible person would ask on hearing Archard's argument. Most of that argument, however, is not occupied with any such practical problems. Its first concern is to demolish supposed grounds for a parental "right to rear."

> Even conceding a limited right to bear children, what relation does this right have to one to rear children? On one account of parentage, the relation is direct and foundational. Those children I bear I may also rear, and do so because I bore them. *This account is a proprietarian one.* It reasons that whatever I produce I justifiably own. Such an account may employ a Lockean theory of property entitlements as grounded upon labour and ownership of one's own body (and rejoice in the felicitous association of the word "labour" with childbirth). Whatever the theoretical foundations, it seems clear that in previous centuries at least the view of children has been as the property of their parents, or more specifically within patriarchal societies, of the father . . . *In the absence of a proprietarian justification, it is difficult to see how the bearing of a child would ground a right to rear it.* (p. 186; emphases mine)

Difficult, is it? Shall we try?

Humans are mammals. For most women, the experience of pregnancy and childbirth is an immense spiritual and psychological upheaval. Physiologically, it involves a tumultuous upsurge in hormonal activity, whose function is to produce deep emotional bonding with the coming child, an attachment strong enough to make the whole grinding effort of rearing possible. It normally does produce that attachment, often transforming the woman's life. Culture does not usually oppose this bonding but backs it by social approval, as it must unless it finds some better way of bringing up the children, which it has not yet done. Even, however, where culture divides mother from child—for instance, over illegitimate births, or for slaves who knew that they could not keep their children—women who have had every external reason to accept separation have often found it agonising, and frequently refused to do it. To bear children is therefore normally to be put in a situation where their removal will cause one great pain and lasting psychological trauma. If that does not ground a "right," it would be interesting to know what does.

About fathers, the situation is certainly different, but less different than has sometimes been thought. Early bond-forming is indeed typically less strong in human males, cultural variation greater, and complete detachment more common than in females. Nevertheless, as the primatologist Jane Lancaster has pointed out,[1] human males do, throughout the species, have a very different emotional relation to children from that of their nearest relatives. Male great apes, while often friendly to infants, never help to support them, do not forage for them nor systematically protect them. They form no strong bonds with them individually. Human males everywhere do do these things, and often share with human females a special deep attachment to those they regard as their own children, an attachment which can, in them also, produce real and lasting self-sacrifice.

This attachment is too deep and widespread to be the product of a particular culture, or of general calculating prudence. It is rather, like the tastes that underlie art and science, one of the innate emotional tendencies that has made possible the success of the human species, and the whole creation of culture. It is not, therefore, something which reformers can reckon on getting rid of.

Worries About Innateness

Is there anything fishy about accepting that there are such innate tendencies? Early twentieth-century theorists were suspicious about innateness, because previous theorists had used distorted ideas of "human nature" uncritically to justify every form of traditional oppression. Behaviourists therefore revived and extended Locke's notion that we are originally mere neutral stuff, blank paper at birth, on which experience may write absolutely anything. This drastic view has, however, not worn much better than its predecessor. The blank paper pattern has not only often turned out unusably remote from the facts, but has also been used to justify further, newly-invented forms of oppression. (*Brave New World* is quite a consistent Behaviourist Utopia).

Both these hasty reactions are, I think growing less common today, as we succeed in separating questions about evidence for the existence of these tendencies from sweeping, unrealistic moral proposals about how they should be handled. For instance, admitting that there is natural bond-forming between parent and child does *not* commit us to believing:

That parents will never behave appallingly,

That children should always obey their parents,

That mothers must always stay with their children, or children with their mothers,

That mothers should do nothing else except look after children,

That children must never be taken from their parents,

or any other silly generalisation. Parental bonds are only part of a rich and wide-ranging system of social and emotional links. All these links involve some innate element, because—as we see when illness or injury damages organs that serve the emotions—all have a bodily basis. All also gain a great deal from experience through culture. But since there are limits to what culture can do to reshape them, it plainly pays for culture to work, when possible, with the grain of nature rather than against it.

The Irrelevance of Property Rights

Obviously these facts about natural bonding do not confer on parents any unconditional "right to rear." But then, the whole idea of such unconditional rights is mysterious and irrelevant. We are discussing a nexus of claims, which can well sometimes conflict. The parents' claim has two aspects. There is the probability, though no certainty, that their bonding will make them more suitable rearers than other people would be. There is also the deep emotional investment which makes separation so painful, both for them, and, after a time, for the child as well.

Neither of these elements needs support from Lockean theories about labour and property rights. Words like "own" and "belong" do have a special use in these topics, but it is one that is far more primitive than any institutions affecting property. If we say "I don't belong anywhere," or "They won't even own him," we are reporting a misfortune. If we say "My own darling" we are not making a property-claim. Bond-forming is a separate topic from property, and one so obviously more relevant to this problem that readers unused to modern academic habits might be surprised to see a writer's back so ostentatiously turned to it, and might suppose that they themselves were being naive in supposing it important. This is the Poker-Face Ploy, a means of ignoring inconvenient everyday topics by recoiling from them with visible distaste.[2]

Archard does indeed notice the idea that strong natural affection gives parents a claim to rear their children, and also that separation can do grave harm to both. But he thinks such views are idle superstitions:

> The . . . claim that separating the child from its parents does irreparable harm is an empirical, psychological one. It is thus no accident that the defenders of the liberal ideal rely heavily on psycho-analytic theories of the parent-child relation, such as those of John Bowlby and Anna Freud . . . "Revisionist" child psychologists such as the Clarkes, Michael Rutter and Jerome Kagan are currently far more sanguine about the adaptability of children to changes in their environments. They have also argued against the alleged importance of the parent-child bonding to the long-term health and development of the child. (p. 189)

That is very interesting; why do we not hear more of it? If this point is seriously meant, it would surely have been better to devote most of the article to making it look plausible. Bowlby's views are indeed empirical, but that is not usually thought an objection to a psychological doctrine. They are not specially psycho-analytic. He and his successors brought much solid evidence about the destructive effects of separation, especially in certain circumstances and at certain ages. Their work has of course produced plenty of controversy, in which exaggerations have been pointed out and sweeping claims refined. But the central thesis, correcting the Behaviourists' crude dismissal of the vital need for strong, lasting personal ties in childhood, has survived criticism. It has earned the acceptance of most professionals who have to deal with such matters, and is now deservedly built into general practice. To wave it away as mere ideology seems to be part of a somewhat desperate campaign to play down the seriousness of an abused child's situation.

The Choice of Evils

If it were not an evil for a child to lose its parents, then the attack on parental rights might have more force. But it is. Of course things are indeed sometimes so bad that it is a lesser evil than remaining with them, and of course later good treatment can often mitigate the ill-effects. But that cannot show that it was not an evil at all. Like most moral problems that cause real trouble in the world, this is a choice of evils, something which the language of rights cannot really handle. When we lose people who have been close to us and played a central part in our lives, we lose a part of ourselves. This is, of course, one of the miseries of divorce, and unluckily it does not stop being true when there is a great deal wrong with those people. Quite apart from Bowlby's work, the testimony of many people who have suffered loss of parents, even not particularly good parents, shows how strongly the natural bond is felt. The difficulties experienced by step-parents—even ones who are really anxious to help and understand the child—underline this point. New attachments, like trees, cannot be instantly created. They call for a surprising amount of time and effort. But children and adults need continuity.

Archard is inclined to wave all confidence in such tendencies away as only part of our culture (p. 188). Even if that were true it would not help much, since we cannot change that culture overnight. Perhaps he is suggesting that we *ought* to change the culture by training people to have a lower opinion of natural affection? This distrust of feeling would accord with his remarkable claim that the only justification for rearing one's own children is that one is specially capable of bringing them up to be mature rational beings exercising rights:

> **If there are any natural rights to rear they derive from duties to bring children into rational maturity where they can exercise rights for themselves. (p. 188)**

This strangely legalistic view of the aims of life, explicitly placing rights at the centre of morality and ignoring all other human values, is not something that can just be taken for granted. Even the Stoics did not hold it, and Kant was never so crude, though selective quotation sometimes makes him seem so. What, for instance, happens in the case of a subnormal child, never destined to reach rational maturity? If Archard is really campaigning for this idea, then he is proposing so large a change in the ideals we live by that it should surely be the central topic of his article. But he does not explicitly propose it.

In any case, however, the claim that our own culture is peculiar on this point does not seem to be true. Though indeed some cultures make more use of adoption and fostering than we do, natural parenting remains central and supplies the model for these other forms. Many cultures lay far more stress on all natural relations than we do. Everywhere, even in those (rather few) places where the mother's brother largely replaces the father, the mother's own position still remains central, and the bond to the uncle is still a natural one. No culture has yet been found to try out the proposal so eloquently argued by Plato,[3] J. B. Watson[4] and Shulamith Firestone,[5] that people should be brought up by outsiders specially qualified to do it, preferably without knowing who their parents are at all.

Practical Measures

So much for how we got here. What, however, should we do next? Archard plumps for "a much closer monitoring of the family," overriding traditional rights of privacy and autonomy, and for testing parents from the start. "We should discount any presumption of natural affection, and assess the capacities of natural parents to rear as we would any potential surrogate guardians" (p. 188).

In what is surely the strongest part of his paper, he describes the terrifying way in which household privacy has served as "a cloak for abuse and neglect" (p. 192), and notes how abused people tend to become abusers themselves, perpetuating a cycle of misery. As he says, children often do not even know that what they endure is not normal; if they do know they are afraid to tell, and harsh threats are used to keep them silent. Accordingly, "the disclosure of abuse will have to involve intrusions on the family proscribed by the liberal ideal."

Somewhat suddenly, however, these intrusions are extended to carry us far beyond the area of abuse in a way that does not seem to be supported by these arguments:

> Closely related to my preference for a greater intrusiveness upon the family is a disliking for the liberal ideal's threshold for statutory action; the occasioning or risk of specific harm to the child. The criterion is essentially "negative." Parents are given the benefit of the doubt, and the onus is upon the State to establish neglect and abuse of a concrete form. I would rather that the State established affirmative duties of care which guaranteed the best possible conditions for the development of the child. This ideal is enshrined within the ancient prerogative of *parens patriae* whereby the State may assume, in the last analysis and the last resort, the protective role of parent to its infant citizens. . . . The liberal ideal requires that parents be shown to be palpably bad before the state will intervene. I would rather that the State requires its parents to be good, and act accordingly when they are not. (p. 193)

When Plato wrote like this, positive moral policing had scarcely been tried—except partially in Sparta—so he had some excuse for not knowing how badly it works. There is surely no such excuse today. Every serious attempt of this kind has resulted in highly confused oppression. It is more or less bound to, because, while there is a good deal of agreement about what constitutes harm, there is much less about which things should be thought good, and especially about what would "guarantee the best possible conditions." Since no government could expect to formulate all the ideals or value-systems that might reasonably appeal to its citizens, what kind of testing would be possible? What religious beliefs if any, for instance, would be judged optimal? What about differences of class, race and temperament? What happens to eccentrics?

Here Archard is surely attacking liberal theory gratuitously on its strongest ground—the need to respect the natural variability of human life. The attack is not needed for his central worry about child-abuse. Abused children need intervention where there *is* actual harm, or risk of harm. Both aspects, however, equally involve the other well-known worry about moral policing—that it cannot work unless it has real public support. Sumptuary laws and regulations to control prostitution or drug use are notoriously ineffective on their own, unless something is also done to change people's attitudes. The same point was well made lately in a newspaper article about a recent financial scandal:

> **If corporate behaviour is to be based primarily on a framework of external regulation rather than on a clear internal perception of the purpose of a company and the duties of the managers who serve it, then we will divorce business morality from individual morality and encourage the belief that law and regulation constitute the whole, not the minimum guide to practice. (Sir Geoffrey Chandler in the *Independent*, September 5, 1990)**

If that is true for commerce, it is surely much more true for something so much less visible than family life. In general, deterrence is less effective than legalists tend to think when it is not supported by shared standards. Eighteenth-century thieves still stole in spite of the prospect of hanging for it. How likely would a child-abuser be to change his ways merely because social workers get a right of entry? He might indeed become more wily in his concealment. But there is no change in the main evil, which is that he was willing to do it in the first place. What sort of attitude to a child makes this kind of thing possible?

This, it seems to me, is the real trouble that we need to think about. A gap has somehow opened between our beliefs and existing practice. Current incredulity about the evidence shows this; it is surely a form of irrational denial. Child abuse, including sexual and ritual abuse, is not—as was, I think, widely supposed till lately—just a survival among people living in specially bad conditions. It is not something that, like tuberculosis, may be expected to clear up as things become more sanitary. Though there are still problems about evidence, it has become clear that a great deal of it goes on, and not just at one social level. The systematic refusal to believe children's complaints was arbitrary and unreasonable.

How are we to understand this, as we must if we are to deal with it? Three questions at once strike me:

1. *Historical and anthropological.* How new is it? Was it always there, or not? We need to go back sharply over our history and folk-lore and that of other societies with this fresh question in mind. As usual, we will probably find a bit of both answers, but the details should help us. My own further questions come one from each department—the timeless and the contemporary.
2. *Psychological.* How does this relate to ambivalence—to the tendency of all strong emotions to combine opposite strains? Any close relationship (and here Freud was right) must involve some hostility as well as affection, because to be very close to someone is inevitably to collide with them in some ways. Because we each have conflicts within our own nature, we cannot act as harmonious wholes in approaching other people. This does not mean that

our affection is not real. But when ambivalence is ignored—when an unrealistic, over-hopeful view of love promises people painless harmony—then disappointment can be bitter and destructive.

Our current idea of love has, I think, been dangerously unreal and sentimental in not taking note of ambivalence. It has also not sufficiently stressed the dangers of being unfamiliar with the kind of person whom one loves before one begins to love them. Men and women who know little of the other sex notoriously have this difficulty if they eventually marry one of these alien beings. But over children, our present way of life makes the situation very common. The generations live much more apart than they do in most simpler cultures. Young adults in particular may be enmeshed in a world of work and play in which children seldom appear, and the real difficulties of dealing with them are concealed. Our official view of life sentimentalises the idea of children and plays down the conflicts. Nobody much wants to face the fact of ambivalence. Yet if it is not faced, it must surely play a central part in what is happening.

3. *Privacy.* Archard is quite right to stress this, and to note how it has grown on us lately. As he says, "the kind of privacy to which the twentieth-century Western family feels entitled and which it has come to expect is historically and culturally very specific" (p. 191). Most human beings do not have it and do not seem to need it. So (he briskly concludes) we do not need it either.

We may, however, need to ask *why* privacy has become so important to us. It has done so in the last two centuries, during the time when towns have been growing ever larger, and while rapid transport has made us all mobile to an extent previously undreamed of. We spend much of our lives in vast, shifting crowds of strangers. This stimulates us, but it easily becomes exhausting. Social responses which are natural to us simply cannot be made to all these passers-by, and we build all sorts of defence-mechanisms to help us ignore them. The Sony Walkman is one recent technological extension of these psychological suits of armour; the private car is another.

However, the most obvious refuge from these troublesome crowds is of course to go home. If there are then no neighbours—as there often are not—this shuts the exhausted commuter up with his or her own family. Ambivalence can then become very obvious, and the strains and struggles of the day can be taken out on one's relatives. The wider circle of people who are friendly and familiar, but not so close as to arouse ambivalence, simply is not easily available. And the way towns are going, it grows less available all the time.

Does this get us anywhere? These are merely lines of investigation. The last two of them, if they prove to have anything in them, might suggest action to revive neighbourhoods and to make towns less brutal.[6] I have an idea, too, that fewer hospital births might help over ambivalence. (The Dutch have much less of them, and also much less child-abuse). But the first step must surely be to understand the present state of things better, which perhaps primarily means getting rid of a lot of self-deception about it. Policing of the kind that Archard demands may indeed sometimes be needed, but it seems unlikely to be much help on its own. And though he is surely right to say, too, that doctors, social workers and other professionals should have training about child-abuse, this need not mean only that they ride in and whisk children away to safety. It could sometimes mean that they can help the whole family out of its nightmare, or enable it not to fall into it in the first place.

Why Philosophy?

What, then, is the philosophers' work? When a large and unfamiliar problem like this looms up, what we all need first is imaginative exploration. We must somehow respond to the world as it is. Our previous conceptual set can block our efforts to do this. The vital help that the great philosophers of the past have given—the work that has made them remembered—has been in shifting and reshaping conceptual sets so as to make new thinking possible. Once this work is done people forget that it was ever needed; they do not know that they once thought in a different way. But that does not make it less necessary.

This means that, though many philosophical techniques go on being enormously useful, there is no single standard way of tackling a new problem. Applying philosophy to the world is not like applying Elastoplast to a cut. It is more like diagnosis; it is applying our skills.[7] We need to see what is wrong with whole areas of thinking and to call in question concepts not yet mentioned in our textbooks. Of course our predecessors' ideas are of enormous use here, and of course life does constantly repeat itself. But it does it continually in new ways. Neither rights-talk nor any other limited conceptual scheme will suit every problem that troubles us.

Notes

1. See Jane Lancaster (1983) *The Evolutionary Biology of Human Reproduction and Parental Investment* (Washington, DC, Smithsonian Press) and (1983) "Parental Investment: The Hominid Adaptation" in: Donald Ortner (Ed.) *How Humans Adapt: A Biocultural Odyssey* (Washington, DC, Smithsonian Press).
2. I have examined this and related ploys further in *Wisdom, Information and Wonder: What Is Knowledge For?* (London, Routledge, 1989), pp. 251–254.
3. As soon as children are born, they will be taken in charge by officers appointed for the purpose . . . These officers . . . will bring the mothers to the creche when their breasts are full, while taking every precaution that no mother shall know her own child . . . Reckoning from the day when he becomes a bridegroom, a man will call children born in the tenth to seventh month sons and daughters, and they will call him father." *The Republic,* Book V, pp. 460–461.
4. "It is a serious question in my mind whether there should be individual homes for children—or even whether children should know their own parents. There are undoubtedly more scientific ways of bringing up children which probably mean finer and happier children." John B. Watson (1928) *Psychological Care of Infant and Child* (New York, W. W. Norton), pp. 5–6. See discussion in: Barbara Ehrenreich & Deirdre English (1979) *For Her Own Good: 150 Years of the Experts' Advice to Women* (London, Pluto Press).
5. (Orphans are) "at present those unfortunate children who have no parents at all in a society that dictates that all children *must* have parents to survive. When all adults are monopolised by their genetic children, there is no one left to care about the unclaimed . . . If *no-one* had exclusive relationships with children, then everyone would be free for all children." Shulamith Firestone (1979) *The Dialectic of Sex, The Case for Feminist Revolution* (London, The Women's Press), p. 197. This oddly hydraulic, quantitative view of affection has been common in people arguing for these arrangements.
6. See, too, the records of the Peckham Health Centre Experiment for the possibility of

building up cheap local centres in which family members could relax and meet other people over interesting occupations without entirely losing sight of one another. Families reported a great improvement in their life at home after joining, because they had something in common to talk about. See Innes H. Pearse & Lucy H. Crocker (1943) *The Peckham Experiment: A Study of the Living Structure of Society* (London, Allen & Unwin), and Alison Stallibrass (1989) *Being Me and Also Us: Lessons from the Peckham Experiment* (Edinburgh, Scottish Academic Press), a very interesting recent reassessment.

7. I have developed these points about the meaning of "applied philosophy" in *Wisdom, Information and Wonder, What Is Knowledge For?*, chapter 23, "Philosophizing out in the world" and in an article called "Homunculus trouble, or what is applied philosophy?" *Journal of Social Philosophy*, San Antonio, Texas, Vol. 21, No. 1, Spring 1990.

Suggested Readings

Blustein, Jeffrey, "Equal Opportunity and the Family," in his *Parents and Children* (New York: Oxford Univ. Press, 1982, Ch. 4).

English, Jane, "What Do Grown Children Owe Their Parents?" in Onora O'Neill and William Ruddick, eds., *Having Children* (New York: Oxford Univ. Press, 1979).

LaFollette, Hugh, "Licensing Parents," *Philosophy and Public Affairs*, 9 (2), 1980, pp. 183–197.

Margolis, Joseph, and Clorinda Margolis, "The Separation of Marriage and Family," in Mary Vetterling-Braggin, F. Ellison, and J. English, eds., *Feminism and Philosophy* (Totowa, N.J.: Littlefield, Adams and Co., 1977, pp. 291–301).

Meyers, Diana Tietjens, Kenneth Kipnis, and Cornelius F. Murphy, Jr., eds., *Kindred Matters: Rethinking the Philosophy of the Family* (Ithaca, N.Y., Cornell Univ. Press, 1993).

Mills, Claudia, "What Would King Solomon Do Today? The Revolution in Child Custody," in Claudia Card, ed. *Values and Public Policy* (Fort Worth: Harcourt Brace Jovanovich, 1992, pp. 521–527).

Okin, Susan Moller. *Justice, Gender, and the Family* (New York: Basic Books, 1989, Ch. 1).

Ruddick, Sara, "Thinking About Fathers," in Marianne Hirsch and Evelyn Fox Keller, eds., *Conflicts in Feminism* (New York: Routledge, 1990, pp. 222–233).

Schoeman, Ferdinand, "Rights of Children, Rights of Parents, and the Moral Basis of the Family," *Ethics*, 91, October 1980, pp. 6–19.

Spiro, Melford E., *Children of the Kibbutz* (Cambridge: Harvard Univ. Press, 1958).

Rights in Education

Cases for Discussion

The Rainbow Curriculum

Joseph A. Fernandes, Chancellor of the New York City schools, introduced a new curriculum into the primary grades in November 1992. The new Rainbow Curriculum emphasizes multiculturalism and includes in its 200 pages instructions to teachers to incorporate references to lesbian-gay people in all curricular areas. Part of the goal of the lessons is to give recognition to the fact that many of the city's children come from families that do not fit traditional patterns.

The curriculum was greeted with strong objections from groups of parents, and in particular the parents expressed their disapproval of several books on the suggested reading lists for first graders, such as *Heather Has Two Mommies* and *Daddy's Roommate,* a book about a young boy who visits his father and his father's gay roommate. The curriculum was withdrawn after heated debate and the controversy resulted in the nonrenewal of Dr. Fernandes' contract.

Many important decisions about the upbringing of their children are taken out of the hands of parents when the state mandates compulsory schooling. Even if parents choose private schools or home schooling, the state sets curriculum standards and requirements. Everyone in a society has a legitimate interest in ensuring that the next generation is educated to take its place in the workforce and to exercise the duties of citizenship, and thus state supervision and compulsory education seem justified.

However, some parents feel that the state has gone too far when it establishes curriculum content that goes beyond basic skills and information, especially when children are being taught things that are inconsistent with many parents' beliefs and values.

School Breakfast Program

Recently the school boards of several communities in Rhode Island provoked a spirited controversy when they proposed eliminating the federally sponsored school breakfast program. The reason for the cut was not primarily financial, since federal funding is provided, but rather the opinion that government should not take over the responsibilities of parents. Some letters to the editor printed in the local paper blamed parents for being lazy or neglectful and suggested that children who come to school without breakfast be placed in foster care, on the grounds that they are being abused. Others took the position that good nutrition is essential to good learning, and that food supplement programs do have a legitimate place in public schools.

Schools, it is said, are increasingly taking over the role of parents. Should school curriculum include sex education, AIDS education, or values and character training, as well as reading, writing, and 'rithmetic? Should public schools have more or fewer social workers, mental health counselors, and health clinics? Should condoms be distributed in the schools? Should Head Start be expanded and after-school care provided at public expense?

Those who defend a larger role for schools in children's lives see this as a desirable equalizing factor, compensating for the wide differences—economic, cultural, intellectual, and emotional—among families. If one's primary concern is for the well-being of the child, they argue, then society must step in to do what parents cannot or do not do. However, others protest against what they see as an encroachment on the right of parents to raise children as they choose. Rights and responsibilities for children should be kept in the family, they say.

The Issues

1. Most people strongly support child labor laws, which restrict the kinds and hours of work that children may do, as well as compulsory education laws, which require children to attend school. As sensible as they may seem, though, it must be recognized that these laws impose requirements on parents and direct the ways they must guide their children's lives. Thus, we may ask: What justifies the state in setting education requirements?

2. Some parents object to the extent or content of state-mandated education, especially if these conflict with religious beliefs. May parents override the state's requirements? Should children be exempted from required education because of their parents' religious beliefs? Is the state taking over decisions and responsibilities that belong to parents?

3. Alternatively, do children have a right to education, a right that cannot be denied them, even against their parents' wishes? Do they also have a right to decide about education for themselves, to leave school at whatever age they choose?

The Arguments

For State Requirements

Several arguments are used to show that the state is within its legitimate power to require school attendance of all children. First, the state has a strong need for citizens who are productive members of society and can take part in the democratic process. Education is a necessary step to these goals. Secondly, the state has an interest in providing, as fully as possible, equal opportunity for all persons to develop their talents and compete for whatever rewards society offers. Tax-supported public education with required attendance, which allows neither children nor parents to forfeit school for paid labor, is a reasonable means of equalizing opportunity.

These arguments can be easily extended to justify the state setting basic curriculum content and standards, as well. If it really is important for all children to be educated about sex or about gay families, then there must be state requirements even against parents' objections, and they should apply to private as well as public schools.

For Parents' Rights

On the other hand, a strong case can be made for parents' rights to decide how their children will be educated and to override state requirements. It is true there are many ways that parents influence a child through informal education at home, parental guidelines about after-school activities and social relationships, vacation trips, enrollment in Sunday school, music lessons, etc. Yet children spend a significant amount of time in formal schooling and the knowledge and attitudes encountered there become an important part of their lives.

Although schools may profess to teach in a neutral way, education is never really value-free. Does the school encourage children to question, to think for themselves, to engage in critical thinking? How does this mesh with a family that wants to bring up children to be quiet, obedient, and accepting of authority? Does the school encourage girls and boys equally? How does this affect families who want to honor their cultural heritage by educating their children to assume traditional gender roles? One may say, "When in Rome, do as the Romans do," but democratic ideals of freedom of religion and respect for differences among people suggest that family differences in educating children should be respected, as well.

Parental objection to school requirements are often based on religious beliefs. This is illustrated in the well-known *Wisconsin* v. *Yoder* court case. In 1972, the Amish community petitioned the court to allow its children to leave school at the end of eighth grade, arguing that high school would expose them to studies they do not need and peer pressures that would tempt them away from the traditional, agricultural ways of their parents. The Amish petition was granted on the grounds of freedom of religion, but many have argued that the decision was wrong.

In other instances, parents of nonmajority religions have asked to have their children excused from sex education or AIDS education classes or birthday celebrations, and in some school districts parents have succeeded in requiring the schools to teach creationism along with Darwinism. Should schools aim at the goal of a "melting pot" America, requiring the same education for all children, or a mosaic of different ethnic, racial, and religious groups whose children are educated according to parents' preferences?

For Children's Rights

Against the claims of parents to determine the nature of their children's education, it can be argued that children themselves have a right to an education that parents should not be able to restrict, and a right to the kind of education that will prepare them well for their future lives. The contemporary philosopher Joel Feinberg claims that every child has the right to what he calls an "open future." By this he means a right to the kind and extent of education that would help children choose how to live their lives as adults. Too narrow or too short an education cuts off opportunities, so presumably the right to an open future implies exposure to a variety of ideas and traditions.

If children have the right to an education and an open future, then someone has a duty to ensure that they get it. Thus compulsory education laws are justified in terms of the children's own interests, as well as by the interest the state takes in having an educated citizenry. Although compulsory education does set limits on the children's right to say no, it is generally considered an act of justified weak paternalism.

The Readings

"Education and Liberty: Public Provision and Private Choice," Brenda Almond, Social Values Research Centre, University of Hull, United Kingdom.

Almond addresses the general issue of who should decide the content and scope of children's education, parents or the state. She advocates giving parents ultimate control of education rather than the state because this control will respect their rights to cultural and religious freedom, provide greater variety, and avoid the threat of state control over people's lives.

"Schooling," Laura Purdy, Professor of Philosophy, Wells College.

Purdy considers the issue of children's right to decide about education for themselves and the issue of parents' right to decide about their children's education. She considers arguments in favor of compulsory education and against children's liberation from it. She also argues against unlimited parental rights by defending public schools against private ones where parents may restrict children's education too narrowly.

"Freedom of Religion and Children," Hugh LaFollette, Professor of Philosophy, East Tennessee State University.

LaFollette considers the issue of religious beliefs that conflict with state-mandated education. He discusses the conflict that may arise between parents' rights to freedom of religion and the interest of the child. He argues against parents' rights in this case, because the adult the child will become is harmed, he claims, if parents limit education by censoring beliefs they do not share.

Education and Liberty: Public Provision and Private Choice

Brenda Almond

ABSTRACT   Conventions on human rights give priority to parents in education but modern states tend to make uniform provision, tending towards a monopoly position. Education itself is not incompatible with liberty but is a condition of it. A three-sided conflict exists, however, between the state, parents and professionals as to who should represent the interests of children. Liberty is best preserved if the conflict is resolved in favour of parents, for only parental decision-making guarantees educational variety and change. In addition, the parental relationship itself generates rights, including one derived from the broader political right to cultural and religious freedom.

I

Irrespective of political colour, most modern States are monopoly controllers of education. Instead of providing a framework for choice, they tend to look for some ideal model or blueprint for education, and to assume, too, that once this has been found, it is to be applied uniformly. Liberal democracies permit the existence of schools outside the framework of public provision, but this private sector, which varies in size in different countries, is nowhere as significant as the mainstream provision. Within the mainstream, an exception is usually made to the general rule of pressure towards uniformity only in the special case of religious or moral belief.

Now there is something odd about this drive to a common education, since the States in question, both liberal and communist, have joined in endorsing various declarations of human rights which are essentially incompatible with it. For these conventions and commitments on human rights give primacy to the individual—that is to say, to individual parents—where education is concerned.

Two statements which make this presumption quite explicit are, first, within the framework of the Universal Declaration of Human Rights' assertion of the right to education:

> **Parents have a prior right to choose the kind of education that shall be given to their children. (26,3)**

and, in the International Covenant on Economic, Social and Cultural Rights, the undertaking to:

From *Journal of Philosophy of Education*, vol. 25, no. 2, 1991.193–202. Reprinted by permission of the publisher.

have respect for the liberty of parents and, when applicable, legal guardians to choose for their children schools, other than those established by the public authorities, which conform to such minimum educational standards as may be laid down or approved by the State and to ensure the religious and moral education of their children in conformity with their own convictions.

There is a similar statement in the European Convention for the Protection of Human Rights and Fundamental Freedoms ruling that:

In the exercise of any functions which it assumes in relation to education and to teaching, the State shall respect the right of parents to ensure such education and teaching in conformity with their own religious and philosophical convictions. (Article 2 of Protocol to the Convention)

So long, however, as consensus prevails on what should be the content and method of education and on how it should be organised, the implicit tension remains concealed. In the case of the United Kingdom, this tacit consensus prevailed for approximately two decades following the 1944 Education Act. Occasionally a case would arise which drew attention to the impotence of the individual dissenter in conflict with authority over some educational issue, but such cases were exceptional. It would have been natural to suppose that only cranks, Seventh Day Adventists or extreme progressives would find themselves in any kind of confrontation with the State over their children's education.

But following comprehensive reorganisation, there emerged an increasing number of cases in which parents who were dissatisfied with the arrangements offered them were prepared to keep their children away from school in an attempt to secure an education that met *their* wishes, rather than social needs as perceived by planners in central Government or in local county-halls. A similar tension emerged in the United States in relation to a different issue: that of bussing to create racially mixed schools. Again, parents who put their own children's needs before what they may well have judged personally to be a worthwhile social and political objective, found themselves placed in the position of having to challenge the law. Finally, to take an example from continental Europe, it is not so long since students and parents in France flocked to the streets to defeat Government proposals to bring private schools under public control.

Now it is typical of parents—although no such truth is of course without exceptions—that they operate on a basis which is altruistic in the sense that they put their children's interests before their own, but is selfish in the sense that on the whole they put their *own* children's interests before that of others, or of the whole community. Although there are undoubtedly some people who place political or ideological principle before personal considerations, it would be generally true that most parents are *not* prepared to sacrifice their own children for the public good—this, even though they may be active in promoting arrangements that are bound in the short-run to have adverse effects for others.

Those who *are* consistent in applying their principles may, in any case, resist the suggestion that this is a sacrifice as far as their children are concerned, arguing that their children are likely to be ultimately advantaged by the transformation of society that is their goal. Even parents in this last category, however, may draw back in the face of a school-phobic child, or a weeping child, or a bullied child. And indeed, casual observation suggests that those with an active interest in education who make a point of accepting the State choice and State arrangements for their children, usually place themselves in a position where that choice or direction is likely to be acceptable, rather than in an area where the local school provides indiscipline, bullying and poor work goals. The State, by contrast, may seek to promote the *public* good, in a sense which is compatible with the sacrifice of some personal or individual interests.

This contrast is of considerable ethical and political importance. The central ethical issue is not, however, whether parents are hypocritical, or ought to be more consistent. It is, on the contrary, the more fundamental question of the legitimate boundaries of State power. This is not only a matter of the dominance of education in a modern State where, as in the United States, more than a third of the population may be involved in the education "industry" at any one time as either consumers or suppliers. Nor is it simply a matter of the shrinking span in the lives of people in wealthy countries between the end of their own education and the start of their children's. Significant though these aspects are for anyone concerned with the totalitarian potential of education, there are two other features of education which affect the individual recipient even more directly. These are: (a) that it is compulsory; and (b) that it is time-consuming—this latter in the important sense that it consumes a child's years from infancy to the frontier of adult life. This means that if the state prescribes not merely education, but also where that education should take place, it becomes difficult to distinguish, at least in principle, between the case of a child in an ordinary educational establishment who must be in a specified place for fixed periods of time, and that of an electronically-tagged prisoner whose movements are similarly controlled, or an offender committed to a progressive open prison with evening and weekend release.

This is not to say that education itself is an invasion of liberty. On the contrary, it is almost universally regarded as a prior condition of liberty by people of every political persuasion, from the anarchist left to the libertarian right. Both of these go on to infer from this the need for some State provision, although their suggestions as to the form this should take are radical. Milton Friedman, for example, offers a justification for at least a minimum of State provision in terms of the "neighbourhood effect" of *not* providing compulsory education for those without personal resources. This, he argues, would be so adverse that self-interest alone provides a justification for it.[1] In terms of the argument from "neighbourhood effect," without universal free education it is as impossible in the twentieth century for a well-off person to maintain a civilised standard of living in conditions of personal security as it was in the nineteenth century for such a person to live a *healthy* life without such public health measures as management of the water supply and sewerage system.

And while de-schoolers, such as Ivan Illich[2] and Everitt Reimer[3], denounce the education system as it is to be found in developed Western countries as a tool of vested interests—a vast industry employing millions of people in a complex web of activities—they offer remedies which in fact allocate educational resources on different principles, rather than rejecting them out-of-hand. They do not present their case as repudiation of the need for education but as an argument for a vastly different method of providing for it. Interestingly, both left and right converge in their practical recommendations: educational vouchers to be spent at choice by the consumer or recipient.

If most people, then, are agreed on the need to constrain children's immediate freedom during the early years, for the sake of education, it is clear that, at least in those early years, children are too young, too inexperienced, and above all too infinitely malleable and adaptable, to determine the conditions and content of their education for themselves. Even those who advocate liberty most strongly see it as necessarily limited in the case of children. J. S. Mill, for example, in his classic defence of individual liberty, specifically excluded from the scope of the liberty principle "children and young persons below the age which the law may fix as that of manhood or womanhood."[4]

Until recently, Mill's view would have been unchallenged by any serious thinker. Kant and Hegel both explicitly included the interests of the child within that of the male head of family; though the latter was concerned to correct Kant's approach to this issue to the extent of insisting that the members of a family retained their individual personhood, and were not to be regarded as mere "things or instruments."

That children themselves may have a perspective and should have a voice is a view of more recent origin and, not surprisingly, it is most often associated with thinkers concerned with educational practice. In particular, it has been "child-centred" theorists such as Friedrich Froebel, John Dewey and A. S. Neill who have pressed the case for children's autonomy. But the kind of freedom in education promoted by these thinkers is an on-the-ground freedom—an adjustment of educational practice which nevertheless takes place within an assumed setting that has been provided by adults. More radical recent proposals for actually providing access to power for children themselves have been, for instance, suggestions that they be given the vote earlier,[5] or that they should be allowed to re-select their own guardians or parental figures.[6]

In the end, however, in the words of another group of commentators, proposals for child autonomy "founder on the physical limitations of the youngest and most vulnerable."[7] It is for this reason that those who believe in personal liberty must see the child's interest at this stage as represented at first entirely by others, only gradually to be replaced with increasing autonomy of choice by the interests and claims of the child or school-age student. So since educational decisions must, and legitimately may, be made by others, whose is the ultimate authority in determining these decisions?

It might be presumed that ultimate authority would lie with the child's parents, natural or adoptive. But professionals—teachers, social workers and others—are alternative claimants in a situation where Government, too, may demand a say in decisions regarding children. So the stage is set for confrontation, or at least for controversy. Attempts may, of course, be made to avoid this: some schools aim at partnership with parents. But it is significant that the initiative for this, and indeed its possibility, tends to lie, at least in the publicly-funded sector, with the school and not with the parents. (Fee-paying schools must, of course, be responsible to parents at least to the extent of attracting them as clients.) But where publicly-funded schools reject parental involvement they are entitled to put up notices, and sometimes do, inscribed, for example: "no parents beyond this point." This example in the United Kingdom taken from the primary or early-grade level, may be paralleled with a recent example there from the secondary or high school level in which a history teacher was threatened with disciplinary action, including possible dismissal, for refusing to obey his headmaster's instruction not to talk to parents about his doubts concerning a new examination—doubts which have subsequently received much public discussion, since they were not confined to this one school or individual. (Parents in this case hired rooms to provide for out-of-hours tuition for their children for a different examination.)[8]

Other examples of this desire on the part of schools to keep parents at a distance by restricting *information* to them arise in situations in which schools are in fact banded or streamed (two different forms of ability-grouping) but where an attempt is made to disguise the fact by successive changes of labelling of classes or groups. These attempts tend to be successful at least to the point of ensuring that the parents of the *incoming* year-group may be unable to see what academic goals have been judged appropriate for their child. Within a few months, however, the children themselves will normally have broken the code. Another example from a United Kingdom context has been the reluctance of schools to publish lists of examination results, on the grounds that parents are not qualified to set these in context and may make invidious and unjust comparisons between schools.

The significance of such examples lies in the conflict they expose between parents, on the one hand, representing the perceived interests of their children, and professionals, on the other, claiming the authority of expertise. This is only one aspect of the general truth, of which the world of education provides a particular example, that people in authority, whether political or professional, tend to see reason to conceal information from those who form their constituency. It is, of course, *simpler* that way. So while few individuals, including those in political or professional life, fail to give lip service to the great moral and political value of freedom, the *information* which is an essential element in choice will be prised from those who control it only with their grudging and reluctant compliance.

When this kind of problem arises in the context of schools, the picture is further complicated by the fact that the goals of those in conflict may differ. In particular, they may be wholly educational or they may be non-educational. The ideal pattern may be imposed for its own sake—because it seems to represent the best form of education—or for the sake of such non-educational outcomes as social justice or equality. In either event a conflict is set up which falls within political party lines, with the ideology of liberalism (emphasising the freedom of the individual, toleration, and the right to be different) confronting the ideology of egalitarianism (emphasising the right of the state to enforce its preferred pattern on its citizens). This in itself justifies a differing moral perception of the imposition of patterns in the two cases.

Where objectives are clearly educational, the issue raised can be stated in terms of paternalism—that is to say, in terms of promoting the best interest of the child. But while there is general agreement that education is in children's interest, there is disagreement about what a good education is, and what it should achieve. One might compare Squire Brown's remark in *Tom Brown's Schooldays:* "If he'll only turn out a brave, helpful, truth-telling Englishman, and a gentleman, and a Christian, that's all I want" with the views of a contemporary working-class parent, who may want a child to be equipped with skills for the job-market, or with the views of a middle-class intellectual who speaks of "education for its own sake," or an educational progressive, who aims only to produce a happy child and a well-adjusted adult. Even clearly educational objectives, then, do not produce unanimity.

But where the objectives are social objectives, the issue is no longer paternalism, with the attendant problems that entails as to what constitutes the child's best interest. It is rather a deeper political controversy about future patterns of society: should it be meritocratic and competitive, or egalitarian and welfare-oriented? regulated or libertarian? redistributive or *laissez-faire?* And since schools also serve to allocate social roles in a future society, questions remain even if the nature of that future society is agreed: of any one child or student it may be asked, how is she, or he, to participate either in that new society, or in society as it is presently constituted?

Disentangling the issues here is an understandably complex matter. One way to view it is as a triangle of competing interests, each claiming competing rights. At the centre of this triangle stands the child, at least until autonomy is reached (and this must be a continuous, not a sudden, process). The child, then, is the *object* of competing claims by State, by professionals, and by parents, and it is a matter of considerable importance to assess the weight of these rival claims.

To begin with, each of the interested parties may present a moral claim. States or Governments have always tended to claim the children within their borders as in some sense "their own." Plato, in the *Republic,* made such an assumption explicit, clearly seeing the ties of family loyalty as in conflict with loyalty to the State, and setting out a pattern of education which depended on complete control of the experience and education of the child. Rousseau too, although he set out a highly individualised system of education in his *Emile,* took a rather different view when he found himself in a position to influence practical policy. In his article on "Political Economy" composed for the Encyclopédie, he wrote:

> If the reason of each individual is not allowed to be the sole
> judge of his duties, still less should the education of children
> be left to the ignorance and prejudices of their fathers . . . The
> state abides: the family passes.[9]

Where the claims of professionals, in particular teachers, are concerned, it is noteworthy that the emergence of this group as an influential body is a twentieth century phenomenon. The contemporary explosion of knowledge has created the age of professionals—people, that is, who claim a prerogative based on superior knowledge, special training and on their professional relationship with their client. In the world of education, they may be particularly confident of their ability to control outcomes, given sufficient scope: as one psychologist, J. B. Watson, is reputed to have said: "Give me the child until he is 7 and I will give you the man"—a claim also made by another group traditionally associated with a high degree of educational control, the Jesuits.

The case for *parents,* by contrast, remains largely unargued in the contemporary setting, sentimental lip-service being given in their case to "the good of the child"—a formula generally used to permit parents to make choices only so long as these conform to professional or political judgment. This has not always been so. Indeed, until recently, the assumption would have been that power in any decision-making relating to children must be exercised by parents. There was no paid army of professionals, and Governments lacked the institutional, financial and bureaucratic apparatus to assert control. Nevertheless, parents have always had duties laid upon them in respect of their children, and it is arguable that duties presuppose rights. If, for example, parents are regarded as having an *obligation* to care for, instruct and protect their child, their *right* to do these things must be simultaneously recognised. It would be inconsistent to admit the "ought" here, whilst withdrawing the "can"—to demand fulfilment of the duty but to deny the practical conditions necessary for fulfilment of the duty. Or, as a contemporary British judge, Lord Fraser, has expressed this: From the parents' right and duty of custody flows their right and duty of control of the child.[10]

In the specific case of education, the British Education Act of 1944 is explicit in this respect. It specifies:

> **It shall be the duty of the parent of every child of compulsory school age to cause him to receive full-time education suitable to his age, ability and aptitude, either by regular attendance at school or otherwise.**

Of course, if what parents want or decide is for the best interest of their child, their moral claim is greatly strengthened. However, parents can be misguided, and do not always do what is in the best interest of their child. This may seem to reduce the legitimacy of their claim. But the issue is complicated by the fact that in assessing the child's interest, an arbitrary judgment must be made as to when it should be calculated. The current under-16 year-old will later be a 20 year-old, a 30 year-old, a 40 year-old, and so on. It is common for a child's own wishes to be over-ruled just precisely in the light of some assessment of what the person at these later stages will then be likely to wish. Where education is concerned, it is assumed that the later person will wish for the benefits that accrue to those who have been educated—or at least wish to avoid the stigma that attaches to illiteracy and inability to earn a living.

But these are minimal goals, and as long as disagreement is possible as to what the later person would desire and what is genuinely in the interest of the child, these considerations do not decide the issue in favor of the professional or the Government rather than the parent. For Government and experts can be mistaken, too, and in their case the potential damage that error can produce is on a vastly larger scale. This is the heart of the argument against educational monopolies, whether of experts or Governments, or of experts working for Governments. It is an argument for damage limitation, and at the same time an argument for social freedom in the widest possible sense. One author has put the point in the following terms:

> **The practice of entrusting children to their parents ultimately limits the control of society to determine the life-style and beliefs of persons.**[11]

It is because of the undoubted truth of this claim that totalitarian blueprints for society, from Plato's *Republic* on, tend to include an attack on the family as part of their proposals for political restructuring. There is no need to see the issue in political terms, however. The consequences are the same even when the motive involved is a disinterested, completely non-political preference for the rule of experts as a way of securing the best possible management of children.

But parents enjoy a unique advantage over experts: this is that their rule is not monolithic. There are as many ways of bringing up children as there are parents. It is also temporary: adult life brings with it exposure to competing viewpoints. Of course, experts, too, and even Governments, may not present a unanimous face. Indeed, they may change their opinions over time. The problem is, though, that the "official" perspective, for as long as it is fashionable, tends to be imposed on everybody. But if this ubiquitous imposition were ever to be achieved on a substantial scale, there would be less scope for change and development, and, in particular, there would be no regression to the norm—something which fortunately appears to happen, on the whole, as a self-correcting mechanism where extreme educational theories are allowed to jostle for space with each other.

But utilitarian arguments—arguments based on assessing the personal and social impact of different ways of settling the question of who should make educational decisions—depend in the end on disputable matters of fact. It is therefore important, in conclusion, to consider what other arguments—in particular, arguments not based on paternalism—might be advanced for assigning the controlling role to parents in children's lives, until they are ready to assume it for themselves.

One strongly non-paternalist argument is that parents do, in a sense, have some claim to ownership of their children. Although not generally acknowledged, the strength of the feeling that this is so tends to be revealed every day in "tug-of-love" cases between divorcing parents for the custody of their children. This proposition was expressed by Sir Robert Filmer, in his *Patriarcha,* in these terms: "the true and first reason of authority is that the father and mother, and simply those that beget and engender, do command and rule over all their children."[12]

The idea that the biological relationship itself generates parental rights is of interest in itself, and is involved in the controversies that surround such issues as surrogacy, *in vitro* fertilisation and the transfer of gametes. These conflicts turn very directly on the differing weighting to be given to biological parenthood on the one hand, and social or nurturing parenthood on the other. It may reasonably be claimed, however, that some qualified notion of at least temporary ownership does apply in the case of the parent–child relation, and that this is linked, however conditionally, to the biological fact of generation. It may be that Hobbes was correct in seeing this as more like the right people have to their own body than their right to ownership of property.[13] If so, the recognition of this right can only be intuitive, and cannot be founded on any consideration more compelling than it is itself.

But whatever the force of the biological argument, it is clear that it cannot stand alone. It is worth turning, then, to some arguments for parental right which do not depend on this deep and intuitive, but nevertheless disputable, assumption.

First amongst these is an argument from cultural and religious freedom. It is clear, to begin with, that there are persisting cultural disagreements as to the extent and limits of parental authority, and that some of these cultural disagreements are based on strongly-held religious views. Some of the differences of opinion that this creates within a modern liberal State can be understood in terms of a requirement of toleration. There is a particular problem of toleration, however, when what is to be tolerated in one person affects the interest of another, whose preferences must ultimately be counted separately. And here it is arguable that if what parents desire on behalf of their child will produce some irreversible physical change (as it does, for example, in the case of female circumcision, footbinding or tattooing) then that absolute power of the parents must be limited by other agencies. But, of course, the issue of education is not so clear-cut.

However, in general, once some necessary exceptions have been made, there is a strong *prima facie* case for the principle that cultural and religious freedom for people of mature years should carry with it a freedom for those same adult people to bring up their children according to their own beliefs, even if to others, perhaps even to the great majority, these beliefs seem in many ways irrational or misguided. Freedom of religion, then, together with freedom to maintain and perpetuate one's culture, provides one kind of independent argument—an argument, in other words, that is not directly linked to a judgment about the well-being of the child—for assigning ultimate authority in educational matters to parents.

A second kind of argument leading to similar consequences may be based on moral rather than religious considerations. An argument of this sort is advanced by Ferdinand Schoeman, when he argues that the right of parents to exercise power over their children is based on their own justifiable moral claim to a certain kind of intimate relationship. He writes:

> Why should the family be given extensive responsibilties for the development of children? Why should the biological parent be thought entitled to be in charge of a family? I believe that the notion of intimacy supplies the basis for these presumptions . . .[14]

Schoeman goes on to argue that intimacy requires privacy and autonomy as its setting, and that a parent's right to this type of private relationship overrides even some limited cost to the child. The focus of Schoeman's argument, then, is not the well-being of children, but the idea of close human relationships. For this reason he rejects the kind of argument advanced by Elizabeth Anscombe in which the legitimacy of an institution arises out of the fact that it is an institution carrying out an important task—an argument, that is, essentially based on utility.[15] On this he comments:

> So long as families maintain their position of being necessary conditions for the performance of such functions, Anscombe's argument captures common sense and preserves family entitlements. But the emergence of alternative, possibly superior (relative to the child), means of rearing children would deprive the family of its position of being necessary and hence undermine its claim to rightful autonomy, except on a customary basis.[16]

This conclusion is particularly important where education is concerned, for here the role of expert opinion may well be decisive. But education does not require a vast centralised and bureaucratised State-wide monopoly of all educational processes. In the last analysis education may be a personal and private enterprise without formal organisation. So the right to privacy is in fact of striking relevance here. It is only by respecting this right that it is possible to guard against the deep invasion of the personality which the compulsory and long-term nature of education would otherwise make possible. Abuse of the education process is something which has taken place under both fascism and communism and its prevention is central to the preservation of a liberal society. The positive ways in which this may be done may now be identified as:

1. permitting individual families to opt out of the education system altogether on reasonable grounds, even whilst recognising the loss this may involve for the small number of children likely to be involved (growing up involves necessary emancipation from possessive or dominating parents, but no process of maturation can guarantee emancipation from a totalitarian state);
2. permitting the existence of independent schools—not providing them with special subsidies, but not on the other hand creating unreasonable obstacles for those who choose to use them (even if their effect is socially distorting and the education they offer less than ideal, this is a smaller price to pay than the socially and politically distorting effect on society of a state monopoly of education);
3. permitting individuals to perpetuate their own ideals and beliefs, particularly religious beliefs, through the family structure by retaining in their own hands ultimate control of the shape and direction of their children's education. This may involve the existence of schools of a particular religious persuasion, and again, while some might see it as preferable that children should not be indoctrinated in a particular religious belief—and some limits must obviously be set—it is even more important that an entire society should be preserved from the possibility of centrally controlled indoctrination either in religion or in anti-religion.[17]

This is an argument, however, for religious education which is funded and provided by either the individuals who want it or the religious groups—

churches, etc.—who promote it. It does *not* provide a justification for the levying of money from the general tax-payer to support beliefs which may conflict with that person's *own* beliefs, values or ideological commitment.

So in order to meet the requirement of religious freedom it is only necessary that a society should permit the establishment of truly independent religious schools, funded by their supporters, and facilitate the limited withdrawal of children in state or publicly-funded schools from ordinary lessons to receive special instruction at their parents' wishes.

Setting aside the special issue of religious education, the view that has been advanced here is that variety itself provides a check—a necessary dispersal of power. Finally, then, this raises a question about the size that schools should be; for clearly the maximisation of choice is related to the number and variety of alternatives available. Clearly, if choice is to be maximised, schools should be as small as is consistent with efficiency. And in practical terms the development of a range of alternatives could be facilitated by a system of direct rather than indirect payment—the voucher system or some variant of it.

II

The British Government has recently embarked on a novel experiment in using the apparatus of centralised Government to hand power back to the people in many areas of life which have increasingly been subject to centralised control. But its new Education Act, acronymically known as GERBIL, is actually a hybrid type of animal. It allows local groups to take control of the administration of their schools themselves, but it also enshrines the principle of a centrally imposed core curriculum for State (publicly) funded schools. It favours the voucher as a means of putting choice in the hands of the individual parent, but it promotes national testing as a way of informing those parents about the performance of schools.

The rationale for this is that State-sector schools will be made more consumer-responsive: unpopular schools will lose students; popular schools will be able to increase in size through unrestricted admission policies. In this way it is hoped that the drift in the British system to the compulsory neighbourhood school, reinforcing social class advantages or disadvantages, will be ended by the abolition of compulsory customers. Strangely, though, the liberated customers will be obliged to consume a compulsory product.

This has to be understood as a reaction to various things that are seen by many as defects in the current system. These include, for instance, the disintegration of the curriculum that has been a feature, though not a *necessary* feature, of the triumph in the state sector of a progressive ideology of education combined with a relativist view of knowledge.

But the structural changes proposed in the 1988 Act could be expected in themselves to correct problems about goals and methods in the schools. In particular, the proposal to conduct simple national tests would in itself make schools more responsive to parental wishes and more directly oriented to the goal of achieving specific standards in literacy and numeracy. This proposal has tended to be seen, however, as a device to test the weaknesses of children rather than a means to make visible the deficiencies of schools. So many are willing to swallow the camel of the compulsory curriculum whilst straining at the gnat of national tests. But a clearer picture of what individual schools are doing, combined with an extension of effective choice, would in itself be a powerful corrective to imbalance. It is a pity, then, that the British Government has not had sufficient confidence in its own remedies to adopt them without transferring monopoly powers to central Government.

In sum, then, the principle that should guide a Government which sets a high priority on liberty is that of leaving the ultimate determination of any child's individual experience to the maximum possible extent in the hands of the child's own family. Within schools, the aim should be to recognise and develop diverse talents and interests, rather than to attempt to produce a uniform product. Those who create a Frankenstein in the shape of centralised State powers for education should not be surprised if, in the future, their creature takes on an unsought and unwelcome life of its own.

Notes

1. Friedman, M. (1962) *Capitalism and Freedom*, Ch. 6 (Chicago, IL, Chicago University Press).
2. Illich, I. (1971) *De-schooling Society* (London, Calder & Boyars).
3. Reimer, E. (1971) *School Is Dead* (London, Penguin).
4. Mill, J. S. (1954) *On Liberty*, p. 73 (London, Dent).
5. See J. Harris (1982) "The Political Status of Children," in: K. Graham (Ed.) *Contemporary Political Philosophy* (Cambridge, Cambridge University Press).
6. See J. Holt (1974) *Escape from Childhood* (London, Penguin).
7. R. Dingwall *et al.* (1983) *The Protection of Children* (Oxford, Basil Blackwell Ltd).
8. Reports in *The Times*, London, 13 and 22 February, 1988.
9. Rousseau, J. J. (1962) "Political economy," in: W. Boyd (Ed.) *The Minor Educational Writings of Jean-Jacques Rousseau* (New York, Teachers College, Columbia University).
10. House of Lords [1985] 3 All ER 402. Quoted in G. Williams, "The Gillick Saga," *New Law Journal*, Nov. 29, p. 1182.
11. Schoeman, F. (1980) "Rights of Children, Rights of Parents, and the Moral Basis of the Family," *Ethics*, 91, pp. 6–19, p. 17.
12. P. Laslett (Ed.) (1959) *Patriarcha and Other Political Works by Robert Filmer* (Oxford, Oxford University Press).
13. See T. Hobbes, *Leviathan*, Ch. 20 (London, Dent).
14. Schoeman, F., op. cit., p. 14.
15. See E. Anscombe (1978) "On the Source of the Authority of the State," *Ratio*, 20, pp. 1–28.
16. Schoeman, F., op. cit., p. 13.
17. These points were argued at greater length by the present author in Cohen, B. (1981) *Education and the Individual* (London, Allen & Unwin).

Schooling

Laura Purdy

Initiation into a band is as rough as the *rite de passage* by which you are moved out of it. Entering a band, you are the youngest, have the least to offer, and have the least physical resistance. You are no asset to the band, and are therefore not much more welcome than you were at home. But at least you will be in the band for four or five years, so it is known that if you survive you will eventually be of some use. Within the band each child seeks another close to him in age, for defense against the older children. These become "friends." There are usually only between half a dozen and a dozen children in a band, so each child is limited to one or two friends. These friendships are temporary, however, and inevitably there comes a time, the time of transition, when each turns on the one that up to then has been the closest to him; that is the *rite de passage,* the destruction of that fragile bond called friendship. When this has happened to you three or four times you are ready for the world, knowing friendship for the joke it is.
—Colin Turnbull, *The Mountain People*

Proponents of children's liberation believe that any difference in treatment between children and adults must be justified by reference to some morally relevant difference between the members of the two classes. Aharon Aviram argues that writers on education and society at large have taken such differences for granted and have therefore failed to provide the necessary justification for subjecting children to compulsory schooling.[1]

Aviram does not deny the possibility that compulsory schooling of some sort could be justifiable; he merely argues that no one has seriously tried to justify the current system, mainly because of assumptions about children's nature that appear to render the task unnecessary. He argues that society has relied on John Stuart Mill's unjustified views about children's incompetence. Aviram rightly argues that the principles of liberal democracy require us to recognize the necessity for defending compulsory schooling. My arguments so far respond to this demand by suggesting that the differences between children and adults warrant different treatment. In particular, I have been arguing that children need systematic teaching so that they may acquire desirable traits; I have also argued that they need parents to do this teaching. But parents need help: they usually can't teach children everything they need to know.

From her *In Their Best Interest? The Case Against Equal Rights for Children,* © 1992 Cornell University Press, Ithaca, N.Y. and London, Chapt. 5, 150–157, 169–174. Copyright 1992 by Cornell University. Reprinted by permission of the publisher, Cornell University Press.

One reason is that life is so complicated that parents can only rarely know everything their children need to learn; most wouldn't have the time to teach them anyway. Furthermore, by recognizing parents' right to rear their children, society chooses a system that gives children (at best) an unequal start in life and (at worst) risks parental abuse. Some such abuse is so serious that children should be taken out of their parents' hands. Many other children continue to be at various kinds of disadvantage from their parents' way of life, however. Poverty, for example, is generally a major source of disadvantage for children; also, some households fail to transmit the kind of self-control and moral concern for others necessary for children's and society's well-being. Universal, compulsory schooling is one way of adding to and reinforcing the useful learning children get at home; for some children it may be the only source of such learning. Such schooling constitutes a reasonable compromise between leaving children's welfare entirely in the hands of their parents and attempting to place it in the hands of other social institutions.

Despite the fact that school can and sometimes does help children to overcome social handicaps, it has been argued that they would be better off if it were not compulsory. Liberationists must, if they are to be consistent, argue for the abolition of compulsory schooling. As we have seen, the right to live where you please implies a right to work; the right to work implies a right to dispose of your time as you choose. Consequently, individuals with a right to choose where they live cannot be required to go to school. In any case, no one requires adults to go to school unless they too are dependent on the state.

This argument would, if sound, justify ending such schooling, although proponents of equal rights also tend to try to strengthen their position by pointing out its overall bad consequences.[2] The issues raised by these questions are many and complicated. I shall seek here only to consider what can be said in favor of compulsory education, without trying to justify the particular forms adopted by any given society.[3]

What would happen if children were not required by the state to go to school? It seems to me that the following claims are plausible. First, some children would get little, if any, schooling, and schooling would more than ever depend on parental interest and income. Second, the public school system might collapse. Third, private schools might well proliferate even if the public schools carried on. Let us consider each of these possibilities in turn.

Some parents, either because they are poor, do not value education, or do not care about their children's future, would want their children to work as soon as they were able; some children might prefer to work and refuse schooling, just as some already undermine their schooling because they work too much. As I suggested earlier, given the current correlation between schooling and income, lack of schooling would probably trap most of these children in unsatisfying jobs.

It is true that some children are now so unhappy in school that they might nonetheless be better off, even in those jobs. Perhaps, if school could not be made more interesting and profitable, letting them go would be a reasonable alternative. I am not so skeptical as some about improving the schools, however, and in any case I would be troubled by the prospect of children stuck for a lifetime in such jobs on the basis of their immature decisions, especially since at present that would simply perpetuate the existing class hierarchy, with women and male minorities at the bottom of the occupational heap.[4]

I also believe that parental income and support would become even more than now the decisive factor in occupational decisions unless society itself were to provide direct help to children who wanted more schooling. It would be ironic if equal rights were to become a mechanism by which economic and social inequality were still further entrenched in American life. That this should occur because of factors beyond the control of the rising generation, or even on the basis of their own immature decisions, should give pause to those who would otherwise favor purely voluntary schooling. Not only is this result undesirable in itself, but it would have seriously negative implications for the future of democracy.[5]

Because of their optimistic assumptions about how children will fare if they are liberated, proponents of equal rights tend to discount the possibility of increased inequality in society as a whole resulting from implementation of those rights. If that optimism is unfounded, as I think I am showing it to be, that prospect should, by itself, sabotage the case for liberation. Greater equality is, after all, the keystone of that case; if treating children more like adults leads to less equality, then the case gets hard to justify even on its own grounds. The damage to democracy would not be limited to this growing gap between rich and poor, however: good democratic decisions depend on an educated citizenry with the kind of self-control and values for which I have been arguing. Given the critically important ecological and political decisions facing us over the next decade, this issue is crucial.

Radical critiques of the educational system point out that the *existing* system already merely legitimates and promotes contemporary inequality in the United States: instead of paving the way for equality, it solidifies the nonmeritocratic hierarchy implicit in our society.[6]

There is a good deal of evidence to support the view that schooling contributes less to social mobility than many have thought and that it has an especially stigmatizing effect on those outside the mainstream. In response to these claims it is important not to throw the baby out with the bathwater, however. First, it's hard to see how weakening schools or letting some children avoid schooling would improve this picture. Second, it is fairly clear how to begin remedying this state of affairs: states must develop school funding arrangements that allocate resources more equitably among schools.[7] To the predictable conservative skepticism that this move would change the situation very much, one might reasonably ask why, then, rich districts spend so much. And if money is so irrelevant, what is the objection to transferring some from the rich to the poor? In short, compulsory schooling is a necessary but not sufficient condition of a better society. That it is not sufficient is no reason to abolish it. The kind of social changes—social changes that liberationists recommend and require—that would be necessary to help children deal with the adult world without education would, if aimed instead at the schools, improve them so much that this criticism would no longer apply. Given the potential value of education, what could then justify giving up on schooling?

The decline (if not collapse) of the public school system, coupled with expansion of private schools, would almost certainly accentuate inequality and other undesirable trends.[8] A universal, compulsory public school system can, in principle, guarantee children's exposure not only to the academic material essential for adult life but, even more important for our concerns here, to the kind of guidance with respect to self-control and the values necessary for optimum development of individuals and maintaining a just, caring society. Parents cannot be counted upon to offer good teaching, and even when they do, reinforcement from other social institutions is needed.[9]

I have been arguing that children need help learning both self-control and morality. In particular, we have seen that there is some reason to believe that children do not learn how to show intelligent concern for others unless they are systematically and deliberately taught. From very early on, children begin to have experiences that encourage them to be self-centered or solicitous of others. Much ought to have been learned by the time they start school, but school can certainly reinforce desirable learning or counteract the undesirable.

An interesting measure of this function is provided by a 1959 study of membership in the American Civil Liberties Union. This organization is a watchdog for civil liberties in the United States; as such it should be of special interest to those who value freedom. Twenty-five percent of its members were teachers; 66 percent listed their last level of schooling as postgraduate university work, 24 percent listed it as college, 7 percent listed it as high school, and 2 percent listed it as grade school.[10] Obviously, these figures differ vastly from the distribution of education in the population at large. It is clear that we cannot assume that additional years of schooling necessarily promote concern for equality or human welfare, given the voting patterns in presidential elections.[11] They do, however, provide an opportunity for learning that supports these values.[12]

Schooling also provides, as I will argue shortly, a crucially important and possibly unique opportunity for children to learn about those who are different from themselves. Only this kind of learning will help eradicate prejudice about such differences as race, sex, and class. Although unjustifiable inequality and discrimination are not based solely on such prejudice, it significantly contributes to the misery of those who are its target. Not only do they suffer from diminished freedom—a fact that undermines arguments based on freedom on their own grounds—but other values (such as fairness) would, in many cases, override the appeal to freedom. Progress on these fronts is slow and fragile: the price of equality, like that of liberty, is probably eternal vigilance. Schools don't necessarily promote equality (or any other value) but they can be more efficient vehicles for such promotion than any other institution.

Universal, compulsory education is our best bet for making sure that everybody is exposed to the perspectives, knowledge, skills, and strategies necessary for dealing with values. Ideally, the public education system would do such a good job that there would be no market or need for private schools or home teaching. These options now sometimes provide better education than the public system, although if they are laxly regulated, they also create loopholes through which some children can slip. The important point is that all children must be decently educated, both for their own sakes and for that of society.[13] Compulsory education is therefore a necessity, even though there is some leeway in what form it shall take. Only compulsory education can ensure that none will be deprived of the unique advantages of the learning it provides, and only compulsory education can ensure society of the kind of citizens it needs to create a fairer, more humane world.[14] . . .

The Importance of Public Schools

It is clear that without compulsory education some children would get little or no schooling; they would therefore be deprived of the school's contribution to the kind of essential learning for which I have been arguing. And if, as I suspect would happen, private schools were to supplant in part or entirely the public school system, it would be much harder to ensure each child's exposure to them unless those schools were very tightly regulated.[15]

Now perhaps they *would* be so regulated. They are not regulated in these ways now, however, and there is no particular reason to think that such regulation would be instituted at the same time as equal rights for children. This conclusion is supported by the fact that the emphasis on freedom that motivates liberation is unlikely to favor stricter controls on schooling.

Tibor Machan believes that the turn to private schooling would be desirable at least in part because of the greater say it gives parents over their children's education.[16] Proponents of equal rights for children could hardly embrace this outcome, however, as they wish to put power in children's hands, not adults'. I think Machan's prediction about parental power is true, however, and it is cause for concern.

Parents may believe a variety of unsubstantiated or dubious claims about children's nature. They may also adopt without critical inquiry whatever is fashionable in the way of popular wisdom about development or education. Thus before the advent of a spate of "gifted and talented" programs a few years ago, the notion of special treatment for those who learn at different rates was anathema.[17] In the teeth of common sense and without a shred of solid evidence, children who were ready and able to learn earlier and faster than their chronological peers were denied the opportunity to do so. Deprived of challenging experiences that might have kindled their thirst for learning, they were instead stupefied by a boredom that often had long-lasting bad effects.[18]

It is plausible that parents' beliefs (if sufficiently popular) would lead to the founding of schools that catered to them, no matter what they were. Reliance on private education would therefore in effect place children's education entirely in their parents' hands. Proponents of children's rights argue that it is children who should determine their educational experiences, not second parties, whether state or parents. But in practice, taking educational policy out of the hands of the state does place it in that of parents. Small children will be schooled according to their parents' beliefs, and this early education will in many cases determine their subsequent attitudes.

Suppose, however, that some parents are persuaded by the argument that reading is no longer necessary in contemporary society because of the all-pervasiveness of the electronic media. Are we prepared to let their children attend schools that follow this notion? Or suppose, not entirely unrealistically, that parents buy the idea that girls have inferior mathematical ability. Are we prepared to let them send their girls to finishing schools that fail to encourage their intellectual development in this area? Such freedom for parents has serious implications for girls and for society, if Lucy Sells's argument that failure to pursue mathematics at the high school level creates a permanent handicap in the scramble for positions of power is sound.[19]

One of the most serious manifestations of this problem would arise with respect to religion. Parents may believe that as a matter of religious freedom they have a right to raise their children in their own faith, even when their "faith" conflicts with widely accepted and defensible secular beliefs.[20] Probably we can agree that parents should be able to acquaint their children with such beliefs at home. If by having their children attend private schools, however, parents can reinforce those beliefs and shield them from critical evaluation, the children are being indoctrinated in an unacceptable way.[21]

A still more fundamental problem arises in the realm of political and social beliefs. It emerges as resistance to genuine inquiry into political theory (concerning such basic issues as capitalism, democracy, communism and feminism), as well as into emotionally, wrenching issues such as sex. Racism provides us with a relatively uncontroversial demonstration of this problem. We know that some Americans are racist, and they want their children to share their derogatory attitudes about the members of other ethnic groups. Should we be prepared to let them sequester their children in schools made in this image?

That people who fear freewheeling critical inquiry are ready to restrict their children's experience (not to mention that of other people's children) is demonstrated by the proliferation of sectarian private schools and the campaigns for censorship in public ones. The witch hunt against "secular humanists" and attempts to remove books, courses, and teachers with "offensive" views do little to engender confidence in a purely private education system. A network of private schools would create new choices, some undoubtedly worthwhile. Others would undeniably tend to narrow rather than enlarge their pupils' vision.

A superficial understanding of this alternative may focus on the increased choices available for those parents who would prefer private schooling but who must now, for financial reasons, send their children to public schools. But greater freedom for some children would be bought at the price of less or no freedom for others. And greater freedom for parents might well mean less for children: being sent to an indoctrinatory private school may please a parent but blindfold the child.[22]

Diversity may be good, but it does not follow that more diversity is always better.[23] Radically divergent world views may tear a society apart by undermining areas of agreement necessary for peace and cooperation. In some respects, the United States is already one of the most heterogeneous societies now existing. Such heterogeneity can be sustained only so long as there is broad agreement on basic principles in regard to human equality, tolerance, and limits on violence. When members of a society fail to agree about such fundamental matters, communities disintegrate: witness the warring factions in Northern Ireland and in Lebanon.[24]

In short, compulsory public schooling can provide a defense against narrowly sectarian education that both constricts children's future possibilities and erodes tolerance and understanding of others.[25] These are not "neutral" aims, as their opponents are the first to point out, but they are the preconditions of any decent society.[26] That the public schools are not now fully successful at these tasks fails to justify dismantling the system unless there are grounds for believing that those values would more reliably be met in its absence. There is little reason to believe in such grounds.[27]

Schools and Parents

One might be tempted to conclude that one of the schools' major tasks is to protect children from parents, and that this conclusion contradicts what I have been saying about the importance of parental authority. I think it is true that we need schools in part to protect children from their parents: there is ample reason to fear that some children would be worse off if their parents had full control of their upbringing and education. This does not detract from my position that parents should be respected unless they have demonstrated their inadequacy.

It may also seem that I have been peering at the schools through rose-colored glasses. This is not the case. As we all know, there are bad teachers who do not know their subject matter, indoctrinate, or are burned out. There are also bad counselors who channel kids into courses, tracks, and programs on the basis of stereotypes. Other problems occur because of insufficient funding, stupidity, incompetence, and political pressures. Our current academic curriculum certainly needs scrutiny, as does the mix of practical and scholastic activities; perhaps we even need to reconsider whether full-time schooling should be compulsory at every level. In addition, I think there is a case for children having more rights within the context of the school.[28]

In short, to argue for universal required schooling is not to say that our present system is ideal. It is to say that we need more than one institution to help keep children on track. Let the best possible circumstances occur as often as possible: loving, responsible, intelligent parents providing what children need, and their schools reinforcing and complementing this care. Let the worst never occur: irresponsible, prejudiced, uncaring parents neglecting or indoctrinating their child, and schools supplying more of the same treatment. With compulsory public education, if a teacher or school is bad, we can hope that a parent will be able to salvage the situation, either by putting pressure on the educational institution or by moving the child to another. But likewise, a good school can help salvage a child who is not being well parented. As in government, it seems prudent to have a system of checks and balances. Equal rights for children would eliminate this particular system of checks and balances.

We have now begun to get a feel for what a world with equal rights for children might look like. The existence of such rights would directly or indirectly affect many areas of life that would appear upon superficial examination to remain unchanged; moreover, exercising them—as opposed to just having them—would have far-reaching implications. These implications and possibilities would to a considerable degree depend on social arrangements as well as social norms. Economic arrangements are particularly important, and require further examination. . . .

Notes

1. Aharon Aviram, "The Justification of Compulsory Education: The Still Neglected Moral Duty," *Journal of Philosophy of Education* 20 (Summer 1986): 51–58. Among the prima facie (but not real) exceptions he cites the following: Ivan Illich, *Deschooling Society* (London: Penguin, 1973); R. S. Peters, "The Justification of Education," in *The Philosophy of Education* (Oxford: Oxford University Press, 1973), and *Ethics and Education* (London: Allen & Unwin, 1980); P. Hirst, *Knowledge and the Curriculum* (London: Routledge & Kegan Paul, 1974); J. P. White, *Towards Compulsory Curriculum* (London: Routledge & Kegan Paul, 1973); and L. I. Kimmerman, "Compulsory Education: A Moral Critique," in *Ethics and Educational Policy,* ed. K. A. Strike (Boston: Routledge & Kegan Paul, 1978).

2. See, e.g., Lindley, "Teenagers and Other Children."

3. A form could be justified only by painstaking analysis of a wide variety of issues that will vary according to circumstance.

4. One might wonder *who* will do these undesirable jobs, since there is no reason to think that everybody will be able to have safe, interesting, and adequately paid jobs in the foreseeable future. At present it is the children of poor and working-class families who are most likely to wind up in them, and I am arguing that equal rights will most likely simply perpetuate this situation. Ideally, nobody should be doing such jobs for very long, and I would hope that in the long run they could eiher be eliminated by automation or spread throughout the population by some rotation system. Furthermore, society ought to balance intrinsic unpleasantness by other appeals, such as high pay. These approaches are obviously utopian at present. Perhaps the most that can be hoped for now is that merit, rather than class, play a larger role in deciding who shall escape them.

5. Amy Gutmann, for example, ultimately derives all our decisions about education from the need to sustain democracy: *Democratic Education* (Princeton: Princeton University Press, 1987).

6. See, e.g., S. Bowles and H. Gintis, *Schooling in Capitalist America* (London: Routledge & Kegan Paul, 1976), and Richard Rothstein, "Down the Up Staircase," in *And Jill Came Tumbling After,* ed. Judith Stacey et al. (New York: Dell, 1974).

7. Funding schools through property taxes means that the resources available on a per capita basis can vary tremendously. According to the U.S. Department of Education, Office of Educational Research and Improvement, *Digest of Education Statistics, 1989,* 25th ed., NCES 89-643 (Washington, D.C.: U.S. Government Printing Office, 1989), Table 146, p. 156, Mississippi spent $2,350 per child on education, whereas New Jersey spent $5,953 and Alaska spent $8,010. Some of this variation is due to differences in the cost of living, but the figures also conceal substantial differences within states. The inadequacy of the resources of poor neighborhoods tends to lead to underfunded schools that can't prepare children well. It's easy to see how a vicious circle is established from which the poor and minorities have difficulty extricating themselves. The obvious inequity here is finally being recognized by some courts. In Abbott v. Burke, 575 A.2d 359 (N.J. Sup. Ct. 1990), for example, Judge Robert Wilentz held both that poor districts had to be assured funding equal to rich ones and that the level of spending had to be sufficient to compensate for the disadvantages of their students.

8. It is plausible that ending compulsory schooling would simply accelerate the trend for

those who can afford it to send their children to private schools, perceived to be superior. I suspect that schooling could be made voluntary only if political support for the schools were still weaker than it is now; repeal of the attendance laws and the resultant drop in enrollments, together with the loss of the promise of equality, would most probably provide sufficient grounds for a taxpayer's revolt.

9. The necessity for consistency is one of Bronfenbrenner's central points: other societies send coherent value messages, whereas we send many contradictory ones. The result is confusion, which contributes to the failure to transmit basic values. See Urie Bronfenbrenner, "The Parent/Child Relationship and Our Changing Society," in *Parents, Children, and Change,* ed. L. Eugene Arnold (Lexington, Mass.: Lexington Books, 1985).

10. This study is reported in Nash, *Authority and Freedom in Education,* p. 77. In general Nash makes a powerful argument for the necessity of schooling. This research, by itself, doesn't make the case, but it is suggestive. In a different society, of course, moral education might conceivably occur in the absence of schooling, but what we need to consider is the likely effect under contemporary circumstances.

11. In the 1989 election, for example, increased income was consistently associated with progressively higher percentages of conservative votes (*New York Times,* November 10, 1988, B6). This pattern of voting is an ongoing phenomenon; see Warren E. Miller and Santa Traugott, *American National Election Studies Data Sourcebook, 1952–1986* (Cambridge: Harvard University Press, 1989), Table 6.5, p. 316. Income is correlated with years of schooling. In the United States it now seems that those who are better off are tending more and more to vote in what they see as their own self-interest, to the detriment of concern for the welfare of those less well off. This trend suggests that people are unconvinced of the importance of concern for others. The present work shows why.

12. Much of the average American's conviction about democratic principle may be superficial. Studies repeatedly show that many citizens fail to recognize or assent to such uncontroversial documents as the Bill of Rights. When Nash asked students about the Bill of Rights, he found unanimous approval for none of its amendments, and two were rejected by a majority. These were the provision in the Sixth for confronting one's accuser and the Tenth Amendment's reservation of rights to the people. As a result of this experience, and of another study of students at nine teachers' colleges, Nash concluded that "they pay lip service to the liberties that they have been taught verbally from elementary school through college, but when faced with specific issues they often take a stand that is more authoritarian than libertarian": *Authority and Freedom in Education,* p. 89. This study, conducted during the McCarthy era, showed that although most of the students said they believed in freedom of speech and thought, they would nonetheless be in favor of censoring speakers in schools and banning textbooks that criticized religious organizations. Furthermore, "a large majority would deport or silence those who do not believe in our form of government": Fay L. Corey, *Values of Future Teachers: A Study of Attitudes toward Contemporary Issues* (New York: Teachers College Press, 1955), p. 46, cited in ibid. Instead of standing up for their rights, they were accommodating pressures to avoid controversial stands and "questionable" groups and individuals. Despite the upheavals of the 1960s, there is little reason to believe that things would be very different now. Lloyd Duck describes a frightening little study: When students circulated part of the preamble to the Declaration of Independence among 252 residents of an Air Force base in Germany, only 16% recognized it; only 27% signed it; and 14% said they agreed with its ideas but wouldn't sign it. Some called the document "a lot of trash." Others thought it advocated revolution or unwarranted changes by "little people"; didn't give enough to the majority class; was too radical, was "pretty" but not workable, or was communistic. The results of this study were placed in the *Congressional Record.* See Lloyd Duck, *Teaching with Charisma* (Boston: Alleyn & Bacon, 1981), pp. 13–15.

13. Only education promises to help us avoid the central moral problem of democracy: unjust or imprudent decisions by the majority.

14. This is not to say that it is being very successful at it now; but there is little reason to believe that ending compulsory schooling would improve the situation, *pace* Ivan Illich.

15. It is plausible to think that schools would continue to exist since many, if not most, parents would doubtless prevail upon their children to continue with school even if the state did not require them to do so.

16. At present, he says, "parents are forced to comply with the State's conception of what is right for their children, not regardful primarily of the individual characteristics, talents, needs, aspirations, interests, qualifications, etc. of any given child." Thus the state can ignore parents' opinions about such matters as when schooling should begin and what kind of material should be taught: "Schools Ain't What They Used to Be," pp. 251, 256. These

claims are not universally true, however, nor would they necessarily be true of any public school system.

17. The history of attitudes toward bright kids is instructive; see, e.g., Gertrude H. Hildreth, *Introduction to the Gifted* (New York: McGraw-Hill, 1966), or Gary A. Davis and Sylvia B. Rimm, *Education of the Gifted,* 2d ed. (Englewood Cliffs, N.J.: Prentice-Hall, 1989).

18. See my unpublished paper "Educating the Gifted."

19. Lucy Sells, "The Mathematics Filter and the Education of Women and Minorities," in *Women and the Mathematical Mystique,* ed. Lynn H. Fox, Linda Brody, and Dianne Tobin (Baltimore: Johns Hopkins University Press, 1980). The same problem would arise for minorities if parents swallowed the myth of Caucasians' superiority in math.

20. For more on religious education see T. McLaughlin, "Parental Rights and the Religious Upbringing of Children," *Journal of Philosophy of Education* 18, no. 1 (1984): 75–83; W. D. Hudson, "Is Religious Education Possible?" in *New Essays in the Philosophy of Education,* ed. Glenn Langford and D. J. O'Connor (London: Routledge & Kegan Paul, 1973).

21. See Alan Peshkin, *God's Choice: The Total World of a Fundamentalist Christian School* (Chicago: University of Chicago Press, 1986), for a frightening example of this problem.

22. We already face this problem to some extent, although state regulations should in principle allay the problem. That they do not now does not mean that we could not do better in the future. But if the libertarian program is realized, such regulation would probably go down the drain along with compulsory schooling. Consider, among other cases, *Wisconsin* v. *Yoder,* 406 U.S. 205 (1972).

23. Our bias in favor of ever-expanding diversity is presumably not unrelated to the intellectual traditions recounted by Arthur Lovejoy in *The Great Chain of Being* (Cambridge: Harvard University Press, 1936).

24. Naturally, it does not follow that we must all agree about everything in order to live together.

25. Tolerance is, of course, a two-edged sword, as extreme tolerance permits oppression of third parties. The exact definition of the limits of tolerance is obviously of major importance. For further development of the political aims of education and the constraints they place on the school system, see Gutmann, *Democratic Education.*

26. This is, of course, a contested assertion, for which I will be arguing later. What it entails also depends on how "equality" and "justice" are defined. Interminable squabbling about the details of such concepts, however, can be an excuse for failure to act even when there are clear cases.

27. For further discussion of this issue, see Ivan Illich, *Deschooling Society* (New York: Harper & Row, 1971), and Arthur Pearl, "The Case for Schooling America," *Social Policy* 2 (March–April 1972): 51–52.

28. Arguing for a specific set of rights is beyond the scope of this work. However, I would not want it to be thought that because I argue against legal emancipation of minors, I think it follows that they should not be granted any particular civil rights. On the contrary, I do think that the burden of proof should be on those who would limit those rights, and that the arguments currently used to do so are indefensible. See, e.g., Justice William Rehnquist's arguments in favor of the right to remove books from school libraries in *Hazelwood* v. *Kuhlmeier,* 479 U.S. 1053, 93; L.E2d 978, 107; S.Ct. 926 (1987).

Freedom of Religion
and Children

Hugh LaFollette

I n a number of recent federal court cases parents have sought to have their children exempted from certain school activities on the grounds that the children's participation in those activities violates their (the parents') right to freedom of religion. In *Mozert* v. *Hawkins County Public Schools* (827 F. 2nd 1058) fundamentalist parents of several Tennessee public school children brought civil action against the school board for violating their constitutional right of freedom of religion. These parents sought to prevent their children from exposure to beliefs or practices opposed to their (the parents') religious convictions. They claim that elementary school readers introduce ideas repugnant to their and their children's deeply held religious tenets.

The district court upheld the parents' claims, but that decision was overturned by the appellate court. Now the U.S. Supreme Court has refused to hear an appeal. The parents' case is dead. I am not entirely satisfied, however, with the resolution of the matter. Though I agree with the decision to overturn the lower court, I think the reasons for doing so are not entirely convincing. More importantly, I think all the judges and the litigants in the case have failed to address significant fundamental questions about the scope of parental authority, especially the authority to teach or indoctrinate children about religious matters. Though I realize this is an extremely sensitive matter—one which the courts are most assuredly loathe to address—that does not, in any way, undermine its importance or centrality. These are issues which must ultimately be faced squarely by the courts. I had hoped that the Supreme Court would have addressed them in this case. I was wrong. Once again the central issues were avoided. Or so I shall argue.

I. The Issues

Most of us presume that freedom of religion is important. We are repulsed at the thought of someone forcing her religious views on us or others. We want the option of believing and behaving as we wish—particularly on matters as significant as our religious beliefs. Although important, these rights are not unlimited. If a person's religious expression harms another, it can be legitimately restricted. Human slavery and sacrifice, for example, are impermissible even if prescribed by one's religion. Likewise for religious beliefs or practices

From *Public Affairs Quarterly*, vol. 3, no. 1, Jan. 1989. 75–87. Reprinted by permission of *Public Affairs Quarterly*.

which might harm one's children. For instance, the courts have consistently held that a parental decision to withhold necessary medical treatment from a child harms that child's interest (*Wallace* v. *Labrenz* 104 NE 2nd 769). In these situations the state may legitimately require necessary medical care even if the parent's sincere religious conviction forbids it.

The courts, however, have been reluctant to interfere with parental decisions except when the child's life or physical health is threatened. Though this reluctance is in many ways understandable, it is unjustified. Children's interests should have more weight than most courts presently grant them. Or so it seems to me.

The crucial (though heretofore ignored) question is: can the parents legitimately demand that the children be shielded from beliefs to which they (the parents) object? Does the fact that the children purport to agree with the parents have any legal weight? The parents claim the constitution gives them the right to have their children opt out of reading these "offensive" books and to be exposed only to texts which express views identical with their own. Are the parents right?

Before I address these questions, let me quickly review the facts of the case: the parents challenged the use of certain readers in elementary reading class. The readers in question depict children who question parental authority, discuss situation ethics, consider the tenability of divergent religious beliefs, and advocate tolerance of opposing views—views to which the parents of the children strenuously object.

Claims akin to these have been previously recognized by other courts. For example, in *Moody* v. *Cronin* (484 F. Supp. 270) children were exempt from physical education classes because their parents thought exposure to students dressed in shorts would incite unwholesome urges. In *Wisconsin* v. *Yoder* (406 U.S. 205), Amish children were exempt from high school since their attendance would presumably undermine the Amish way of life advocated by their parents.

However, even in these cases where the courts have ruled against parental claims (as in *Mozert*), they did not justify the decisions by express appeal to the interests of children. In most cases, they did not even mention the children's interests. Instead they cited some "compelling state interest" which presumably justified overriding the parental claims. Nonetheless, I think we can discern a deep and pervasive confusion about the scope of parental rights and the children's interests.

A Confusion

This confusion is evident even in the parents' brief in *Mozert*. The parents claim that their children agree with them, thereby implying that the school readers conflict with the children's religious beliefs. They thus suggest that being exposed to these readers violates both the children's and the parents' rights to free religious expression. This claim is intermingled, though, with the contention that the parents have a constitutional right to *control* their children's religious development. These claims are clearly in tension, if not outright contradictory. Yet the possibility of conflict between the interests of children and their parents is never mentioned by the courts or by any of the litigants in *Mozert*. Moreover, it is a conflict which, as far as I can ascertain, has been noted by a single federal judge: Justice Douglas in *Yoder*.

All parties seem to agree that parents have the right to control the religious upbringing of the child, yet also think it is important to determine if the children find the readers offensive. However, if parents have the right to **control** their children's religious beliefs, as the parents aver, then the children cannot have any rights in this matter which need to be or could be protected. The fact that children agree with their parents—if they indeed do—is legally irrelevant; even mentioning the children's agreement is a diversion from the presumed fundamental legal issue.

On the other hand, if children have rights which merit mention in these legal proceedings, then the parents cannot have a right to control the children's religious upbringing. If the children have rights, these may need protecting not only from state intrusion, but, at least in some instances, from parental indoctrination. The parents cannot consistently argue for both rights; nor can the judge consistently recognize both. Yet that is exactly what the district judge did.

Setting this inconsistency aside; what exactly is wrong with the parent's position? It is undeniable that it has some legal merit. Nonetheless, I think their claim is seriously misguided though the only way to demonstrate that has consequences which many will find objectionable.

Courts Need Not Decide If a Religious Belief Is Reasonable

Most lay people will quickly reject the parents' contention since they find the parents' religious beliefs unreasonable if not irrational. The parents think *Macbeth* is objectionable because it discusses witchcraft. They consider *The Diary of Anne Frank* heretical since it suggests diverse religious beliefs might be correct. They are offended by any story, television show, or movie which encourages tolerance, openmindedness, respect for differences, feminism, or children who question parental decisions—for example, most fairy tales, Aesop's Fables, "Sesame Street," etc. Most people find these claims preposterous. Even many who share the plaintiff's religious perspective would reject the contention that a child's exposure to these views is religiously forbidden.

It is insufficient, however, to find the parents' religious convictions unreasonable. The constitution protects their right to religiously instruct their children, they claim, and that protection cannot depend upon a judicial decision that those beliefs are reasonable or plausible (see *Thomas* v. *Review Board;* 450 U.S. 710, 718). The constitution does not protect only expression deemed reasonable by the court, it protects religious expression period; that is, at least expression which does not harm others. If the courts were empowered to determine which religious beliefs were reasonable, then legal protections would likely be accorded only to those whose views meshed with, or were at least vaguely similar to, those of the sitting judges. That would undermine the very purpose of these constitutional guarantees.

The bill of rights is strongly counter-majoritarian.[1] It insures that the beliefs or views of the majority cannot automatically override individual choice. To that extent, the plaintiffs' position is tenable. Judges need not determine that a religious belief is plausible before they decide that it merits legal protection. This is not the way to undermine the parents' case. Consequently, to reject the parents' arguments, one must show that their freedom of religious expression is more limited than they and the district judge supposed.

There is, I think, both a direct and an indirect way to show that. The first begins with the claim that everyone should have the same right to free religious expression—regardless of the right's rationale. It then notes that the parents are striving to effectively deny to the children the same right they (the parents) find so dear. The second argues that the right to free religious expression is justified by concern for personal autonomy. This more basic concern will constrain the control parents can legitimately exercise over their children. Though these arguments differ, they are clearly interrelated.

To set the stage for these arguments I must first describe the most common rationale for freedom of religion. Moreover, it is a rationale frequently cited by courts in defense of freedom of speech and religion (see, e.g., *Dennis* v. *United States,* 341 US 494, 71, S.Ct. 857 and *New York Times Co.* v. *Sullivan,* 376 US 255; 84 S.Ct. 710). The rationale will help us understand both the force and the limitation of the parents' position and the lower court's ruling. Though a detailed and sophisticated defense of this rationale would require volumes, it is sufficiently illuminating for our purposes to briefly summarize John Stuart Mill's argument in *On Liberty* for freedom of religion (and for other rights of personal choice and action).

Why Freedom of Religion Is Important

Mill claims that freedom of thought and belief (including religious belief) is essential because it is the best avenue to truth. That is not to say freedom guarantees truth, but it is to say it provides the most reliable means for attaining it. Suppressed views, Mill points out, frequently turn out to be true, and even when they aren't, they still contain elements of truth (or insights)—elements which might have escaped notice had the view been repressed. Moreover, even when the view the majority desires to suppress is completely false (something which is rarely the case, he urges), something vital is lost by suppressing it. The majority would have benefitted from discussing the mistaken view; they would have better understood the strengths (and weaknesses) of their own beliefs. Unless balanced by serious consideration of opposing and even false views, the majority's received beliefs cease to be living truths for them and become instead dead dogmas—items of belief which make no real difference to their lives. The presence of divergent religious views enlivens discussion about important issues, thereby increasing the opportunity for finding truth and for determining one's personal beliefs.

Mill is not concerned merely with freedom of belief; he is equally concerned with freedom of action, with the *exercise* of one's deeply held beliefs, including one's religious beliefs. It is better, on Mill's view, for someone to live according to her own lights—even if she is wrong—than to engage in the "ape-like quality of imitation." A person's life is her own even if it is, from some external perspective, misguided. She will be better off making her own mistakes than in mimicking other people's "correct" views. She has a better chance of discovering what really is best for her.

Furthermore, if her life is self-directed, she can see and learn from her mistakes; something she cannot do if she merely follows someone else's life plan. The freedom to exercise one's religion, to engage in experiments in living, is as essential as freedom of belief. Freedom of religion, then, is legitimate since it increases the chance of finding the truth and because it gives each individual the means to a self-directed and satisfying life. It does not guarantee these worthy goals, but it is a vital social mechanism supporting them.

I recognize there are plausible objections which can be raised about aspects of Mill's account. Nonetheless, I think the broad outline of the account is correct. Moreover, something like this justification has been offered by the courts in defense of individual rights of conscience (see citations above). Consequently, it will provide a means to assess the legal merits of Judge Hull's decision in *Mozert*. It will enable us to discern its initial plauibility as well as its defects.

II. What's Wrong with the Parents' Claims

Children's Interests Have Been Ignored

As mentioned earlier, all of the litigants in the case have assumed that the only constitutionally recognized interests are those of the parents and the state. This is demonstrated clearly in Judge Hull's decision:

> . . . The parents claim their religion compels them not to allow their children to be exposed to the Holt series. Plaintiffs have also alleged that the Board's policy interferes with the inherent right of the parents to 'direct the upbringing and education of children under their control' (Pierce). . . . the court FINDS that the plaintiff's beliefs are sincerely held religious convictions entitled to protection under the Free Exercise Clause of the First Amendment.

In short, according to Judge Hull, the only legal issue is: "What do the parents want?" What they want, they get. The children's interests are irrelevant.

The appeals court decision was not much better. Justice Lively, in issuing the court's opinion, rejects the parents' claims because the children were not required to **believe** what they were reading, and thus, the reading program did not burden anyone's constitutional rights of freedom of religious expression. In a consenting opinion Judge Kennedy comes closest to identifying what seems to me to be the fundamental issue. She claims that even if the parents' rights of free religious expression were constitutionally burdened, that such a burden would still be legitimated by a compelling state interest, namely, the interest in having an informed citizenry. Apparently, though, this interest applies only to children who attend public schools, for there is no such expectation of children attending private schools. Thus, she does not recognize that all children have interests which may be harmed by overly zealous parents.

Judge Boggs, on the other hand, claims the school board should have accommodated the parents, though there is no constitutional requirement that they do so. School boards may, on his view, lay down virtually any requirements they wish, and unless these abridge the establishment clause, they are constitutional. All these decisions, though, skirt the central issue, namely, what to do if a parent's practice of religion harms the interests of the adult that the child will become?

In other situations where the parent's religious beliefs or practices directly and physically harm the child, the courts have ruled that the parent's wishes (even when the child claims she concurs) may legitimately be overridden. For instance, when parents have refused to allow treatments thought to be medically necessary for their child's health, for example—blood transfusions and some surgery—courts have intervened and authorized them (see, for example, *Wallace* v. *Labrenz*).

We must remember, though, that not all harm is physical. Repressing political speech, for example, does not physically damage anyone, but it can harm them. Slandering a person harms her even if it doesn't cause physical damage. Admittedly it is easier to identify physical rather than psychological harm; but the law must sometimes make difficult decisions. I want to suggest that the judge's decision in *Mozert* ignores non-physical harm to children. Parental indoctrination, normally thought well within the scope of legitimate parental authority, can harm the child. Children have interests which should constrain that authority; interests which legitimate the state's intervention on the child's behalf.

However, I need not assume that children's interests or rights are more important than or are even equal to those of parents. Nor do the judges in aforementioned cases like *Wallace* v. *Labrenz* make this assumption. I need only hold that children's significant interests may not be legitimately ignored; they must be taken into consideration and in some cases may override parental interests.

Parents Should Have Extensive Authority

Let us consider, for a moment, the central claims of the parents' case, namely, that they have a right to control the religious, moral, and political upbringing of the child (see *Pierce* v. *Society of Sisters* 268 U.S. 510, 534). I think most people will agree that parents do and should have wide-ranging influence over the religious and moral instruction of their children. In fact, I would go further. Even though parental authority is limited, as I shall argue in a few pages, I would contend parents not only have a right to teach their children moral and religious beliefs, they have a solemn duty to do so. To instruct a child—even if the beliefs she is taught turn out to be wrong—is preferable to not instructing her at all.

Some parents, out of a fear of giving their children wrong beliefs (or possibly out of indifference), fail to provide them with any moral, political, or religious guidance. Though this decision may be well-motivated, it is usually disastrous for the child. If a child is not taught any substantive beliefs she comes to think that ideas and beliefs are largely irrelevant. "If they are important," the child might think, "why haven't my parents taught me their beliefs?" Conversely, if a parent teaches their children religious, political, and moral views, then the child will learn a vital lesson, namely, that one's beliefs and ideas are not insignificant appendages; they are essential parts of who and what she is. Even if her beliefs change, she is likely to retain the general conviction that a person's beliefs are important.

Conversely, if a child is brought up in an environment without parental instruction, the child fails to acquire an initial set of beliefs. One's initial beliefs set the stage against which she can compare beliefs she later encounters—to see how they are similar and how they diverge. Without these, there is no point of comparison. When confronted with opposing views later in life, an individual reared without parental instruction will likely be indifferent to the alternatives. Since she has no strongly held beliefs, the alternatives don't conflict with anything she deems important.

Consequently parental instruction is probably essential for a person's genuinely considering alternative views, and thus, is essential for the child's full development. This is exactly what Mill's view would suggest. However, parents may legitimately instruct their children not because they have a God-given right to mold them, but because instruction is vital to the child's long-term interests. Yet the same considerations which explain the need for parental instruction also constrain it. But neither the parents nor the courts seem to recognize that.

Why Parent Authority Should Be Limited

First, we should note that the parents are not asserting a right to religious expression *per se*. No one has proposed limiting their religious expression; nor has anyone told them they cannot instruct their children as they wish. What is at issue is whether they should or could obtain state support to limit the child's access only to views which are consonant with their own. The parents asked for that support and the district judge obliged. Though the appeals court rejected the parents' legal arguments they did not, I am sad to say, challenge this presumption of parental control.

Of course, inasmuch as the parents think they know the truth about how their children should live, it is not surprising that they want this control. They think there is one and only one way for their children to attain salvation, and salvation, for them, is the most important good in the world. It is a good which they think will be blocked by the corrupting influence of the textbooks.

However, the intensity of the parents' beliefs is insufficient to bar state intervention. For instance, if a child needs a blood transfusion, the state will and should authorize it even if the parents think the transfusion will hinder or even block the child's search for salvation. The child's interests demand it.

We are now in a better position to see the direct objection to the judge's decision. If the parents have a right to free religious expression, then no one should force them to hold any particular religious belief. No one should compel them to espouse a belief. More relevant to the present point, no one should brainwash them so that they are "compelled" to adopt a particular belief. Their children have the same right—even if not as children, then as the adults the children will become. However, the parents have requested and been granted court permission to indoctrinate their children, thereby undermining the child's ability to freely choose, and thus, abrogating their right of free religious expression. That makes the parents' right more important than the children's. That is unjust.

A parallel argument can be mounted in a somewhat more circuitous fashion. The claim that the parents should morally instruct their children is based on a Millean argument that such instruction is in the child's best interest. However, it is not the child's immediate interest which explains (or justifies) the need for parental instruction; it is the interests of the adult whom the child will become. The child may somewhat benefit from parental instruction now. The primary benefit, however, is that it helps her develop into a fully functioning adult. By instructing her the parents enable the child to become an enlightened citizen and an autonomous individual. Concern for the future of the child explains the parental right to instruct; the right does not emerge in a vacuum.

This same concern, however, also serves as a brake on the parental right. Some teaching aids the child while some could harm her. Certainly there are ways in which indoctrination can harm the child, most notably by effectively closing off the alternatives for the adult the child will become. An individual can choose only among the options of which she is both aware and can consider seriously. If parents limit the child's exposure to religious and moral views identical to their own, then the child will see only one option and choose it; she will likely hold the same beliefs when she becomes an adult.

Of course the parents in *Mozert* realize this. That is exactly why they are so adamant. They know that if their children are aware of alternatives, they might eventually choose them. *That* is most assuredly what they don't want. They wish to be not only the primary instructional influence on their children; they should be the *sole* influence. They think they should determine the beliefs of the adult the child will become.

"But what," the parents might ask, "is wrong with that?" Parents understandably desire that their children grow up to be certain kinds of people, among other things, people who live up to parental ideals. True. But that does not show that the state should take steps to help them realize these desires at the expense of the child's interests. Parental indoctrination, particularly when coupled with an absence of exposure to alternative views, can limit the options of the adult whom the child will become. It can limit her options as much as, if not more than, legal prohibitions against the adoption of those views. Let me explain.

The parent's complaint is based on the claim that adults should be able to control and direct their own lives, particularly in those matters they deem important, for example, in their religious beliefs. To say that one has rights of religious belief and free religious expression is to say that no one else should limit her options of belief and expression. Yet there are multiple ways in which the options can be limited. They can be limited by explicit prohibitions—that is the parents' fear. They can also be limited by certain kinds of indoctrination or brainwashing—that is my fear.

Interestingly enough, the parents in *Mozert* recognize this latter possibility; they make essentially this very point in stating their case. They cite approvingly the U.S. Supreme Court's ruling in *Tinker* v. *Des Moines Independent School District* that public school students 'may not be regarded as closed-circuit recipients of only that which the state chooses to communicate' (393 US 503, 111). Moreover, in their initial brief before the federal district court they also include a long citation from "The Manipulation of Consciousness," originally printed in the *Harvard Civil Rights Civil-Liberties Law Review* (Vol. 15, p. 309). That quote deserves reiteration:

> **Free expression makes unfettered formulation of beliefs and opinions possible. In turn, free formulation of beliefs and opinions is a necessary precursor to freedom of expression. If the government were to regulate development of ideas and opinions through, for example, a single television monopoly or through religious rituals for children, freedom of expression would be a meaningless right. The more the government regulates formation of beliefs so as to interfere with personal conscience, the fewer people can conceive dissenting ideas or perceive contradictions between self-interest and government sustained ideological orthodoxy. If freedom of expression protected only communication of ideas, totalitarianism and freedom of expression could be characteristics of the same society.**

There is no doubt, I think, that what the authors claim and the parents aver is true. A one-sided presentation of views by the state is bad. If the government allowed only the expression of one view, the individual's chance to develop her own views would be greatly reduced. Moreover, from a broader perspective, government indoctrination would be detrimental to the entire society. It would block the means for progress, it would hinder the search for truth.

The judge, parents, and the state, however, seem oblivious to the fact, that *for the individual child,* governmental indoctrination is not *nearly* as likely as is carefully orchestrated parental indoctrination to make freedom of expression meaningless. If the state teaches one view in the school, the child might still be exposed to variant beliefs by her parents. But if the parents push a unitary view, and the state supports the parents' decision to stop their children's exposure to alternatives, then the child will doubtless grow up without genuine freedom of expression. That is, she can, without overt constraint, express the views she holds; it is just that the views she holds won't be freely chosen. She will only be able to mimic the views she learned. By substantially altering the child's ability to reason and choose, the parents will effectively control her actions as well as, if not better than, if they tried to overtly control them.

Successful indoctrination is at least as much a limitation on her freedom as is an explicit rule backed by law. That seems obvious. If indoctrination would not have this effect, why would we take the trouble to oppose governmental propaganda? And why would any government even be tempted to indoctrinate its citizens?

Objectionable indoctrination is likely to occur, however, only when there is a single view to which the child is exposed. Parental instruction is not likely to have this disastrous effect (though on occasion it might) if the child is eventually exposed to alternatives. If a child attends school where alternatives are presented, then she will have an opportunity to adopt them, even if, in the end, she doesn't. Her chance to develop into a mature, self-directed adult is enhanced by exposure to alternative views.

Since the parents in *Mozert* are asking the state to keep the children from being so exposed, then the parents' claim should be denied, the appellate court's ruling sustained. It should be sustained, though, not because the decision will place a burden on the school system (which it doubtless would), but because it will harm the children.

So both the direct and the indirect arguments lead to the same result. If we assume freedom of religious expression is justified by the value of autonomy, then we must reject the judge's decision because it supports parental decisions which damage, if not completely undermine, the child's budding autonomy. Or, if we assume freedom of religion is a non-derivative, intuitively grasped right which is not supported by an appeal to autonomy, we may reject the judge's decision because it gives parents justifiable power to violate their children's rights.

We may hold this conclusion without undermining parental authority. Parents will still have wide-ranging control over their children. Nor need we conclude that children's interests and rights are more weighty than those of their parents; I do not think that we even need hold that the children's rights are as strong as those of their parents—though perhaps they are. I have only argued that the children's interests cannot be completely ignored as they were in this case and as they have been typically within the American judicial system.

A Radical Implication

This argument undercuts the judge's decision, but it may have radical implications. The argument has stated that children should be given a meaningful right of free religious expression, regardless of the parents' wishes. This requires allowing the child to be exposed to alternative views. Otherwise the child will not have genuine freedom of choice or derivatively, meaningful freedom of expression. Hence, it seems that **any** system that prevents such exposure is suspect.

Consequently, not only should the state not support the efforts of parents of public school children to deny their children exposure to alternatives; they should not do so for the parents of private school children either. Children who attend private religious schools may well be denied access to alternatives. If they are—and that would have to be determined by careful study—then those schools should be banned or forced to change. Of course if such schools don't block children's exposure to alternative views, then nothing I have said shows they are objectionable.

Note

1. See Ronald Dworkin, *Taking Rights Seriously* (Harvard University Press, 1977). Also see Justice Jackson's decision in *Barnette* v. *West Virginia:* "The very purpose of the Bill of Rights was to withdraw certain subjects from the vicissitudes of political controversy, to place them beyond the reach of majorities and officials and to establish them as legal principles to be applied by the courts . . . [they] may not be submitted to vote, they depend upon the outcome of no elections."

Suggested Readings

Feinberg, Joel, "The Child's Right to an Open Future," in William Aiken and Hugh LaFollette, eds., *Whose Child? Children's Rights, Parental Authority, and State Power* (Totawa, N.J.: Rowman and Littlefield, 1980, pp. 124–53).

Gutmann, Amy, *Democratic Education.* (Princeton: Princeton Univ. Press, 1987).

——— "Should Public Schools Teach Virtue?" in Claudia Card, ed., *Values and Public Policy* (Harcourt Brace Jovanovich, Fort Worth: 1992, pp. 493–498).

Jencks, Christopher. "Whom Must We Treat Equally for Educational Opportunity to Be Equal?" *Ethics,* 98, April 1988, pp. 518–533.

Kozol, Jonathan, *Savage Inequalities, Children in America's Schools* (New York: Crown, 1991).

Pritchard, Michael S., "Families, Schools and the Moral Education of Children," *Denver University Law Review,* Vol. 69, No. 3, 1992, pp. 687–704.

Who Decides About Health Care?

Cases for Discussion

Refusal of Treatment

In 1989 an Illinois teenager who was being treated for leukemia was allowed to refuse a blood transfusion. Like her parents, she was a committed Jehovah's Witness whose religious beliefs prohibit the use of blood or blood products. Doctors brought the case to court, as is customary when parents refuse lifesaving therapy for a minor, expecting the court to issue an order for transfusion. The lower court complied, but on appeal the Illinois Supreme Court held that if there is convincing evidence that the minor is mature enough to appreciate the consequences of her actions and to exercise the judgment of an adult, then she has the right to consent or to refuse medical treatment, even if her life is at stake. A psychiatrist testified that this 17-year-old had the maturity of an 18–21-year-old person. As the result of her own choice, the teenager died.

When parents refuse lifesaving therapy for their children, the most common response is for the state to invoke its role as *parens patriae,* that is, guardian of children, and set limits on parental authority. Health care is considered a basic necessity and failure to provide it can be considered parental neglect. However, forty-five states have religious immunity laws that excuse parents from charges of neglect if they refuse standard medical care and substitute prayer, faith healing, or other religiously sanctioned means for treating disease. The American Pediatric Society has challenged such laws, and recent court decisions such as the Twitchell case in Boston (1990), the Hermanson case in Florida (1989), and the Hamilton case in Tennessee (1983) have been decided against parents whose children have died because of Christian Science practices which permit only spiritual healing.

The situation of an older teenager raises in a special way the general question of who decides for minors. For completely utilitarian reasons, even young teens are permitted to consent to their own medical treatment in the special cases of venereal disease, AIDS testing, and alcohol or drug abuse. Unless such treatment can be given without parental involvement, it is feared, many teens would not come for treatment at all. In the case of refusal of treatment, however, questions about the competency of minors to know their own best interests or to have stable and serious religious commitments become relevant. When is a child no longer a child for the purpose of making important life decisions? Should the legal age of consent for all medical care be lowered?

Anencephalic Baby As Organ Donor

When Laura Campo was eight months pregnant, tests revealed that her fetus was anencephalic—that is, formed without vital material in the brain. Anencephalic babies can suck, swallow, and breathe on their own, but they can never develop most ordinary human functions such as walking, talking, understanding language, or recognizing people. There is no cure or treatment for this condition, and the babies usually weaken and die within a short time.

Many couples choose abortion when a diagnosis of anencephaly is made, but this baby's parents decided to carry the pregnancy to term, hoping to be able to donate the infant's organs to help other children. However, in order to maintain healthy organs that would be usable in transplant, their baby would have to be supported with heart-lung machines and thus would not die a "natural" death. To avoid this situation, the court refused to permit the use of the infant's organs, although in Canada such use is permitted.

This case demonstrates the classic dilemma between two conflicting ethical principles: the Kantian theory of respect for persons, which precludes using an infant or any person as a means to someone else's good, and the utilitarian principle of doing what is best for the greatest number of people. It is always difficult to make decisions for newborns, since one cannot know what they would want if they were able to choose. It is also difficult to decide whether approving the use of an anencephalic's organs would lead to a "slippery slope" of devaluing human life, or whether, as the baby's grandmother said, "Taking one and helping two, three, five—that's pro-life."

The decision to donate organs for transplant is altruistic, and it is considered virtuous to choose altruism or self-sacrifice for oneself. But, one might ask, can one "volunteer" a child to be altruistic? Or must decisions be made for a child solely on the basis of what is in the best interest of that particular child?

The Issues

1. Considering issues that arise about the health care of children introduces a fourth party into the arena of decision making. In addition to parents, the state, and children themselves, there is a role for physicians and other medical professionals. All medical treatment requires the informed consent of the patient, but since children, as minors, are by law considered incompetent to give consent for themselves, others must be the official decision makers. Thus all consent for children in health care is proxy consent—that is, consent by one person for another. Parents are generally designated as proxies for their children, but in special cases this may be challenged. Thus the first issue in health care for children is: Who should decide?

2. A second issue concerns the standards to be used in deciding for children. Whoever it is who decides, how should the decision be determined? A common answer to this question is to say that decisions should always be made on the basis of the best interest of the child. There are problems with this standard, however, for judgments about what is in the child's best interest may differ.

For example, in cases of severely handicapped newborns, parents may feel that nontreatment is best for the child who would suffer through weeks or months of painful treatment that has only a small chance of success, whereas the infant's physicians may think it is worth the risk, even though the odds are against it. The best-interest standard may also be questioned by asking whether it might not be justified in some cases to consider the best interests of the family as a whole, even giving it precedence over the interest of the child. For example, if the drain on a family's emotional and financial resources to help one child would result in serious harm to other siblings, should that be considered?

For an older child, a subjective standard is often proposed. Using what is referred to as substituted judgment, adult decision makers choose as they think the child would choose, if that child were adult, taking into account the child's own values, preferences, and personality.

The Arguments

For and Against Parents

Legally and morally, parents are generally assumed to be the best proxies for their children because most parents are loving and well-intentioned and have the best interests of their children at heart. It is also said that parents know their own children best and thus are most likely to know what is good for them. Parents, then, are expected to use the best interest or the substituted judgment standard. And finally, the point is often made that parents are the ones who will have to live with the decisions that are made about their children, and this seems especially important when decisions involve treatment vs. nontreatment of handicapped infants who will require a lot of long-term care.

On the other hand, health care decisions often require medical expertise that parents do not have, and decisions often must be made quickly in the midst of emotional shock, as in the case of unanticipated birth defects or a school child's serious accident. Further, the assumption of loving and well-intentioned parents is rebutted by the high incidence of physical and sexual abuse by parents.

Much of the challenge to parental authority in health care decisions concerns parents whose religious convictions prohibit commonly used medical treatments or substitute methods thought by doctors to be ineffective or harmful. Whereas competent adults can always use or refuse any medical treatment for themselves, it is problematic when they refuse it for their children. Although courts are reluctant to interfere in families in everyday matters, where it is a matter of life or death for the child, common practice is for physicians to petition the courts for permission to treat, and the courts generally agree.

For and Against Doctors

Unlike parents, physicians have the expertise required to make appropriate health care choices for children, and they are not emotionally involved with the individual child in ways that might cloud their judgment. The goal of medicine is always to do what is best for the patient, and medical personnel are likely to use objective standards, thus ensuring the same treatment for all children in similar circumstances. In these cases, doctors are seen as knowing and using the best interest of the child standard for decision making. For these reasons many argue that physicians should be primary decision makers concerning health care for children.

However, health care decision making involves not only factual expertise but values. It is not a question of facts but values to decide, for example, whether a child should have plastic surgery for severe facial deformities, which would improve his social relations but incur risk from anesthesia, a period of physical discomfort, and absence from school. Parents cannot make good decisions in the absence of information from doctors, but doctors should not impose their own values on their patients.

The Role of the State

The state, through legislation, judicial decisions, and the courts, becomes involved in health care decisions for children either when the issue is one of public health, as in mandating vaccinations, or when appealed to in cases of serious conflict between physicians and parents, especially when physicians feel that parents are unreasonably refusing permission for treatment that could be lifesaving. Less frequently, physicians and hospitals can appeal to the courts when parents insist on continuing treatment that physicians judge to be futile and causing suffering to the child.

Judges and courts are asked to decide because they are presumed to be objective, neutral, and have the best interest of the child in mind. It is, further, a way of overcoming or sidestepping the inequalities that children inherit by being members of families that may make decisions on grounds different from the mainstream.

Courts are not ideal decision makers, however, because judges generally lack medical expertise and must rely on a physician's judgment of what is life threatening and what is not, and generally they have little or no knowledge of the individual child or of the family. Also, courts use the model of rights, thus casting parents and physicians as adversaries in a win/lose situation, and this may not serve the interests of the child well.

The Child As Decision Maker

For young children, there is little question that they cannot have a significant role in deciding about medical treatment. Without the capacity to envision the consequences of refusing treatment, or to endure present pain, say of injections, to achieve future good, their judgment would often not be in their own best interest. Some form of the incompetency argument is generally accepted to justify overriding children's objections to treatment. Paternalism in the form of requiring children to submit to medical treatment protects their future as adults.

As children become more mature, however, and especially if they have had a good deal of experience with a chronic disease, they become much more like adults in their decision making.

Arguments in favor of allowing adolescents the right to consent or refuse are based on claims that they are competent and on the argument that it is their lives and their bodies. The law recognizes some older teens as emancipated minors, capable of giving consent for themselves, if they are financially independent of parents, in the army, or married. Physicians are also allowed by law in some states to recognize some teenagers as mature minors and accept their consent or refusal of treatment without parental authority. Accepting a teenager's consent for abortion with parental approval or notification, however, remains a very controversial issue.

The Readings

"Making Decisions—Whose Choice?" Edwin N. Forman, Professor of Pediatrics, Brown University, and Rosalind Ekman Ladd, Professor of Philosophy, Wheaton College.

Forman and Ladd introduce the issue of who should decide about health care for minors. They offer a summary of arguments for and against parents, doctors, or children as decision makers with special discussion of the competency of adolescents.

"Children's Competence for Health Care Decisionmaking," Dan W. Brock, Professor of Philosophy and Director, Center for Bioethics, Brown University.

Brock discusses the issue of who should decide by reviewing the literature on the competency of children and adolescents to make medical decisions. He defends parents' role as decision makers because he thinks parents have an interest in deciding for their child which should be respected, even if the child is competent.

"Parental Discretion and Children's Rights: Background and Implications for Medical Decision-Making," Ferdinand Schoeman, who was Professor of Philosophy, University of South Carolina.

Schoeman answers both the question of who should decide and what standard should be used to make a decision. He offers a defense of parental rights, arguing for limits on state intervention on the grounds that families are characterized by intimate relationships that are not governed by the usual moral principles. Thus, parents need not always choose according to the best-interest standard for their children.

Making Decisions—Whose Choice?

Edwin N. Forman and Rosalind Ekman Ladd

Parents' Rights

"It really is time to consider surgery. Six urinary infections in the last 12 months, and the tests show vesicoureteral reflux. This can be repaired with surgery, and she'll be as good as new."

"No, no surgery. Annie's only 8, and I know her father wouldn't agree to it."

"Well, we can't go on treating it with antibiotics. It will cause terrible problems for her in the future—hypertension, renal failure, lots of discomfort and even a shorter life span."

"No, no surgery. That's final."

What should the physician do when parents refuse standard care for their child?

Discussion Questions

1. What rights do parents have in making medical decisions for their children?
2. What is the moral basis of parents' rights? Why do parents, not others, have rights over children?
3. What are the legal and moral limits of parents' rights?

I n the past few years, we have seen the question of parents' rights to make medical decisions for their children raised with dramatic intensity. It is the stuff of newspaper headlines and TV specials.

It began in 1975 with the case of Karen Ann Quinlan, whose parents had to plead with a judge to be allowed to remove ventilator support from their comatose daughter. The Chad Green case gained national attention in 1978, when the court appointed a legal guardian in the place of his parents to assure continuation of chemotherapy instead of the Laetrile and vitamin therapy they had chosen for him. The Baby Doe cases in 1982 were hotly and publicly debated and prompted an attempt by the federal government to take decision-making power away from parents who refused aggressive therapy for seriously handicapped newborns. Then in 1989 there was the father in Chicago who held hospital staff at bay with a shotgun while he unplugged the respirator from his nearly brain-dead young son.

Cases that gain public notoriety are not the everyday fare of the pediatrician's practice, yet the issue of the rights of parents lies at the heart of many everyday

From their *Ethical Dilemmas in Pediatrics: A Case Study Approach,* Springer-Verlag, New York, 1991. Chapt. 1, 2, & 3, 7–17. Copyright 1991. Reprinted by permission of the authors.

management decisions. The moral foundation of parents' rights as well as the limits society places on them need to be understood in order to operate effectively in the branch of medicine where the patient does not stand alone but is intimately linked—physically, legally, emotionally, and economically—with one or both parents.

The Rights of Parents

Suppose that the doctor is convinced that Annie should have surgery. Does she have the obligation to honor the parents' decision, even if she believes it is wrong? Given her greater medical knowledge, experience, and objectivity, does she have the right to continue to try to persuade, cajole, or even coerce Annie's parents to change their minds? If they remain adamant, should she consider appealing to a state agency or to the courts, as one would in cases of refusal of life-saving therapy? Why shouldn't parents be required to choose the best medical treatment for their child? Why should they be allowed the liberty to make mistakes at their child's expense?

Medical paternalism is the view that the doctor knows best and the patient (parents) should not be allowed to choose. The problem with this view is that it assumes that the only relevant factors are medical. It confuses medical knowledge, in which the physician is clearly superior, with knowledge of a person's own best interests, which may be based at least in part on personal values.

For example, in a simple case of choosing between liquid or capsule vitamins for a small child, the physician knows that they are equally effective but the pills are cheaper; the parent weighs the time and trouble to be sure that each pill is swallowed successfully as more burdensome than the extra cost. Values may be weighed differently by different families, and respect for pluralism in values cautions against an unexamined medical paternalism.

Thus, Annie's physician should try to discover the family's reasons for their choice in order to know whether it is owing to a difference in values as opposed to a lack of understanding of the medical facts.

The Foundation of Parents' Rights

The most basic and fundamental question is why parents' values may be imposed on the child; that is, why parents have the moral right to decide for their children.

Proxy consent is generally obtained from biological parents or legal guardians. Why parents are assumed to be proxies for their children is answered in part by historical precedent: rights of parents over children are grounded on the property rights of fathers. This idea gives parents a good deal of latitude to mold children as they see fit.

More popular reasons for recognizing parents as decision-makers are: 1) they are the ones charged by society with responsibility for the welfare and upbringing of children, and responsibility for children requires having the rights for decision-making over them, 2) parents are the people who live most directly with the consequences of their child-rearing, and 3) they have a genetic tie to their children.

A pragmatic view is that parents make the best qualified decision-makers because they know the child best. The parents who are helping to form the child are in the best position to know his or her needs and wants. Sensitive parents observe minute changes in their children's physical and mental states and know almost intuitively what is right for them.

Finally, an even newer theoretical position is that the intimacy of family life is among the greatest personal values. The special relationship between parents and child can be achieved only by protecting it from interference by others.

Whether or not parents do make the best decision-makers has been disputed. Some argue that parents, especially under the emotional stress of sudden accident or serious illness, are incompetent to make decisions. Moreover, the existence of child abuse and neglect by parents is evidence that not all parents always act in the best interest of their children.

The Limits of Parents' Rights

The physician in this case believes that Annie's parents are not making the right decision for their child. She believes that there are limits to the autonomy or freedom of parents to choose for their children. What are the limits set by law and by society's moral standards?

Legally, there are certain things society has decided parents cannot choose. Their liberty is limited by such things as required vaccinations, required school attendance, and the various criteria for child abuse and neglect. Although there is wide latitude given to families to allow them to practice various religions and lifestyles, courts have intervened to protect children and not allowed refusal of standard medical treatment in life-threatening situations by Jehovah's Witnesses and Christian Scientist parents.

In less than life-threatening situations, for the reasons given above, society is more reluctant to intervene between parents and child. Thus, the physician could not count on a court requiring surgery for Annie against her parents' wishes. On the other hand, society's interest in healthy children seems to be leading to an increasing willingness to intervene more.

For example, currently courts are being asked to intervene to protect a fetus by requiring a caesarean section even without the woman's consent and to restrict the freedom of drug-using women during pregnancy to prevent the birth of so-called cocaine babies. Strict laws requiring report of even suspected abuse or neglect also reflect an apparent trend toward greater limits on parents' rights. On the other hand, no one has ever required that parents make "the very best" choice, but only that they meet some acceptable standard.

Morally, good conscience requires the physician to pursue the idea of surgery for Annie, discussing it at each future office visit. Good communication requires her to be patient and to continue to give information, trying to elicit and understand and then respond to the parents' reasons for not choosing surgery. Good doctor-patient relationship requires that she not be coercive or condemnatory. Respect for parents' rights and their concern for their child offer hope that they will choose surgery if and when they become convinced that it is, indeed, the best medical treatment for their child. In a case such as this, where nonsurgery is not a life-threatening harm, it can be postponed safely. When the time comes that the child's life is threatened or serious and irreversible morbidity is likely, then the physician will rightly feel compelled to call in legal authorities.

Consulting the Child

"But I don't want to stay in the hospital overnight, Dr. Hartman. It always ends up longer than you say, and anyway my ear doesn't even hurt that much."

"Benjie, let's go through it again. I explained to you what happens with a bad ear infection. It doesn't seem so bad to you now, but when I look into it with my light, I see all kinds of red. With your low white cell count, if I let you go home with it, it might get worse in the middle of the night. You wouldn't want to have to come back here then, would you?"

"Oh, for heaven's sake, doctor, you've been at it for 20 minutes. Why bother with all that explanation? You know he has to be admitted, and we'll do it whether he agrees or not."

What are the reasons for trying to get a child's agreement for necessary medical treatment?

Discussion Questions

1. In general, should children be given a voice in decisions affecting them? If so, why?
2. Are children competent to make decisions for themselves?
3. Is it in the child's interest to be involved in decision-making?

It used to be said that children should be seen and not heard. Historically, children were considered chattel or property, completely under the control of their parents. In contrast to this, our generation has seen a real movement toward greater rights for children. Theories of child-rearing now describe parents' roles as including teaching, guiding, and encouraging the development of decision-making skills. Adults are encouraged to offer choices even to very young children when possible and to give reasons for decisions when choices are not possible. The influence of John Dewey is profound: he argued that children learn by problem solving and that the goals of education in this country should be to develop skills in making thoughtful decisions, in order to develop adults who will be good citizens in a participatory democracy. Although parents and physicians are still obviously authority figures, they should not operate in an autocratic way.

Why Consult the Child?

Dr. Hartman's conversation with Benjie reflects his commitment to the view that Benjie, although a child, is deserving of respect. He is entitled to explanations and should have a role in decision-making. He is applying in therapeutic practice the policy recommendations now generally in effect in the context of research, which require child assent in nontherapeutic research and encourage attempts to obtain assent in therapeutic research from all children ages 7 years and older. . . . But, why bother to do this when, as his colleague rightly points out, the outcome is a foregone conclusion, and the child is not really being given a choice? What is the point of obtaining assent, when the real consent must still come from the parents? And, could it do harm to consult the child but then not comply with his wishes?

Dr. Hartman's colleague may be questioning not only this instance of obtaining assent, but the whole trend toward greater independence for children. Would he really allow Benjie to veto a hospital stay? He wants to protect him from harm, including his own bad choices, but that can be accomplished only by restricting his liberty.

Children's Competence

This protectionist position rests on certain assumptions about children's competence. Benjie is not fully rational: he tends to see only pleasure, he is not mature enough to choose a present pain in order to achieve future benefits, and he has not had enough experience to be able to imagine what an impairment permanent hearing loss would be. The skeptical physician may have read Locke, who says that to turn a child loose to an unrestrained liberty before he has reason to guide him is to "thrust him out amongst Brutes," and Bentham who claims that the child is "too sensitive to present impulses, too negligent of the future."

The evidence about children's lack of competence can be challenged, however.

1. If one looks at decision-making as a developmental process, then one cannot treat the 18th birthday as a magic milestone at which competence and rationality spring full-born from children's heads. The 9-year-old can be expected to understand and contribute more to the process of decision-making than his 7-year-old brother, and the older teenager can contribute as an almost-adult.

2. There is some empirical evidence showing that although young children cannot give sophisticated rationales for their choices, they generally make the same treatment choices as adults.[1]

3. From a practical point of view, insofar as making decisions is a form of practical reasoning, it depends not only on cognitive capacities but to a large degree on life experience, practice in making moral judgments, and practice in disciplining oneself to act according to one's principles. Those who work with children with chronic and fatal illness find that they are much more mature in their ability to understand and make choices about their treatment than Benjie is with his very first serious ear infection.

Some people are skeptical about the value of consulting children because even if they agree to something, it is impossible to be sure that it is voluntary. This is particularly troublesome because a child is almost always in a vulnerable position toward adults. Not only are they weaker physically, for even a 10 year old can be simply carried off, but they have no power to impose their decisions on adults: all the institutions of society and access to them are controlled by adults. Even the child who needs protection from abuse from an adult needs the intervention of another adult.

There are subtle and not so subtle psychological pressures working as well. In general, children want to please their parents and may have well-hidden anxieties about being abandoned if they do not cooperate with them. The physician may be viewed as a kind friend, but even the most independent adults know that their welfare lies in the physician's hands and older children know that they need to keep the physician as a friend against the mysteries of illness and medicine. Thus, one has reason to question voluntariness even when, or perhaps especially when, assent seems to be willingly given.

A final note on voluntariness: for assent to be genuine, there must be the possibility of dissent. Children who need treatment do not really have the choice of effective dissent. Thus, their assent, one might say, is essentially meaningless. Nonetheless, there are benefits in trying to get child assent. Talking and explaining helps them to see the reasons for the medical decision and understand why they should agree. It provides a model of human relationships that are not autocratic and treats them with respect, it helps train them in decision-making, and finally, it often achieves compliance and cooperation.

Even if Benjie is not the ultimate decision-maker and does not have veto power, he can be accorded some role in decision-making. There is room for negotiation, bargaining, or even compromise. Perhaps he would settle for being able to go to MacDonald's for supper and being admitted right after that. Having a voice in deciding reinforces his sense of himself as a person and helps prepare him for the independent decision-maker he will some-day be.

Adolescent Age-Specific Values

"Out of the question! I won't wear a brace. I'll do the electrical stuff at night and anything else you want, but no brace."

"The brace is the best option for your scoliosis. Your back curvature has reached 30 degrees, and if we can't prevent it from getting to 40 degrees, it means surgery. No one wants that for you, Celia."

"But the brace is so obvious. How would you like to start high school with a big ugly brace? That's what's important to me."

How should an adolescent's values be ranked against "adult" values?

Discussion Questions

1. What are a person's "real" values and goals?
2. What weight should be given to age-specific values?

Adolescent choices are typically characterized by what might be called age-specific values, that is, values that are held only during the teen-age years or given high priority only during that time. Chief among these are concern with body image: "How do I look to others? Am I too fat, too thin, wearing the right clothes?" Also of importance is acceptance by peers and striving for independence, especially of parents.

The developmental tasks of adolescence seem to require that the individual be able to fulfill at least some of these needs. According to some psychologists, adolescents develop their own identity precisely by being concerned with their bodily image, finding a peer group that accepts them, and being able to act independently from family. Achieving these goals in adolescence paves the way for a mature and responsible adulthood.

"Real" Values and Goals

Adolescent age-specific values, however, often hold little appeal for the parents whose ultimate responsibility it is to make decisions for their child. They may see concern with body image as trivial, especially when compared with concern for good health. Even if they are sympathetic to the acute embarrassment their child would suffer from wearing a bulky back brace, they are more likely to weight long-term permanent benefits more heavily than immediate, short-term unpleasant experiences.

Age-specific values are temporary: children outgrow them and, in their own adulthood, will most likely repudiate them. So, if one were to override the adolescent's wishes, it could be justified by saying it is simply imposing the child's own later, adult values on his or her own earlier, adolescent self. Imposing a decision on another person for that person's own welfare is always a form of paternalism. As such, justification is required. Some say paternalism is justified if the person will thank you for your intervention later on. Another version of this principle is that it is justified to prevent people from choosing for themselves if they are choosing something inconsistent with their own values. Thus, if Celia's true values are those that she will have as an adult, then she should not be allowed to choose now according to her transitory adolescent values. From this it would follow that the adolescent's preference should be overridden when it conflicts with typically adult judgments of value.

It might be objected here that one cannot assume universality of adult values, which is why paternalism toward competent adults is generally not considered justified. So, why allow typical adult values to override adolescent values? If the argument is that these are the values the adolescent will later adopt, this is problematic; this adolescent may not adopt typical values.

The answer to this objection needs to be framed in practical terms. If one does not and cannot know what adult values a particular adolescent will adopt, but one does know pretty clearly that they will be different from the typical adolescent values, the best one can do is appeal to typical adult values. This is like appealing to the "reasonable person" standard: in carrying out proxy consent for those who have not had a history of well-defined values, for example for infants or severely retarded adults, one chooses for them as a reasonable person would choose.

Choosing for adolescents against their wishes assumes that their own stated preferences are not their "real" values. Of course, some adolescents do know what adult values they will adopt. Their age and behavior suggests maturity. They already have well thought-out life plans that are not transitory and that guide their choices. Unlike young children, who need protection from decisions that would preclude their having an open future, that is, the possibility of making a wide range of choices later in life, some adolescents have goals that require commitment and narrow choices. One usually does not have much of a chance of becoming a professional musician or athlete if one keeps all options open until 18 years. In such cases it seems right to let adolescents choose for themselves or, if parental consent is needed, to use the subjective standard for substituted judgment; that is, to choose as that adolescent would choose.

On the other hand, some adolescents retain their adolescent values into adulthood. To put it another way, some typically adolescent goals and values are shared by some adults. For example, successful movie stars have great concern with bodily image, no less as an adult than as an adolescent. The difference is that they retain them as adult values for good reasons, not out of developmental need.

Difficult judgments must be made by the would-be paternalist about the seriousness of an adolescent's life plan and the relation between medical choices now and the possibility of fulfilling that plan in the future. Whereas it may be irrational to allow an adolescent to refuse an appendectomy on the slight chance he may someday want to pose for the centerfold of *Playgirl* magazine, it would not be irrational to allow a high school soccer star to choose knee surgery, which carries some risk but also the promise of continued play.

Adolescent Versus Adult Values

Every stage of life has its own age-specific values. Those in the prime of life may see adolescent values as trivial or shallow, but those approaching old age may regret the workaholic nature of their midlife years and criticize their own former values.

Although it is natural enough to discount adolescent values in favor of adult or prime of life values, it should not go unquestioned. One cannot argue that later is better or that values that are transitory and likely to be changed or repudiated at a later stage are to be weighted less, for then it would follow that the values of old age should be the standard by which we judge others, not prime of life values.

Adolescent values are to prime of life values as prime of life values are to old age values. We need a better justification to impose adult age-specific values on adolescents, especially when these values do not lead to choices that are irrational in the sense of being incompatible with the adolescent's own perceived life goals or so idiosyncratic that no sane adult would choose them.

One last argument against allowing children and adolescents to make decisions for themselves should be considered. It is that they suffer from lack of knowledge; that is, they do not have enough experience to be able to anticipate the future realistically; they do not know human nature well enough to know how they will feel and react in changed circumstances. This concern is well founded, but it holds, to some degree at least, against any form of advance directive. If life is a series of stages, individuals are a succession of selves, and any promise, contract, or living will one enters into binds one's future self according to present vision and values. Thus, the adolescent's decision binds her for the future in ways similar to those of more mature people. Parents and doctors may choose to keep trying to persuade Celia to accept the brace, but they should give serious consideration to her concerns, even though they may seem misguided to them.

Note

1. Weithorn, L. A. and S. B. Campbell. "The competency of children and adolescents to make informal treatment decisions." *Child Dev.* 1982; 53: 1589–1598.

Children's Competence for Health Care Decisionmaking

Dan W. Brock

What role should children play in decisionmaking about their health care?[1] The doctrine of informed consent requires that medical treatment only be given to adults with their competent, informed and voluntary consent. The law, as well as common medical practice, presumes that adults are competent to decide about their medical treatment, though this presumption can be rebutted in particular instances. On the other hand, the law presumes that minors, who in most states are persons below the age of 18 years, are *not* competent to decide about their medical care; though with some exceptions to be noted below. For minors, the law generally holds that others, usually parents or guardians, are to decide for them about their medical treatment. The general presumption then in legal policy is that adults are entitled to decide about their medical care while children are not. However, medical practice, as we shall see, for good reason has often involved minors in decisionmaking about their care to a greater extent than the law seems to require.

One purpose of this paper is to address whether the general policy presumption of minors' incompetence for health care decisionmaking is sound, or whether it ought to be revised. Questions about the competence of both adult and minor patients arise not just at the level of general legal policy, however, but also in concrete circumstances concerning a particular patient's decision for or against a specific treatment. The other broad purpose of this paper is to clarify the nature of judgments about the competence of a minor to make a particular treatment decision. Clarity on the nature and basis of competence judgments is important both for assessing whether current legal policy concerning minors' competence to make health care decisions is sound or ought to be revised and for managing the many cases in medical practice in which even current legal policy permits an assessment in the individual case of a particular minor's competence.

I note here that my concern throughout this paper is with minors' competence to decide about their medical therapy or treatment and not with their competence to participate in research. While much of the analysis presented here could be applied to minors' consent to research, research raises some distinct issues of its own that I do not address in this paper.[2]

From *Children and Health Care: Moral and Social Issues*. Loretta M. Kopleman and John C. Moskop, ed., Kluwer Academic Publishers, Dordrecht, 1989, 181–189, 200–211. Copyright 1989 Kluwer Academic Publishers. Reprinted by permission of Kluwer Academic Publishers.

There are both conceptual components and empirical components of the issue of children's competence. The conceptual components concern the nature of the concepts of competence and incompetence, and in turn of determinations about competence. The empirical components concern the degree to which children at particular ages possess the various decisionmaking capacities the conceptual analysis shows to be necessary for competence. I believe it is not unfair to say that much current legal and medical practice displays both considerable confusion about the conceptual issues concerning competence determinations, whether of children or adults, and an inadequate appreciation of the empirical evidence from developmental psychology about children's capacities. My discussion in this paper will be structured around the conceptual issues, integrating the relevant empirical data into the analysis at appropriate points. The argument and analysis are complex and I forego drawing conclusions for legal policy and medical practice until the analysis is completed. Readers who want a preview of these conclusions before setting out should consult the final section, Section VII of the paper.

There is one final preliminary point of considerable importance. I will be addressing the standards in particular cases and general policy for children's competence to decide about their health care *when they wish to do so.* Nothing in the analysis to follow implies that children should be pressured, forced, or even encouraged to decide about health care for themselves when they do not wish to do so but wish instead to have others, such as their parents, decide for them. If a child, for example, does not feel psychologically ready to take responsibility for a difficult treatment decision, then even if his or her other decisionmaking capacities appear well-developed it could be harmful to the child to have to take responsibility for the decision. Waiver by competent adults of their right to give informed consent and their transfer of that right to others is well recognized in medical practice, medical ethics, and the law, and deserves to be equally well recognized for competent minors.[3]

I. The Concept of Competence

Any person is competent to do some things and not other things. Thus, all judgments about a person's competence are task-specific. The task in question here is health care decisionmaking, but, for either children or adults, that still suggests too broad or global an understanding of competence. An adolescent under severe stress or suffering the effects of some medications may be incompetent, whereas when those stresses or effects are removed the adolescent may then be competent to make health care decisions. Competence thus varies over time with changes in the person's condition and so may be intermittent or fluctuating. Over longer time frames, children's competence will vary with developmental growth and any judgment about a child's decisionmaking competence must be relative to both a particular time as well as the particular conditions in which the decision is to be made. The task in question must also be specified more precisely than decisionmaking, or even health care decisionmaking, since even a particular child at a specific time with specified decisionmaking capacities may be competent to make some health care decisions but not others.

Different health care decisions vary in the demands they make on the decisionmaker, for example, in the complexity of the information that must be understood or the balancing of risks and benefits of different alternatives that must be weighed. Where a number of closely competing and complex alternative treatments exist for a condition such as bone cancer, the understanding and reasoning required may be much greater than when there is only one standard relatively simple, low-risk, and clearly beneficial treatment for a less serious condition. Competence determinations, therefore, involve matching the capacities of a particular person at a particular time and under particular conditions with the demands of a particular decisionmaking task. Competence determinations are decision-specific because both the capacities of the person as well as the objective demands of the decision can vary substantially. Throughout this paper, when I speak of children's decisionmaking competence, I do not mean, of course, their capacity to make decisions on their own without the collaboration of health care professionals. What is in question, just as with adults, is their capacity, with the help of their physician, to understand the nature and consequences of alternative treatments sufficiently well to be able to give or withhold informed consent to a recommended treatment alternative.

Up to here I have appealed to the ordinary understanding of competence without elucidating it. For many cases this is adequate. With infants and very young children there is no question that they lack competence for all health care decisionmaking; perhaps, there might be no controversy as well that an exceptionally mature 17-year-old is competent to consent to a relatively simple and straightforward medical treatment imposing no significant risks. But adolescents and pre-adolescents constitute one of the largest and most important classes of patients of questionable or borderline competence for the health care decisions they commonly face. In order to clarify these cases of uncertain competence we require a more careful analysis of the competence determination.

II. The Capacities Needed for Competence

What are the capacities needed, whether by a child or an adult, for competence in health care decisionmaking? There are many possible ways of breaking down what is needed and no one correct way, but at a quite general level I find it helpful to distinguish three broad sorts of capacities:

1. capacities for communication and understanding of information;
2. capacities for reasoning and deliberation;
3. capacity to have and apply a set of values or conception of the good.

The first category of communication and understanding includes the various capacities that enable a person to become informed for a given decision. These include linguistic, conceptual, and cognitive capacities necessary for an understanding of the information relevant to the decision at hand. Combined with these must be sufficient life experience to appreciate the meaning of particular outcomes, what it would be or feel like to be in possible future states or to undergo particular experiences.

The second category of reasoning and deliberation, which obviously overlaps the first category to some extent, includes some capacity to engage in hypothetical or if-then reasoning necessary for drawing inferences about the consequences of making a particular choice and for comparing alternative outcomes. Some at least limited capacity to employ probabilistic reasoning about uncertain outcomes is commonly necessary, as well as the capacity to give appropriate weight to probable future outcomes in a present decision.

The third category—the possession of a set of values or a conception of one's good—supplies the standards by which to evaluate treatment alternatives and their various features as either benefits or risks, and to assign relative weights or importance to these features. The conception of one's good needs to be sufficiently consistent and stable at least to permit arriving at a treatment choice and maintaining that choice long enough for treatment to be carried out. The conception of one's good should also take account of one's future interests so that they will be given appropriate weight in one's present decisions, as well as reflect the predictable ways that one's values and goals will change over time. However, here as elsewhere, we must be careful not to demand more of children than we do of adults who are standardly deemed competent.

All of these capacities necessary for competent decisionmaking are possessed by different persons, as well as by a single person at different times, in different degrees. We will address shortly how the appropriate *levels* of capacities for competence should be determined, but it is fair to say that for most health care decisions normal adults generally possess these capacities in sufficient degree to be deemed competent. In particular cases, the effects of physical or mental illness, medications, alcohol, or other conditions may diminish or eliminate these capacities, either temporarily or permanently. Such conditions, however, represent impairments of otherwise normally sufficient capacities for decisionmaking competence in adults; this is, of course, the basis for the legal presumption of competence in adults. Children, on the other hand, begin life entirely lacking these capacities and then progressively develop them from the very earliest stages of childhood through adolescence. The presumption of decisionmaking incompetence of minors would seem to reflect the assumption that children generally lack these capacities in sufficient degree to be permitted to make their own medical treatment decisions. To what degree is that assumption justified?

III. The Developmental Evidence About Children's Decisionmaking Capacities

As a philosopher, and neither a developmental psychologist nor an empirical researcher, I have no new or original data or evidence to offer on children's decisionmaking capacities. What I shall do instead is to summarize very briefly a number of results from child development studies and theory that are relevant to general assessments of these capacities in children.[4] Though I will assign age ranges to the development of a number of capacities, I emphasize at the outset that these age references are only rough generalizations and that there is considerable variation among children, including variation outside the bounds of these age ranges, in the ages at which they reach particular stages in the development of the capacities needed for decisionmaking.

We can consider the capacities for understanding and reasoning together since the relevant empirical evidence and theory often does not distinguish clearly between them. At a minimum, the capacity for communication and understanding requires sufficient linguistic and conceptual development to enable the child to understand the semantic content of the information relevant to a particular treatment decision. As Grisso and Vierling conclude in their excellent review from a developmental perspective of minors' capacities to consent, "we have practically no systematic information regarding children's understanding of the meanings of terms likely to arise in situations in which consent to treatment is sought" ([10], p. 417). Physicians and other health care professionals often do use terms and concepts in decisionmaking contexts that are difficult or even impossible for many patients, whether children or adults, to understand. However, the question is whether it is possible to put information relevant to patient's treatment decisions in terms that children can understand. The principal understanding children need for most treatment decisions is not of technical medical data, but of the impact that treatment alternatives will have on their lives. While admittedly we lack systematic data on this, I believe there is little reason to hold that children who otherwise have the capacities to consent are barred from doing so by inadequate semantic understandings of necessary information. Even for difficult concepts like "death" there is probably an adequate understanding by early adolescence.

The major issues lie in the capacities I have lumped under reasoning and deliberation. As Grisso and Vierling note, among the capacities that may be needed for the reasoning process are the ability to sustain "one's attention to the task, ability to delay response in the process of reflecting on the issues, ability to think in a sufficiently differentiated manner (cognitive complexity) to weigh more than one treatment alternative and set of risks simultaneously, ability to abstract or hypothesize as yet nonexistent risks and alternatives, and ability to employ inductive and deductive forms of reasoning" ([10], p. 418). Developmental theorists posit that the degree to which children perceive the locus of control in a particular matter as internal and subject to their decision, or external and a subject of fate, will affect their attentiveness to the decision, awareness of its details, and the effort they will exert to gather information about it. Children below the ages of 12 to 13 are significantly more prone than older children or adults to see the locus of control as external to them. Lewis [16] found that children in the 6 to 9 age range often did not perceive themselves as deciding even when they were doing so. Role-taking skills are also thought to be necessary to enable a child to entertain a position presented to him by the physician as well as his own different position as both potentially valid, so that the alternatives can be weighed against each other. These skills are undergoing substantial development in the 8 to 11 age period, and are often quite well-developed by 12 to 14.

Perhaps most important for reasoning are several capacities Piaget [20, 21, 22] identified in what he called the formal operations stage of cognitive development. As characterized by Grisso and Vierling, "this stage includes the development of an increased cognitive capacity to bring certain operations to bear on abstract concepts in problem-solving situations." Included is the ability to "perform inductive and deductive operations or hypothetical reasoning at a level of abstraction that would be represented by many consent situations involving treatment alternatives and risks" ([10], p. 419). These capacities are related to children's understandings of the causation of disease and illness, which also appear to follow a developmental pattern. Beginning with quite magical views of causation of disease at around age 5, it is not until around age 12 to 13 that "most children begin to understand that there are multiple causes of illness, that the body may respond variably to any combination of agents, and that the host factors interact with the agent to cause and cure illness" [15]. Further, "emergence of the formal operations stage allows a child to become sufficiently flexible in thinking . . . to attend to more than one aspect of a problem at once—for example, to entertain alternative treatments and risks simultaneously."[5] In the formal operations stage children's general problem-solving abilities increase markedly, as does their ability to consider novel data and to use logic in the solution of problems. With the usual qualifications about the variability with which different children reach a particular developmental stage, it is generally in the 11 to 13 period that the various skills and capacities of the formal operations stage appear in children.

What are some of the limitations of children related to their values or conception of their good? An important issue is whether their values adequately reflect their future interests. While children in the 7 to 13 age range have largely left the earlier magical stage of thinking and now view the world in concrete terms, they can have great difficulty anticipating their future ([11], p. 96). This can lead to two important problems: children may give inadequate weight in their valuing to the effects of decisions on their future interests and also fail to anticipate future changes in their values that may be predictable to others. Related is the instability in children's values in this period, particularly as they concern the child's future goals, and due in part simply to limitations in their experience, especially with adult rules. (Some features of this category of capacities for competence overlap the reasoning category, since limits in anticipating the future will result in prudential irrationality in reasoning when present effects receive disproportionate weight in comparison with future effects.) All of these factors, and others, underlie the concern about relying fully on the values or life plans of children below the age of 14. I reiterate again that the presence of these factors varies significantly among children of the same age, that, other things being equal, these limitations become progressively more prominent the younger the child, and that their impact can vary greatly depending on the nature of the treatment choice before the child.

In adolescents above the age of 13, a heightened concern with physical appearance in comparison with adults or children at earlier stages of development can have a substantial effect on treatment choices [15, 29]. It is important to avoid the mistake of judging such values mistaken or distorted simply because different from those of adults. Children quite properly will commonly have age appropriate values different from adults that reflect their current stages of development. Thus, for example, the effects of a treatment on the physical appearance of an adolescent may properly be given more weight than they might be given by an adult. The adolescent's incapacity may reside only in his or her failure to appreciate how the importance of that effect may often recede later as an adult.

As a very broad generalization, I believe the developmental evidence briefly summarized here supports the conclusion that children by age 14 or 15 usually have developed the various capacities necessary for competence in health care decisionmaking to a level roughly comparable to that attained by most adults. The policy implications of this are developed in the last section of this paper. However, there is an additional factor besides competence in decisionmaking that is necessary for valid informed consent—consent must be voluntary. Children's capacities to give voluntary consent also bear on whether they should have decisional authority about their treatment, and there is significant developmental evidence about these capacities as well. I have already noted above that whether children perceive the locus of control on a matter as internal to themselves or external in the environment affects their capacities for understanding and reasoning. This perception is relevant to voluntariness as well in its effect on children's understanding of whether the choice is really theirs or whether it rests with others, making opposition pointless. A related point is that "children (particularly young children) are unlikely to perceive of themselves as having rights . . . children learn that they should 'obey thy father and mother—and anyone else bigger than they are'."[6] More generally, development theorists have observed that children below the age of 14 or 15 do not assert themselves well against authority figures, and of course the other parties involved in the consent process—parents and physicians—are likely to be perceived as strong authority figures. Indeed, children in the 11 to 13 age range have been found to be more conforming in their behavior than younger children of ages 7 to 9. On the other hand, for children in strong oppositional stages during later adolescence, the voluntariness of their *dissent* to the treatment recommendations of authority figures is in question. Grisso and Vierling conclude that below the age of 15 there is at least significant question about children's capacities to give voluntary consent. . . .

VI. The Variable Standard of Competence

We began discussion of the values at stake in the competence determination in the hope of clarifying the proper standard of competence. If in setting a standard of competence at least the three values of protecting the child's well-being, respecting his or her self-determination, and honoring legitimate parental authority are all at stake, and must often be balanced against each other, we can now draw several conclusions about the proper standard. First, there is no reason to believe there is one and only one objectively correct trade-off to be struck between these competing values, even for a particular decision under specified circumstances. Determining the proper trade-off goes beyond an empirical investigation of the child's decisionmaking capacities and is not simply a scientific or factual matter, but a value choice. The proper standard is thus an essentially controversial matter concerning the proper weight to be accorded these different values.

Second, while there may be no single, objectively correct balancing of these values, we can see that some standards of competence that have been proposed clearly fail to represent a reasonable balancing of them. At one extreme is a minimally paternalistic standard requiring only that the child be able to express a preference for some alternative. Since this standard would respect every expressed choice of the child, it fails to be any criterion of *competent* choice, and so fails either to provide any protection of the child's well-being against the harmful consequences of its decisionmaking incapacities or to give any weight to the parents' interest in deciding. By giving absolute weight to the child's present self-determination under all circumstances, it fails to balance the several values at stake. This standard is insufficiently paternalistic and fails to find incompetent some children who should be so judged.

At the other extreme are standards that are excessively paternalistic and that too readily and often find children to be incompetent. Perhaps the most important example of standards of this type are standards that look simply to the content or outcome of the decision and then apply some "objective" measure of the correct decision which is not based at all on the child's aims and values; for example, the standard that the choice be a reasonable one, what other rational persons would choose, or what the child's parents would choose. Using such standards, failure of the child's choice to match the allegedly objective standard of choice entails that it is an incompetent choice. Any such purportedly objective standard for the correct decision will ignore the child's own emerging and distinctive conception of the good and will substitute another's conception of what is best for the child; it will sanction so-called hard paternalism. Such standards maximally protect the child's well-being—according to the standard's conception of well-being—but fail adequately to respect the child's self-determination. Moreover, even such a standard's claim maximally to protect the child's well-being is only as strong as the objective account of the child's well-being on which the standard rests.

Objective standards of the "best" choice raise complex theoretical issues that cannot be explored here. For normal adults, I believe any standard of well-being that does not ultimately rest on their informed preferences is both problematic in theory and subject to intolerable abuse in practice. With children, however, there is more room in an account of their good for appeal to the objective conditions necessary for the development and preservation of the abilities and opportunities that will enable them later, as adults, to be self-determining agents with choices from among a reasonable array of life plans. The younger the child and the less well-developed and mature his or her values, the less weight others reasonably give to those values in their assessments of the child's good. Other things being equal, the younger the child, the stronger the basis for discounting his or her expressed values and substituting an opportunity-based objective conception of value. To the extent that children's good is defined in terms of developing the capacities and opportunities for determining the course of their own life as adults, their good also *cannot* be determined by the particular values and goals that their parents have chosen for themselves and might wish to apply to them.

An appropriate standard of competence, whether for adults or children, should focus on and address the *process* of their reasoning. The more mature the children's development of their values or conception of their good has become, the more the competence evaluation should seek to determine the extent to which their decisionmaking accurately assessed the available alternatives in terms of those values. Only by examining the process of children's reasoning can others determine whether and where children's choices may fail to secure *their own* aims and values, as opposed to fail to secure another's conception of what is best for them. The question remains for a process standard of competence: how defective should a child's decisionmaking be on a particular occasion for the child to be judged incompetent to make that decision? We can now see clearly the extremely important point that no single answer to that question is adequate. This is simply because both the effects on the child's well-being, as well as the importance of his or her exercise of self-determination, can vary greatly depending on the choice the child has made. The most important variable is how the expected consequences of the choice for the child's well-being may vary from clearly and substantially beneficial (for example, preventing serious, irreversible disability or loss of life) through trivial or negligible, to seriously harmful (for example, causing serious, irreversible disability or loss of life). The more adverse the expected consequences to the child of accepting his or her choice, the higher both the level of decisionmaking capacity and the certainty that level is attained that are reasonably required.

There is an important implication of this view that the level of competence required ought to vary with the expected benefits or harms to the child of acting in accordance with his or her choice—namely, that just because a child is competent to consent to a treatment, it does *not* follow that he or she is competent to refuse it, *and vice versa*. For example, consent to a low risk, life-saving procedure by an otherwise healthy child should require a minimal level of competence, while refusal of that same procedure by the child should require the very highest level of competence. This very same variability applies to adults as well.

Because the appropriate level of decisionmaking competence properly required for a particular choice must be adjusted to the consequences of acting on that choice, no single standard of decisionmaking competence is adequate for all cases. Instead, the level appropriately required for decisionmaking varies along a full range from low/minimal to high/maximal.[7] Table I illustrates this variation.

The presumed net balance of expected benefits and risks of the child's choice in comparison with other alternatives refers to the physician's assessment of the expected benefits in achieving the goals of prolonging life, preventing

Table I

Presumed net balance of expected benefits and risks of child's choice in comparison with other alternatives.	Level of decisionmaking competence required.	Grounds for believing child's choice best promotes/protects own well-being.
Net balance of expected benefits and risks from child's choice is substantially better than for possible alternatives.	Low/minimal	Principally the benefit/risk assessment made by others.
Net balance of expected benefits and risks from child's choice is roughly comparable to that of other alternatives.	Moderate/medium	Roughly equally from the benefit/risk assessment made by others and from the child's decision that the chosen alternative best fits child's conception of own good.
Net balance of expected benefits and risks from child's choice is substantially worse than for another alternative(s).	High/maximal	Principally from child's decision that the chosen alternative best fits own conception of own good.

injury and disability, and relieving suffering from a particular treatment option as against its risks of harm. The table also makes clear that the relevant comparison is with other treatment alternatives, and the degree to which the net benefit/risk balance of the alternative chosen is better or worse than that for other treatment options. A choice might properly require only low/minimal competence, although its expected risks exceeded its benefits, because all other available alternatives had substantially worse expected benefit/risk ratios.

Table I also indicates, for each level of competence, the different grounds for believing that a child's own choice best promotes his or her own well-being. For *all* treatment choices of children, the persons responsible for deciding whether those choices will be respected should have grounds for believing that the choice, if it is to be honored, is reasonably in accord with the child's good and does reasonably protect or promote the child's well-being. When the child's level of decisionmaking competence is only at the low/minimal level, those grounds are only minimally that the child has chosen the option, but are principally others' positive assessment of the option's expected effects for the child's life and health. At the other extreme, when the expected effects of the child's choice for life and health appear to be substantially worse than an available alternative, the requirement of a high/maximal level of competence provides strong grounds for accepting the child's decision as establishing that the choice best fits the child's good (his or her own particular aims and ends). The very highest level of competence is required to rebut the presumption that if the choice seems not best to promote life and health, then the choice is not in fact reasonably related to the child's well-being. When the expected benefits for life and health of the child's choice are approximately comparable to those of the best alternative, a moderate/median level of competence is adequate to provide reasonable grounds that the choice promotes the child's good and adequately protects his or her well-being.

I have spoken above of levels of competence in a manner that suggests that it can be measured, perhaps on some single quantitative scale. In competence evaluations of adults the use of tests such as the Mini Mental Status Exam may further reinforce the notion that competence is formally testable and admits of a quantitative measure. To assume this, however, would be misleading if not outright mistaken. There are no simple tests in widespread use for children like the Mini Mental Status Exam for adults. But even if there were, such tests could not measure competence for a particular treatment decision. Instead, they could only serve as an initial crude screening of the patient's general capacities for understanding, memory, and reasoning. In any case of borderline or questionable competence the patient's understanding and reasoning in the decision at hand must be examined, and that will inevitably involve an informal process of discussion with the patient about that decision and his or her reasons for it. Any tests or exams for measuring general capacities for understanding and reasoning, whether of adults or of children, cannot measure how well a person's decisionmaking capacities are exercised in a particular decisionmaking situation, though they can sometimes serve as useful guides for defects to look for in the decision at hand.

This necessity for more specific and informal evaluation of the child's decision does not mean that competence does not admit of measurement at all. Competence evaluations are often criticized as intuitive, arbitrary, and lacking any sound theoretical basis because they are based on no single, uniform, and precise measure of competence. Moreover, lacking any such measure, they are particularly susceptible to evaluator bias and variability. The fact that there exists no single unified scale or numerical measure of competence applicable to every decision and decisionmaker does not imply, however, the competence evaluations are arbitrary and lack any sound theoretical basis. Instead, the lack of such a scale merely reflects the reality that competence involves too complex a meshing of various capacities and skills of each decisionmaker with the demands of a specific decision situation to yield any single, unified, formal summary. The potential situations are too numerous and the potential arrays of patient decisionmaking abilities and disabilities are too varied. In any particular case, however, the various capacities and skills of understanding and reasoning necessary to competence in decisionmaking could each be measured on a relative scale and reasons offered for the relative importance of specific deficiencies that limit a child's overall competence to make that decision. Thus, while competence evaluations are not amenable to any simple measure, they do have a sound theoretical basis and need not be merely intuitive, subjective, or arbitrary.

VII. Implications for Medical Practice and Legal Policy Regarding Competence

My prinicipal concern to this point has been with the nature of the competence determination, with the relevant data, largely from developmental studies, concerning children's possession of the various capacities on which that determination should be based, and with how an appropriate level of competence required in a particular decisionmaking situation can be determined. I want now to consider some issues of general legal and medical policy regarding children's competence.[8] As noted at the outset of this paper, in most states the law presumes that minors (in most states, persons below the age of 18 years) are incompetent to give informed consent for their own health care. Most states also have statutes enabling children of specified ages, usually ranging between 12 and 17 years, to give informed consent for treatment for specific medical conditions. The conditions covered by such specialized consent statutes include alcoholism, drug abuse, emotional disturbance, mental illness, pregnancy, rape, sexual assault, transplantation, blood donation, and sexually transmitted diseases. Which of these conditions are covered by specialized consent statutes varies from state to state as does the age at which consent by a minor is permitted. These reductions in the age of consent, however, do not seem usually to be based on assumptions about the minor's competence. Instead, their rationale usually is to permit minors to seek and obtain treatment when requiring parental consent and/or notification for treatment would likely discourage many minors from seeking treatment important to their own and/ or others' well-being.

Many states also have statutes specifying conditions in which minors are considered emancipated from their parents or guardians for the purposes of giving informed consent to medical treatment, including marriage, pregnancy, self-management, self support, being a parent, military service, and being a high school graduate. The conditions establishing emancipation vary considerably from state to state. Some states also have what have been called subjective rules permitting consent by minors of two general sorts: "(1) Conditional Minor—a minor may consent if he will be in serious danger unless health care services are provided: (2) Mature Minor—a minor may give consent if he understands the nature and purposes of the proposed treatment" ([6], p. 94). The conditional minor rule may be intended to be restricted to emergency or quasi-emergency conditions, and in any event in Alexander Capron's 1982 survey of state laws it had been adopted in only two states ([6], Appendix).

The mature minor rule has also been adopted in statutory law in only a small minority of states, though it probably has a broader basis in case law.[9] It retains the presumption that minors are incompetent to consent to their own treatment, and requires that their "maturity," that is, their understanding of the nature and purposes of the proposed treatment, be demonstrated in any particular instance to rebut that presumption. Moreover, the application of the mature minor rule has generally been restricted to minors very close to the age of majority, usually not less than 15, independent of the particular minor's general capacities to decide. Despite these limitations, the mature minor rule does come closest to rejecting the general legal policy that minors are not permitted to give informed consent to their own treatment. Does our analysis of competence and the available empirical data concerning children's decisionmaking capacities support further revision in legal policy and/or in medical practice, insofar as it is guided by legal policy?

Because I have been unable to assess here the merits of the various strands of argument identified earlier as commonly offered in support of parental authority to make treatment decisions for their minor children, I want first to address the policy question about children's competence independent of the claims and value of parental authority. Thus, if we look principally to children's interests both in having their well-being protected and in having their emerging self-determination respected, what ought legal and medical policy be? One relatively clear implication of our conceptual analysis of the nature of the competence determination together both with empirical studies of children's decisionmaking capacities and with development theory is that the general presumption that all minors are incompetent for health care decisionmaking is very difficult to defend.[10] As we saw above, there seem to be no differences of significance between adults and children of roughly ages 15 (some would say 14) to 17 years in their general capacities that are needed for health care treatment decisionmaking. This suggests that the presumption of competence for health care decisionmaking that holds for adults should be extended to minors in this age range as well. The most direct way of doing this would be through statutes that explicitly lower the age of majority for medical decisionmaking. At the time of Capron's 1982 survey, three states had enacted such statutes: Alabama, age of majority for medical decisionmaking set at 14; Oregon, at 15; South Carolina, at 16, with restrictions on consent for operations. It bears emphasis that a presumption of competence extended to 15- to 17-year-olds would be, just as with adults, only a presumption and so rebuttable in any particular cases by evidence concerning the child's decisionmaking in that case. This presumption of competence would cover both consenting to treatment without the need for parental consent, as well as refusing treatment to which the child's parents might or might not be prepared to consent.

Below age 15, there seems good reason to maintain the current presumption of incompetence because of the extent to which various general decisionmaking capacities then are usually still undergoing significant development and are appreciably more limited than for most adults. Nevertheless, in the 9 to 14 age period some children will demonstrate sufficient capacities to make particular decisions to be deemed competent to make them. Since the younger the child within this age period, the less often is competence likely to be demonstrated, the presumption of the children's incompetence for medical decisionmaking in the 9 to 14 age range should be understood to be increasingly strong the younger the child. Grisso and Vierling go somewhat further in concluding that "there may be no circumstances that would justify sanctioning independent consent by minors under 11 years of age, given the developmental psychological evidence for their diminished psychological capacities" ([10]), p. 424). While this would be correct for the vast majority of cases, I believe the very great variability among children of this age in decisionmaking capacities, as well as the very great variability in the demands made by different decisions, justifies allowing for the possibility that the very strong presumption that 9- and 10-year-olds are incompetent to decide about treatment for themselves might on occasion be rebutted.

The principal implication of the fact that children in this 9 to 14 age range sometimes demonstrate competence may be for medical practice rather than legal policy. Physicians treating children in this age group should always explore treatment alternatives with children, as well as with their parents, in an effort to determine the children's preferences regarding treatment, to understand the reasoning on which their preferences are based, and to assess their competence for decisions. If parent and child are in agreement with the physician's treatment recommendation and the parents' competence is not itself in question, then the physician will have both the parents' consent and the child's assent and can proceed with treatment.

If the child is in disagreement with the physician's recommendation and/or the parents' choice, the first response, as always, should be to seek to resolve that disagreement through further discussion. When disagreement cannot be resolved, whether the child's disagreement is with the physician, the parents, or both, the physician should be obliged to seek to assess the child's competence in this decisionmaking situation. If the physician judges the child to be competent, it should be his responsibility to accede to the child's wishes if the parents are also in agreement with the child, or to serve as his patient's—the child's—advocate in pursuing further steps to enable the child's wishes to be heard and respected. Such a practice would insure that treatment of children in this age range would never proceed without either the child's assent to the treatment or an evaluation by the physician of the child's reasoning in the case in question that affirmed the presumption of the child's incompetence.

While the preceding suggestions concern medical practice, they would require some change in the law in virtually all states. What is needed is clearer legal authority, and in turn legal procedures, for rebutting the presumption of incompetence of children in this age group and for establishing their competence. I have no special suggestions about what those mechanisms should be, but, plainly, if they are desirable, it would not be impossible to develop them.

For children below the age of 9 it is probably reasonable to maintain the practice of treating the presumption of their incompetence as irrebuttable. Despite the significant variation in different children's decisionmaking capacities at any particular age, it is hard to imagine the circumstances in which this young a child's refusal of a treatment on which both the physician and the parents were agreed, or request for a treatment that both physician and parents opposed, evidence sufficient decisionmaking capacities to be honored in the face of this opposition. However, just as with incompetent adult patients, such children should always have their treatment explained to them before they receive it in a manner appropriate to their abilities to understand. This is a way of respecting their dignity appropriate to their limited decisionmaking capacities.

Finally, while assessing the various complex arguments in support of parents' independent interest in deciding about their children's health care is beyond the scope of this paper, we can at least add one suggestion to remedy slightly this incompleteness. A minimal recognition of this interest, which is desirable as well on other grounds, would be provided by a policy for all dependent minors of encouraging joint decisionmaking between parent and child about the child's treatment. Even in the absence of a willingness of children to engage in joint decisionmaking with their parents, a general policy of parental notification before proceeding with treatment to which a competent child has consented is probably desirable except when treatment is needed under emergency conditions, when parental notification would seriously threaten to make the child's decisionmaking involuntary, or when parental notification would substantially discourage children seeking a particular kind of treatment. While this would certainly not satisfy some advocates of parental authority, it would at least go some small way in recognizing parents' quite legitimate concern about their children's health care.

Notes

1. The analysis in this paper extends to the case of children the account of competence and incompetence of adults that I have developed elsewhere. While on the staff of the President's Commission for the Study of Ethical Problems in Medicine and Biomedical and Behavioral Research, I was the principal author of the account of competence and incompetence in the Commission reports, *Making Health Care Decisions* [23] and *Deciding to Forego Life-Sustaining Treatment* [25] and of its discussion paper, "Patient Competence to Make Decisions About Medical Therapy" [24]. I was also the principal author of the chapter, "Competence and Incompetence," in the longer study, "Surrogate Decisionmaking for Elderly Individuals Who are Incompetent or of Questionable Competence" [5] and in [4]. I have drawn freely on both the ideas and, in some cases, the specific statement of them in these works in developing the basic framework of competence in the present paper. I am especially indebted to Allen Buchanan and to the other Commission staff members with whom I worked in what was truly a team effort on the two reports cited above: Alexander M. Capron, Joanne Lynn, Marion Osterweis and Alan J. Weisbard, Edwin N. Forman, Rosalind Ladd, and Peter M. Smith generously provided written comments on an earlier draft of the paper, and Robert Holmes provided a very helpful written commentary at the conference at East Carolina University School of Medicine at which this paper was first delivered. Many others have provided helpful comments and criticisms of my views on this subject, though none can be held responsible for any misuse I may have made of their good influences.

2. A good source of data and discussions on research involving children is the National Commission for the Protection of Human Subjects of Biomedical and Behavioral Research [19].

3. See Alan Meisel, "The Exceptions to the Informed Consent Doctrine: Striking a Balance Between Competing Values in Medical Decisionmaking" [17].

4. For the account in this section of the developmental evidence about children's capacities, I rely heavily on the excellent review by T. Grisso and L. Vierling, "Minors' Consent to Treatment: A Developmental Perspective" [10] and also on: G. B. Melton, "Psychological Issues in Increasing Children's Competence" [18], C. E. Lewis, "Decision Making Related to Health: When Could/Should Children Act Responsibly?" [16], M. A. Grodin and J. J. Alpert, "Informed Consent and Pediatric Care" [11], L. A. Weithorn, "Involving Children

in Decisions Affecting Their Own Welfare: Guidelines for Professionals" [28], L. A. Weithorn and S. B. Campbell, "The Competency of Children and Adolescents to Make Informed Treatment Decisions" [29], and S. Leiken, "Minor's Assent or Dissent in Medical Treatment" [15].

5. Grisso and Vierling ([10], p. 194). This is also consistent with the findings of Weithorn and Campbell [29] that 9-year-olds were able to reach reasonable conclusions, but were not able to attend to all relevant factors in complex cases and instead focused on a few prominent factors.

6. Melton ([18], p. 24), quoting Keith-Spiegel [14].

7. Among other explicit defenses of a variable standard of competence are J. Drane, "The Many Faces of Competency" [7] and W. Gaylin, "Competence: No Longer All or None" [9].

8. Capron's "The Competence of Children as Self-Deciders in Biomedical Interventions" [6] contains an excellent review of the law regarding children's competence, as well as a very useful appendix detailing the standards in the different states.

9. Cf. Holder [12], pp. 133–135.

10. Capron [6] argues that as a matter of law this presumption is undergoing change and erosion.

Bibliography

1. Aiken, W. and LaFollette, H. (eds): 1980, *Whose Child? Children's Rights, Parental Authority, and State Power,* Littlefield, Adams, Totowa, NJ.

2. Blustein, J.: 1982, *Parents and Children: The Ethics of the Family,* Oxford University Press, New York.

3. Brandt, R.: 1982, "Two Concepts of Utility," in H. Miller, and W. Williams, (eds.), *The Limits of Utilitarianism,* University of Minnesota Press, Minneapolis, pp. 169–185.

4. Buchanan, A. and Brock, D. W.: 1986, "Deciding for Others," *Milbank Memorial Quarterly* 64: Suppl. 2, 17–94.

5. Buchanan, A., with Gilfix, M. and Brock, D. W.: "Surrogate Decisionmaking for Elderly Individuals Who are Incompetent or of Questionable Competence," National Technical Information Service, Washington, D.C. (forthcoming).

6. Capron, A: 1982, "The Competence of Children as Self-Deciders in Biomedical Interventions," in W. Gaylin, and R. Macklin, (eds.), *Who Speaks for the Child,* Plenum Press, New York, pp. 57–114.

7. Drane, J.: 1985, "The Many Faces of Competency," *Hastings Center Report* 15: 2, 17–21.

8. Erikson, E.: 1963, *Childhood and Society,* 2nd Ed., W. W. Norton, New York.

9. Gaylin, W.: 1982, "Competence: No Longer All or None," in W. Gaylin, and R. Macklin, (eds.), *Who Speaks for the Child,* Plenum Press, New York, pp. 27–54.

10. Grisso, T. and Vierling, L.: 1978, "Minors' Consent to Treatment: A Developmental Perspective," *Professional Psychology* 9, 412–427.

11. Grodin, M. A. and Alpert, J. J.: 1983, "Informed Consent and Pediatric Care," in G. B. Melton, G. P. Koocher, and M. J. Saks, (eds.), *Children's Competence to Consent,* Plenum Press, New York, pp. 93–110.

12. Holder, A.: 1985, *Legal Issues in Pediatric and Adolescent Medicine,* 2nd Ed., Yale University Press, New Haven.

13. Houlgate, L.: 1980, *The Child and the State,* Johns Hopkins, Baltimore.
14. Keith-Spiegel, P.: 1976, "Children's Rights as Participants in Research," in G. P. Koocher, (ed.), *Children's Rights and the Mental Health Professions,* Wiley, New York, pp. 53–81.
15. Leiken, S.: 1982, "Minor's Assent or Dissent in Medical Treatment," President's Commission for the Study of Ethical Problems in Medicine, *Making Health Care Decisions, Volume III: Appendices,* U.S. Government Printing Office, Washington, D.C., pp. 175–191.
16. Lewis, C. E.: 1983, "Decision Making Related to Health: When Could/ Should Children Act Responsibly?" in G. B. Melton, G. P. Koocher, and M. J. Saks, (eds.), *Children's Competence to Consent,* Plenum Press, New York, pp. 75–91.
17. Meisel, A.: 1979, "The Exceptions to the Informed Consent Doctrine: Striking a Balance Between Competing Values in Medical Decisionmaking," *Wisconsin Law Review,* 413–488.
18. Melton, G. B.: 1983, "Decision Making by Children: Psychological Risks and Benefits," in Melton, G. B., Koocher, G. P., and Saks, M. J. (eds.), *Children's Competence to Consent,* Plenum Press, New York, pp. 21–40.
19. National Commission for the Protection of Human Subjects of Biomedical and Behavioral Research: 1977, *Research Involving Children, Appendix Volume,* U.S. Government Printing Office, Washington, D.C.
20. Piaget, J.: 1965, *The Moral Judgment of the Child,* Free Press, New York.
21. Piaget, J.: 1972, *The Child's Conception of the World,* Littlefield, Adams, Totowa, N.J.
22. Piaget, J. and Inhelder, B.: 1969, *The Psychology of the Child,* Basic Books, New York.
23. President's Commission for the Study of Ethical Problems in Medicine and Biomedical and Behavioral Research: 1982, *Making Health Care Decisions,* U.S. Government Printing Office, Washington, D.C.
24. President's Commission for the Study of Ethical Problems in Medicine and Biomedical and Behavioral Research: 1982, "Patient Competence to Make Decisions About Medical Therapy," unpublished.
25. President's Commission for the Study of Ethical Problems in Medicine and Biomedical and Behavioral Research: 1983, *Deciding to Forego Life-Sustaining Treatment,* U.S. Government Printing Office, Washington, D.C.
26. Rawls, J.: 1971, *A Theory of Justice,* Harvard University Press, Cambridge, MA.
27. Schwartz, T.: 1982, "Human Welfare: What It Is Not," in H. Miller, and W. Williams, (eds.): 1982, *The Limits of Utilitarianism,* University of Minnesota Press, Minneapolis, pp. 195–206.
28. Weithorn, L. A.: 1983, "Involving Children in Decisions Affecting Their Own Welfare: Guidelines for Professionals," in G. B. Melton, G. P. Koocher, and M. J. Saks, (eds.), *Children's Competence to Consent,* Plenum Press, New York, pp. 235–260.
29. Weithorn, L. A. and Campbell, S. B.: 1982, "The Competency of Children and Adolescents to Make Informed Treatment Decisions," *Child Development* 53, 1589–1598.

Parental Discretion and Children's Rights: Background and Implications for Medical Decision-Making

Ferdinand Schoeman

This paper argues that liberal tenets that justify intervention to promote the welfare of an incompetent do not suffice as a basis for analyzing parent-child relationships, and that this inadequacy is the basis for many of the problems that arise when thinking about the state's role in resolving family conflicts, particularly when monitoring parental discretion in medical decision-making on behalf of a child. The state may be limited by the best interest criterion when dealing with children, but parents are not. The state's relation with the child is formal while the parental relation is intimate, havings its own goals and purposes. While the liberal canons insist on the incompetent one's best interest, parents are permitted to compromise the child's interests for ends related to these familial goals and purposes. Parents' decisions should be supervened, in general, only if it can be shown that no responsible mode of thinking warrants such treatment of a child.

Key Words: proxy medical consent, children's rights, state's protection of children, parental authority and the state's intervention, paternalism, liberalism and parental values.

Thinking about families raises a dilemma for those enamored of a liberal social and moral philosophy. It has been well argued in the literature on the family that in a society committed to distribution based in large part on merit, respect for the autonomy of the family interferes with efforts to provide effective equal opportunities for children, and hence for the adults into which those children mature (Fishkin, 1982; Blustein, 1982). What I shall concern myself with here are some reasons for puzzling over liberalism from the perspective of the parent-child relationship. I will argue that liberal tenets do not suffice as a basis for analyzing parent-child relationships, and that this inadequacy is the basis for many of the problems that arise when thinking about the state's role in resolving family conflicts, particularly when monitoring parental discretion in medical decision-making on behalf of a child.

From the liberal perspective, individual autonomy and social well-being share the honors for ultimate value, it being agreed that either taken by itself leads to excesses (Sen, 1982; Hart, 1979). Roughly, freedom of choice is to

From *The Journal of Medicine and Philosophy*, vol. 10, 1985. 45–61. Copyright © 1985.
Reprinted by permission of Kluwer Academic Publishers.

be limited only by concern for the rights of others and for important features of social efficiency. Less roughly, it is not all choices, but significant choices that we are concerned with protecting. Individual discretion may often be limited for the sake of merely marginal social gains, so long as the limitations imposed are themselves incidental to important life choices (Dworkin, 1977). The more important the social objective is perceived to be, the greater the limitation on individual discretion permitted, although some domains of choice are not to be actively restricted short of threat of catastrophic consequences. Despite the fact that details of this liberalism are difficult to elaborate precisely, for liberals, limitations on important choices must be justified by something of paramount and pressing significance.

Thought about families challenges the adequacy of this perspective. Children in families are not accorded the same rights as adults. Indeed, children are denied most of the significant autonomy rights adults enjoy. If this denial were merely the result of a judgment that children were incompetent to exercise reasonable discretion, such a status would not seem to violate the vague tenets of liberalism adumbrated, for within liberalism an exception is made for those not competent to show mature discretion. Paternalistic interference with a person is regarded as legitimate when limited to those who are unable to deliberate maturely and when the interference is exercised for the sake of promoting the well-being of those who would otherwise be endangered. In so far as an authority like the state limits a child's freedom, this criterion probably supplies a necessary and sufficient condition for depriving children of adult status. Though some of the limitations parents impose on the free choice of a child surely are aimed at promoting the child's welfare or protecting the legitimate interests of others, many limitations imposed by parents are not aimed at such ends at all. Mundane examples include requiring children to help with family chores, to go on vacations which will surely strike them as boring or inconveniently timed, or limiting the occasions on which they can invite friends over. As these examples illustrate, limitations on children are not made solely on the basis of concern for the welfare of the child and are not solely legitimized by having this end in view.

Suppose we want to answer the question: Why does any given individual have authority over his own child? Few persons would believe that the answer could be that he has this authority because he is uniquely positioned to promote the child's best interest. It is in the child's interest, at least at birth, to be placed with the most loving, patient, caring, devoted, enlightened, and affluent persons to be found. Obviously, not all parents, and not even all good parents, can make this claim about themselves. Although we may concede that someone should have authority over the child, we cannot say that the biological parents should typically be this person if the basis for this authority restricts eligibility to those who are among the class of persons who will promote maximally the welfare of the child.

Furthermore, there are legitimate decisions parents can make concerning a child which actually and significantly harm the child without offering some compensating benefit (see *Hart* v. *Brown* (1972)). If a child is critically ill and the only potentially hopeful means of saving the child is to operate on its healthy sibling, say to remove bone marrow for a transplant, even though it may cause a serious, though not life threatening, risk to the healthy sibling, most people would consider such an operation legitimate.

When pressed with examples like this, people rush to point out that it would actually benefit the healthy sibling to be in a position to assist the ailing sibling, and that if it were not really in the interests of the healthy sibling, the transplant would not be permissible. There are some legal decisions which seem to support this response. In the case of *Strunk* v. *Strunk* (1969), a court permitted the removal of a kidney from a healthy twenty-seven year old mentally retarded ward of the state to save the life of his brother. The court argued that the transplant would be beneficial to the donor because of his great emotional dependence on his brother and because, upon the death of his aging parents, his sole active family relationship would be to his brother. In the context of the prospects of the operation being successful and of the low long-term risk to the donor, the operation would be less harmful to the incompetent than would be the death of his brother. In another case dealing with a potential donor who was severely retarded and whose sister was in need of a kidney transplant the court did not approve (*In re Richardson,* (1900)). Here the court claimed that for the seventeen year old to donate his kidney to his thirty-two year old sister was not in his best interest. The court observed that the kidney transplant was not an absolute necessity for the sister since she did have dialysis as an alternative and that there was little expectation that the sister would care for her incompetent brother after their parents were no longer in a position to do so. As in the previous case, this person was a ward of the state. Though it seems as if what differentiates these two cases is the extent of benefit to the potential donor, the decision and the concurring opinion in the Richardson case both emphasize the absence of a life-threatening urgency in the case of the needy sister. This suggests that even if the prospects of long term benefits for the potential donor were not improved, had there been a life and death situation for the sister, the court might have allowed the transplant and qualified some of its scruples about protecting the interests of immature family members.

Exploring our thinking about such situations suggests that some impositions which would be unthinkable outside the family context are acceptable within an intimate context. The state may be limited by the best interest criterion in its dealings with children, but parents are not. This difference between what parents are traditionally permitted and what the liberal state is permitted in its treatment of children is significant. While the state occupies a formal relationship with the child, the parents occupy an intimate relationship—one in which a different range of principles and objectives applies. It would be a mistake to think that the state could occupy an intimate role with the individual or that the parent's role is properly conceived as ideally doing for the child what practically the state is unable to perform. The parent is not performing a function for the state when raising his child, even though we recognize that there are certain limits on what is permissible to parents because of concern for the child's or society's welfare.

The parent's responsibility is fundamentally different from that of the state. The parents' responsibility is partly characterized as providing opportunities for the emergence of meaning, intimacy, identity, and character—altogether inner qualities and not the kind of thing that can develop from abstract relationships. The point of an intimate relationship is not just to supply some necessary ingredient in a needy child's life. The relationship within a family typically has an inner focus and an independent meaning which results from sharing of life and its intimacies. While the relationships within a family may be very complex and in some ways dependent upon the wider social context, responsibilities are aimed at making the family as such a working entity. They are not typically concerned with the maximization of individual welfare or the promotion of social interests.

This leaves us in an awkward position. In cases of conflict between the state's and the parents' objectives for the child, which should dominate? Is it not the state, after all, which tolerates, permits, and even sanctions parental authority? If so, then it seems as if the state is enforcing what we have just described as impermissible for the state—limitations on a child not justified by liberal principles. It is tempting to think that all authority really does come from the state or from principles that are liberal in character. In recognizing parental authority which goes beyond promoting the child's interests, broadly understood, the state has seemingly authorized others to do what is beyond its legitimate scope. Parents frequently deprive children of rights and in other ways exercise authority over children that would be impermissible in other contexts between citizens or even between incompetents and state appointed guardians. So it seems as if the state must have the attitude that such exercises of authority as parents maintain over their children must be for the benefit of the child, for the protection of society, or be altogether too trivial to warrant outside interference. For while the state may acknowledge parental control over children for the benefit of the child or for the protection of others, as a liberal state it cannot recognize as legitimate any other objectives of parental discretion. This inability does not mean that there are no other bases, but only that such others as there may be are not recognizable as legitimate by a liberal state.

If the state is limited by liberal principles in its structuring of relationships involving children, does that mean that the state should deal with conflicts that arise within a family in the same way as it deals with conflicts between citizens generally? In the case of adults, though there may be some financial responsibilities that the state requires individuals to meet, the liberal perspective would warrant individuals to decide for themselves to what extent they wish to maintain their moral ties to other members of the family. This attitude would leave family relationships in the domain of individual virtues, not state policies. Were this stance taken toward children, so long as parents and children agreed, there would be little occasion for state interference. But were the child to disagree with the parent and seek state protection, or were someone to demand state protection on behalf of the child, the latter thought not competent to judge its own interests, then either the state would have to regard the child as mature and thus in a position to determine things for himself or it would judge the child immature and make its own determination as to what actually promoted the child's interest. Alternatively, the state could adopt the attitude that family matters are essentially private and impose upon itself high threshold conditions before it intervenes to protect the rights of various members, or before it recognizes the right of anyone else to intervene on behalf of the child.

While there are numerous practical reasons why the state has tended to adopt the latter stance, there is a specifically moral reason for this stance as well. If the family is to be thought of as an intimate arrangement having its own goals and purposes, it is inappropriate to impose upon that arrangement the abstract liberal principles we have discussed above. This is not to say that these liberal principles do not have any moral weight in the context of the family, but that they are not exhaustive of the principles which may legitimately bind people together and structure their relationship.

Might we utilize the notion of the separation of powers to characterize the relationship between parents and children on the one hand and the relationship between the state and the family on the other? What is beyond the state's authority to impose on children is, or may be, within the parents' authority. Recognition of this by the state does not mean that the state authorizes or legitimizes such parental rights. It means only that the state recognizes another authority with powers it itself lacks. The state intervenes when a serious violation of parental authority has occurred perhaps because no one else is designated to monitor such transgressions and it is desirable that someone should. The state may, at times, supervise family affairs not because it has final authority over family matters as such, but because in extreme cases someone should be given this authority and by default it has fallen to the state. There is a difference between saying that the state has a right to step in when an urgent situation emerges and saying that the state has ultimate authority in the domain of child-rearing, delegating some powers but reserving some supervisory powers for itself. Compare: If you see a neighbor attacking one of his children with a knife, it is appropriate for you to intervene. This does not mean that under normal situations the neighbor derives his authority over the child from you. The right to intervene does not presuppose possession of ultimate authority.

Problems still remain. What stance should the state take if a child asks the state to intervene in a case where a parent has deprived the child of autonomy and where admittedly such a deprivation does not promote the child's interests, present or future? What stance should the state take if someone other than the child, but acting on behalf of the child, asks the parents' authority to be limited because the child's interests are being ignored or misinterpreted? There is a whole host of cases which reflects this latter difficulty: Parents believe that a child with a serious medical condition is best served by something other than medically recommended life-saving treatment. The parents may think that prayer, and not medical treatment, is the only appropriate response to life-endangering conditions, as was the situation in the case of Pamela Hamilton, a twelve year old girl, suffering from Ewing's Sarcoma. Her father, with her concurrence, believed that medical treatment would not work and that any approach besides expressions of faith would be religiously prohibited. (*In re Pamela I. Hamilton* (1983)). Or the parents may think that medically recommended treatments are harmful and should be replaced by Laetrile and megadoses of certain vitamins, a course of treatment doctors find to be positively toxic. The famous Chad Green case illustrates a situation like this (*Custody of a Minor* (1979)). Or the parents may feel that the child's life, if prolonged by emergency treatment, will fall below a certain threshold requisite for worthwhile living, perhaps because there would be no higher brain functioning or because the child's existence would be a torment to the child due to the pain the child's condition would engender. The Baby Jane Doe case involved a situation like this where a child was born with spina bifida and other serious complicating disorders, and in need of life saving treatment. The parents refused to authorize such treatment after consultation with neurological experts, nurses, religious counselors, and social workers, all of whom concurred with the parents' decision. (*Weber* v. *Stoney Brook Hospital* (1983)). Each of the cases just mentioned involves a life-or-death dilemma.

In reflecting upon such cases, it is important not to fall subject to a kind of distortion that such high-stakes issues predispose us to. The fact that we think that the child's life is more important to protect than the choices of the parents, and possibly even the child, does not show that when the situation is less urgent it is still only the child's welfare that carries any moral weight in judging the appropriateness of any particular exercise of parental discretion.

Gerald Dworkin (1971) differentiated two types of mistake that might trigger paternalistic intervention generally: mistakes about facts in the context of agreement about principles; mistakes about principles. He argued that we should be more indulgent of individuals who disagree with us about principles than we should be of individuals who agree with us about the general norms that apply but disagree with us about the facts. We have more authority to intervene in the affairs of another if we know that he is aiming at some approved end but benighted about how to achieve it than if we are trying to impose our values on someone unwilling. Dworkin's discussion was focused exclusively on intervention for the benefit of the restricted party. In the case of exercises of parental authority, we can ask ourselves how much difference this distinction makes. Parents may agree with the rest of society about the proper ends to achieve in childrearing, but get the facts wrong, as in the Chad Green case, or they may just disagree about what ends are proper. Short of subjecting a child to extreme, irremediable, and obvious harm as a result of parental discretion, I do not think that parental discretion ought to be legally undermined whatever the source of the mistake. However, in case of impending danger resulting from parental discretion, whatever its typology, intervention is desirable. The difference between these different sources of error in judgment relating to discretion will, perhaps, bear on what alternatives there are for remedying the situation, but not on the legitimacy of the intervention.

If we adhere to the liberal rationale for parental control over the child, we must support only those limitations on childhood discretion which actually promote the child's present welfare and future autonomy or which are necessary to protect others. This raises the prospect of expertise. Presently, child-rearing is not the kind of domain in which there is technical expertise that goes beyond informed common sense. If this picture changes and people came to invest some professionals with expectations of expert judgment concerning child welfare, it would then seem as if the only legitimate discretion allowable to parents or guardians would be in the *application* of guidelines that were themselves outside of the control of the parent. If the only bases for limiting the discretion of an incompetent were the well-being of the person restricted or the protection of others, then parents would be under a duty to follow the advice of experts on what was really beneficial for the child. Discretion in the structuring of individual family aims would be permissible only for those domains in which such could have no adverse bearing on the child, as determined by the experts. Parents would not have rights with respect to their children, but only duties or virtues. This principle lies at the core of the liberal attitude toward parental authority (Gutmann, 1980). In the Chad Green case mentioned above, part of the opinion reads: "Parents' right to control a child's nurture . . . is rather akin to a trust, subject to a correlative duty to care for and protect the child. Where a child's well being is at issue it is not rights of parents that are chiefly at issue" (*Custody of a Minor* (1979)). Parents would not have authority to limit their children unless their objective were the child's welfare. Recent Supreme Court decisions emphasize that when state laws require that parents be given some role in important decision making processes concerning their children, as in the case of an abortion decision, the parents must be put on notice that they may be guided exclusively by concern for the best interest of their child (see *Baird* v. *Bellotti* (1977)). Once persuaded that there were right ways of rearing children, from the liberal perspective there would be no excuse for not following recommended patterns in any field in which limitations on children were being legitimately imposed.

People are able theoretically, and to a certain extent practically, to differentiate between imposing a rule because it is what the parents desire or value for a variety of reasons, and imposing a rule because it will promote the child's welfare as the parent conceives it. From the liberal viewpoint, only the welfare of the child, or the protection of the rights or the welfare of others serve as a basis for limiting the child's choices. Suppose, for instance, that a parent wants to require a certain life style for his child because the parent's religion requires this, but not because the parent thinks that this is best for the child. Recently, a New York City family court judge reported that in her years of experience hearing parents of pregnant teenagers explain why their daughters should not be permitted to have an abortion, she had not even heard cited the rationale that continuation of the pregnancy would be in the child's best interest. Instead, parents invoked reasons like: "It is against God's will"; or "People should pay for their mistakes"; or "I could not have an abortion when I got pregnant out of wedlock, so why should my daughter be able to have one?" (Dembitz, 1980). Were the parents more sophisticated, they surely could have recast their reasons in terms of the child's welfare. But the fact remains that the actual reasons parents often have for imposing restrictions on their children have little to do with the child's welfare and more to do with the parent's values and preferences.

Parents rear their children to participate in diverse social units. Perhaps at one time the ends of such units were largely complementary. Western society, however, seems full of sources of conflict between family ties and religious duties, family ties and social duties; between codes of conduct which favor narrow societal virtues and codes of behavior which favor universal, trans-societal loyalties. Although families function to mediate an individual's connection to society, they do this by instilling wider loyalties than to the self but narrower than to all other citizens, and in so doing generate distinct sources of conflict. Even what we think of as familial loyalty is itself bifurcated into loyalties to the individual members of the family and loyalty to the family unit itself as an organic and enduring entity. The values and virtues which generally promote the well-being of family members can at times encourage sacrifice of family members for the ideals of the family, just as religious virtues can at times function to promote the extinction of all active members.

Family loyalties present two sources of potential conflict with social welfare: extra weight given to concerns of those in the family, and extra weight given to the promotion of the family either at the expense of those outside the family or even at the expense of those within. If the family is seen functionally as purely an instrument of society's aims, such conflicts will seem to be a pathological development. But why should we suppose that the point of a family is solely to promote some agreeable social end? Being uncomfortable with conflicts in loyalties is not a good reason for thinking that families are to be thought of as functional in a narrowly social way. There are institutions like the family in which people find meaning in their relationships with others and to an ideal or practice. Such meaning equips individuals with goals independent of the grand social objective of maximizing social welfare. From an evolutionary perspective, we can expect that few institutions which are disastrous for social well-being will survive. This provides us with an explanation of why institutions found in viable societies will be limited in the extent to which they generate conflict. It does not, however, demonstrate that such institutions as are indifferent or hostile to social welfare are wrong in their very point. There appear to be many sources of value that conflict with, and that cannot be made to fit into, the social welfare mold without loss of something essential. It would strike many as a decimation of the moral realm to include in the moral pantheon only those values, ends, and virtues which promote social welfare or individual rights. Much of what we now think of as *moral* tragedy would not be expressible without acknowledgement that what is in conflict are indeed conflicting moral concerns. (See Williams, 1973; Wiggins, 1976, Marcus, 1980; Conee, 1982.)

We can expect to find principles of decision making within a family that, under certain circumstances, conflict with the welfare of members of the family and society at large. The interests of individuals both related and unrelated to the family can be endangered by decisions which may seem legitimate from the family perspective. Examples previously cited to illustrate this were: not reassigning children at birth and permitting operations on healthy children for the benefit of ailing siblings. Other examples, such as recognizing testimonial privileges for spouses of the criminally accused, and the recent extension of this privilege to cover child-parent communication, illustrate how willing we are to tolerate increased social risk for the sake of protecting certain family-based loyalties (see *In re Agosto* (1983)).

Here is the dilemma: certain decisions seem legitimate when made within the context of a family, even though they seem to violate the liberal principles for treating incompetents. Yet we want to account for the treatment of children in the context of a family using the same principles we use in dealing with individuals generally. Welfare and autonomy provide parents with ideals or values to keep in mind when raising their children. But these are by no means complete as family virtues. The other values that parents recognize may limit and redirect some of their familial objectives. But these other values do not replace, or even always fit comfortably with, familial values. Major proponents of contemporary versions of liberalism, like John Rawls (1971, p. 511) and Ronald Dworkin (1977), acknowledge the inadequacy of border principles of liberalism at both the individual and the familial levels. For both of these theorists, part of the point of liberalism is to enable individuals to find their own versions of the good life, with the meanings, connections, and identifications we all recognize as lending life its value. What we find when we read discussions of the moral basis of parental control over the child, however, is the perspective that the liberal principles suffice for a full exploration of the domain. Seeing families and societies as institutions with independent ideals and as invested with meanings of their own is necessary to understanding what is so important about them. Recognizing this explains why experts on the promotion of child welfare and autonomy, if there are any, are not to be seen as making parental authority anachronistic. Welfare and autonomy of the child are only part of what should be considered when judging how children may be limited in the range of their discretion. It is also only part of what the parent must keep in mind in making medical decisions for a child.

There is a tendency to think that children's rights or autonomy should be recognized as soon as their competence to exercise such rights is developed (Schoeman, 1983). Interestingly, an entirely different perspective has historically dominated thinking about such matters. Individuals were subject to the authority of a household, not until they demonstrated maturity, but until they sought to establish a family of their own. It was not the gaining of competence, but the character of their relationships, which lifted the dominance of parental authority from their children. David Flaherty describes the historical attitudes toward autonomous living as follows:

> The seventeenth-century custom of forbidding persons to live alone and ordering them to submit to family government is another significant instance of the state's regulation of private lives. When it became necessary to enact a statute on this matter, the law was primarily directed against young single persons, although it was enforced against widows on occasion. . . . The opposition to the solitary life, however, was motivated, not by lack of concern for privacy, but by traditions, practicality, and an underlying fear of sin.
>
> The English immigrants did not come from a tradition that encouraged solitary dwelling. Even in Greece, Rome, and the

medieval world one was expected to belong to a family. Living under a family roof was considered essential to a healthy economy and an orderly society in the sixteenth and seventeenth centuries (Flaherty, 1979, p. 175).

Vestiges of this way of thinking are still evident and powerful. In Joseph Goldstein's (1977) discussion of medical decision-making for children at risk, for example, we find combined an extreme form of parental discretion with an automatic exception for pregnant teenagers, even though none of the conditions which he sets out for overriding parental discretion are necessarily engaged just because of pregnancy. Before his discussion of adolescent pregnancy, Goldstein had argued that the state is warranted in overriding parental discretion only if the child's life is in imminent danger, if the parental decision would deprive the child of prospects of a relatively normal life, and if medical authorities all agree that there is a reliable procedure for translating the child's condition from one of extreme danger to one of probable well-being. It is in being ready to head a family, and not just being in possession of mature capacities, that qualifies one for full autonomy rights.

As liberals, we like to represent a child's moral and social development as legitimizing parental authority with the consequence that such authority lasts only so long as the child lacks adult moral competence. In actual practice, however, it is the role as a member of a family unit that defines an individual's responsibilities and rights, at least as much as does his level of mature capacities.

The discussion thus far provides us with sets of values which, though unharmonious in form, remain true to moral consciousness to a far greater extent than strictly and consistently liberal canons. From the liberal perspective, an individual is either competent or not. If he is competent, then his own decisions about medical treatment, for example, are to be respected. If he is not competent, then his preference for treatment or for non-treatment is not decisive. What becomes decisive in this instance is another person's judgment of what is in the best interest of this individual. I have argued that the contextual isolation suggested by such principles does not in fact accord with our considered judgments about intimate situations.

In looking at decisions within a family that concern a child, I have suggested that factors other than the parents' responsibility for promoting the child's interests may be taken into account legitimately. These other factors can roughly be characterized as concerns emerging from the desire to promote the family's welfare or character. Such a perspective does not entitle parents to sacrifice their children's lives or welfare, although it does permit parents to compromise the child's interests for ends related to family welfare. Such a perspective recognizes the child as having a status within the family by virtue of which certain liabilities and responsibilities accrue. Such liabilities and responsibilities are not exclusively based on the ideal of preparing the child for his eventual role as a citizen, but instead on his place within the family.

I suggest that when we think about medical decision-making, at least with respect to children, we broaden our understanding of the context of the decision and acknowledge that interests are at stake in addition to those of promoting the child's best interest. It is difficult to set explicit limits on what parents may decide for their children when such a decision does not accord well with accepted public standards. While cultural bias abounds, there are genuine dilemmas we must face, as when we try to compare the significance of cultural identification, when practices which promote that involve mutilation of the body of the child or serious deprivations, and our interests in protecting children from gratuitous harm. (See Korbin, 1977.) While certain limits must be set, an effort must be made to appreciate the meaning of such practices for those involved.

The legal liability of minors is based in large measure on their social dependence as well as on their varying degrees of incompetence. Regarding medical treatment (or non-treatment) of children, unless the parental decision would seem from most perspectives as shockingly reckless or negligent, these decisions should count as decisive. What should be thought of as shockingly reckless or negligent is largely dependent on social practices, but not exclusively so. For instance, while courts have been reluctant to convict a parent or medical personnel for failure to treat defective newborns with life-threatening but treatable complications, such decisions seem very much out of line with other practices regarding children—even defective children—so long as one can say that for them life is better than death (Robertson, 1975). If a parent's decision is challenged by the concerned child or by someone advocating for the child, then the parent's decision should be supervened, in general, only if it can be shown that no responsible mode of thinking warrants such treatment of a child.

Since state scrutiny of, and intervention into, family affairs is highly disruptive of familial relationships, high threshold conditions should be met before an investigation into the propriety of familial decisions is even appropriate. Once the case is made that there may be abuse of parental discretion, then the courts must judge the legitimacy of the decisions. Even here, however, the terms for the decision need not be restricted to the best interest of the child, but may include concern for family relationships in addition to those which directly impinge on the child thought to be at risk.

In the Baby Jane Doe case mentioned above, the New York Court of Appeals took what strikes me as a disingenuous approach to the situation they confronted. They argued that the plaintiff was unauthorized to advocate for the child since he was unrelated to the child and was not authorized by the court or by child protection services to intervene on her behalf. While the court's concern for protecting the privacy and intimacy of the family is admirable, the chief reason they seemed to regard the plaintiff as unauthorized is because they thought the parents were acting acceptably in electing not to have surgery performed on their daughter. The court did say that there are cases in which the intervention of "unauthorized" persons would be heard more sympathetically, but declined to specify what would distinguish such cases from the case at hand. Since the case seemed like a straightforward life and death case, it is difficult to see what would have to be altered about the case to make intervention more appropriate except the addition of the assumption that the child's life would be worth saving. It seems as if the court was unwilling to acknowledge that for the judges the real issue was the desirability of saving the child's life, and not familial privacy, except as that becomes important *after* the evaluation of the child's life is made. It is the court in this instance which has been oblivious to the distinction between conditions for scrutinizing parental discretion on the one hand and conditions for imposing its own judgment on the other. It is unclear what would trigger third party scrutiny of parental discretion if not the failure to save a child's life through treatment that would ordinarily be required in the case of a normal child.

Allen Buchanan (1979) has recently advocated the view that family members be presumptively entitled to make medical decisions for incompetents, in accord with principles laid out by an Ethics Committee established in the hospitals. Buchanan recognizes that such a committee cannot limit itself to procedural issues when defining its principles, and suggests that as a substantive principle the committee insist that decisions made on behalf of incompetents either reflect what they (the incompetents) in fact wanted when they were competent, something not applicable in the case of a child, or be something which is in the patient's best interest (Buchanan, 1979, p. 112). I have been suggesting that using this as a substantive moral standard is misguided at both levels of inquiry. It is incorrect to suggest to parents that in making their substantive decisions relating to their children that they only concern them-selves with their child's best interest. Second, when a presumptive case is made that further inquiry is warranted by an outside body, they too may take into account matters in addition to the child's welfare. While preserving the child's life or physical and emotional integrity from imminent and obvious danger will usually override the other concerns that could normally arise, it is wrong to suggest that these other concerns have no role to play in parental decision making generally.

In defining the scope and limits of parental discretion over the medical and other decisions of their children, large scale utilitarian concerns also carry weight. Thus public health measures like inoculation, provision of confidential birth control planning or abortion services, and treatment for venereal disease, may also limit the range of parental control.

While such a conclusion may seem indecisive in that no algorithm for adjudi-cating hard cases is provided, the virtue of the present conceptualization of the issue is that it does not treat a multifaceted issue as if it were one-dimensional. It accounts for what seems morally compelling about opposing positions in diffi-cult cases. Without this kind of account, explaining why the difficult cases raise real dilemmas would be troublesome. The proposal here places the presump-tion for decision making with the parent and incorporates the prospect for parents making a real contribution from their very selves to the child and to decisions relating to the child. It is not just because the parent provides the best services for the child that the parent is authorized to make decisions for the child. It is because the parent and the child are presumed to be intimately related that the parent is given authority over the child. Because of this pre-sumed intimacy, state scrutiny and interference is warranted only after a good case is made for imminent and serious harm befalling the child as a result of parental discretion. Only those decisions which reflect gross ineptitude in moral resolution, widely interpreted, should be scrutinized and counter-manded.

Note

The author would like to express appreciation to Robert Veatch, Sarah Schechter-Schoeman, and Linda Weingarten for substantive and stylistic suggestions responsible for making this paper better than it would otherwise be.

References

Baird v. *Bellotti,* 428 F. Supp. 854 (1977).

Blustein, J.: 1982, *Parents and Children,* Oxford University Press, New York.

Buchanan, A.: 1979, "Medical Paternalism or Legal Imperialism: Not the Only Alternatives for Handling *Saikewicz*-type Cases," *American Journal of Law and Medicine* **5**, 97–117.

Conee, E.: 1982, "Against Moral Dilemmas," *The Philosophical Review* **91**, 87–98.

Custody of a Minor, Mass., 393 N.E. 2d 836 (1979).

Dembitz, D.: 1980, "The Supreme Court and a Minor's Abortion Decision," *Columbia Law Review* **80**, 1251–1263.

Dworkin, G.: 1971, "Paternalism," in R. Wasserstrom (ed.), *Morality and the Law,* Wadsworth Publishing Co., Belmont, pp. 107–126.

Dworkin, R.: 1977, "Liberty and Liberalism," in R. Dworkin (ed.), *Taking Rights Seriously,* Harvard University Press, Cambridge, pp. 259–266.

Fishkin, J.: 1982, *Justice, the Family, and Equal Opportunity,* Yale University Press, New Haven.

Flaherty, D.: 1972, *Privacy in Colonial New England,* University of Virginia Press, Charlottesville.

Goldstein, J.: 1977, "Medical Care for the Child at Risk: On State Supervision of Parental Autonomy," *Yale Law Journal* **86**, 645–670.

Gutmann, A.: 1980, "Children, Paternalism and Education," *Philosophy and Public Affairs* **9**, 338–358.

Hart v. *Brown,* 29 Conn. Supp. 368, 289 A.2d. 386 (1972).

Hart, H.: 1979, "Between Utility and Rights," *Columbia Law Review* **79**, 828–846.

In re Agosto, 553 F. Supp. 1298 (D. Nev. 1983).

In re Richardson, La. App., 284 So.2d 185 (1900).

In re Pamela Hamilton, 657 S.W.2d 425 (Tenn. App. 1983).

Korbin, J.: 1977, "Anthropological Contribution to the Study of Child Abuse," *Child Abuse & Neglect* **1**, 7–24.

Marcus, R.: 1980, "Moral Dilemma and Consistency," *The Journal of Philosophy* **77**, 121–136.

Rawls, J.: 1971, *A Theory of Justice,* Harvard University Press, Cambridge.

Robertson, J.: 1975, "Involuntary Euthanasia of Defective Newborns: A Legal Analysis," *Stanford Law Review* 27, 213–270.

Schoeman, F.: 1983, "Childhood Competence and Autonomy," *Journal of Legal Studies* 12, 267–287.

Sen, A.: 1982, "Rights and Agency," *Philosophy and Public Affairs* 11, 3–39.

Strunk v. *Strunk,* Ky., 445 S.W.2d 145 (1969).

Weber v. *Stoney Brook Hospital,* 456 N.E.2d 1186 (N.Y. 1983).

Williams, B.: 1973, "Ethical Consistency" and "Consistency and Realism," in B. Williams (ed.), *Problems of the Self,* Cambridge University Press, Cambridge, pp. 166–206.

Suggested Readings

Forman, Edwin N., and Rosalind Ekman Ladd, *Ethical Dilemmas in Pediatrics: A Case Study Approach* (New York: Springer-Verlag, 1991).

Gaylin, Willard, and Ruth R. Macklin, ed., *Who Speaks for the Child? The Problems of Proxy Consent* (New York: Plenum, 1982).

Group for the Advancement of Psychiatry. *How Old Is Old Enough? The Ages of Rights and Responsibilities.* (New York: Brunner/Mazel, 1989).

Koocher, Gerald P., *Children's Rights and the Mental Health Professions* (New York: Wiley, 1976).

Kopelman, Loretta, and John Moskop, ed., *Children and Health Care* (Dordrsecht: Kluwer, 1989).

Mahowald, Marcy Briody, *Women and Children in Health Care: An Unequal Majority* (New York: Oxford Univ. Press, 1993).

Manion, Maureen D., "Parental Religious Freedom, the Rights of Children, and the Role of the State," *Journal of Church and State,* Vol. 34, Winter 1992, pp. 77–92.

Melton, Gary B., Gerald P. Koocher, and Michael J. Saks, ed., *Children's Competence to Consent* (New York: Plenum, 1983).

Stinson, Robert, and Peggy Stinson, *The Long Dying of Baby Andrew* (Boston: Little, Brown & Co., 1983).